DEMOCRACY AND DEVELOPMENT

This book is a thorough investigation into the requisites of democracy. Based on data from all 132 sovereign states of the Third World, it first establishes a scale to measure the level of democracy existing in these countries. The author discusses various interpretations of the meaning of political democracy, and emerges with a specification of its essential principles which includes such elements as the holding of elections to central decision-making organs, and the maintenance of certain fundamental political liberties. Theories concerning the requisites of democratic government are then examined in order to explain the manifest differences in the level of democracy among the states of the Third World. The author employs statistical techniques including regression analysis to test theories related to socio-economic conditions, demographic and cultural factors, and institutional arrangements.

This book thus provides a uniquely wide-ranging examination both of the elements which constitute democracy, and of the factors which explain its varying prevalence.

DEMOCRACY
AND DEVELOPMENT

AXEL HADENIUS

CAMBRIDGE
UNIVERSITY PRESS

Published by the Press Syndicate of the University of Cambridge
The Pitt Building, Trumpington Street, Cambridge CB2 1RP
40 West 20th Street, New York, NY 10011–4211, USA
10 Stamford Road, Oakleigh, Melbourne 3166, Australia

First published 1992

Printed in Great Britain at the University Press, Cambridge

A catalogue record for this book is available from the British Library

Library of Congress cataloguing in publication data

Hadenius, Axel, 1945–
Democracy and development / by Axel Hadenius.
p. cm.
Includes bibliographical references and index.
ISBN 0 521 41685 X
1. Developing countries – Politics and government.
2. Democracy-Developing countries.
I. Title.
JF60.H33   1992
321.8′09172′ 4 – dc20   91–30815   CIP

ISBN 0 521 41685 X hardback

For Karin

Contents

Tables

Figure

Acknowledgements

For detailed reading and comments on parts or on all of the manuscript at one stage or another, I wish to express my gratitude to Stefan Björklund, Hans Blomkvist, Bengt-Ove Boström, Jörgen Hermansson, Göran Hydén, Leif Lewin, Folke Lindahl, Carl G. Rosberg, Giovanni Sartori, Tatu Vanhanen, Evert Vedung and Anders Westholm. Important research assistance was rendered by (in chronological order) Annika Molin, Per Nordlund, Kristina Karlsson and Peter Johansson.

I am most grateful to the Bank of Sweden Tercentenary Fund, whose financial support made this study possible. For helping me to put my thoughts into English, I am particularly indebted to Teodosia Gray, and also to Folke Lindahl and Alexander Davidson. I owe special thanks to Laila Grandin, who typed all my drafts with speed, accuracy and great patience.

Uppsala
May 1991

Introduction

When this study began, my purpose was to execute a review of theories and empirical studies concerning the requisites of democracy in the Third World. My ambitions were to present the different explanatory hypotheses which had been put forward, and report the extent to which these had been confirmed by the extensive empirical research done on the subject. In other words, by utilizing the available research literature, I intended to produce both an interpretation and an evaluation of the current theories.

Working along these lines I soon realized, however, that I would not be satisfied with the outcome. For several reasons, it was in many cases difficult to draw any distinct conclusions from the empirical research at hand. In certain interesting fields no studies had in reality been executed; at least not on a broader, comparative scale. And in other cases, where investigations of such a kind existed, the empirical indicators used as measurements of the potentially explanatory factor sometimes seemed doubtful. In addition, there was a significant variation with respect to the selection of countries – both in terms of the size of the sample and its geographical profile. What is more, the treatment of the issue to be explained – democracy – involved many problems. First of all, the general indicators of democracy that have been used by different researchers vary to a considerable extent. Furthermore, the information on the actual circumstances in the countries at issue is in many studies taken directly from available data catalogues which, when examined, convey – at least for this purpose – a most unreliable impression. The classifications made are frequently very crude and, in addition, sometimes wholly unspecified.[1]

For the shortcut to an empirical material which these catalogues indeed constitute – it is just a matter of transcription – one must, in my view, pay a high price in the form of uncertainty of what the information really represents.

Instead of drawing on other's work, as I at first attempted to do, I decided to undertake my own empirical study. The object thereof would still be the Third World. The reason for this was simple: it is there that we find the greatest variation with respect to democracy. In order to obtain as large a sample as possible, I chose to include all the sovereign states[2] in Latin America, the Caribbean, Africa, Asia and Oceania, with the exception of the OECD countries (Australia, New Zealand and Japan). These amounted to 132 in all; they represent some 80 per cent of the number of independent states in the world.

It is worth emphasizing that the issue to be discussed in what follows is the varying *level* of democracy at a certain point in time (1988), which should not be confused with the question of the *stability* or the *duration* of democracy.[3] In the latter case, it is a matter of how long certain standards of democracy have been maintained. Had this been our object, we would endeavour to produce a time scale based on a dichotomy; we should seek to grade (in terms of, e.g., number of years) the states which during a certain period attained a level acceptable from a democratic viewpoint.[4] For the part of the world here in focus, we could then obtain a fairly limited sample: applied to, let us say, the last twenty years, roughly 25 per cent of the states would be of interest. But for the purpose of this study, we are interested in the variation along the whole scale concerning the level of democracy – from the very lowest degree to the highest – at a certain time. Thus, obviously, all the states should be included.

Part 1 of the book is devoted to the establishment of such a scale, on which could be read the countries' relative performances from a democratic point of view. This involves a discussion of the very meaning of democracy, including a concrete specification of its essential elements. With this as the basis, a number of theories pertinent to the requisites of democracy are examined in Part 2 – thus the purpose in this part is to find explanations for the manifest differences concerning the level of democracy among the states of the Third World.

PART ONE

Determining the level of democracy

CHAPTER I

Points of departure

The first task of the study consists in the establishment of the attribute which is to be explained, i.e., the degree of democracy in the countries under discussion. In purely practical terms this is a matter of compiling a wealth of data on the situations in these countries. But before this can be achieved, we must, of course, decide on which information we shall seek, and how this in turn is to be weighed and interpreted. We need a number of empirical indicators which to a reasonable extent reflect the degree of democracy in the different states. The question is, what should these measures be?

The simplest and, in view of the cumulative nature of science, most fruitful approach is to relate to a firm, well-founded tradition within the field of research – that is, if such a tradition exists. As was mentioned earlier, however, this is hardly the case. When we survey the fairly extensive research hitherto pursued we are immediately struck by the variation which prevails regarding the indicators of democracy which have come into use.[1] In the face of this motley assortment we can only state that whoever undertakes this task must make his or her own choice of indicators and give reasons for his or her stance. Such, in brief, is our starting-point.

How are we to proceed? It is clear that if the choice of empirical indicators is to be convincing it must relate to, and reflect the fundamental criterion of the theory of democracy, namely the general principles which characterize democratic government. This link 'backward' (or 'upward' if this is preferred) may be rendered more or less explicit and circumstantial. The common feature of the great majority of the studies is that the most convenient approach was chosen; the author takes the underlying criteria more or less for granted and instead concentrates on explaining which empirical measures and methods of enquiry will be used.[2] This strategy is understandable since it is thereby possible without further ado to plunge into work and tackle the practical issues. The disadvantage is that we do not really know whether we are measuring what we set out to measure; the variation regarding indicators unquestionably gives grounds for general doubt on that point.

The problem is inherent in the issue: the very concept of democracy is a difficult (and perhaps also frustrating) one to tackle. As Robert Dahl says: 'Perhaps the greatest error in thinking about democratic authority is to believe that ideas about democracy and authority are simple and must lead to simple prescriptions.'[3] The distressing fact is that the principles of democracy are not wholly unequivocal and unchallenged in their implications; indeed in some respects they are even highly controversial (e.g., a recently published book on the subject bears the significant title 'The Battle of Democracy').[4] Is it then possible to do anything at all about the matter? Is not the concept of democracy so ambiguous and open to diverse interpretations that every attempt firmly to define it only becomes one voice among many in the large (and discordant) 'democratic chorus'? Not necessarily. I would maintain that it is indeed possible to give the concept of democracy a fairly clear content, at least at its heart. For everything is not in dispute and, although opinions differ, it is nevertheless feasible to spell out the main content – and we can hardly, in the social sciences, require much more of an investigation of a complicated concept.

It goes without saying that the definition which I shall present derives from certain premises. Firstly, it is based on a core formula concerning the principles of democracy (which I believe to be generally accepted). Secondly, it is framed by certain supportive arguments of methodological character which – in order that they may be clear from the outset – I will now introduce.[5]

(1) Definitions are commonly required to relate to accepted linguistic usage. While this requirement is very reasonable in terms of practical communications, we must admit that it does not lead us very far in our field. The Greek word *demokratia* means 'government by the people'. But we cannot define it further with the help of the conventions of linguistic usage.[6] Even if we confine ourselves to the scholarly debate we must admit that the concrete significance of the term has varied considerably. Indeed, as is well known, the principles of democracy have been championed in both Eastern and Western Europe. At the same time the forms of government which have been applied are radically different. In the controversy which

ensued linguistic usage can be of little help – for this is the crux of the problem.[7]

In order to escape from this and other, similar, disputes we could, as Robert Dahl suggested, resort to another term. For his part Dahl recommends the designation 'polyarchy' for the form of government which he analyses.[8] Yet he has met with little success.[9] The new designation has not won general acceptance, and even Dahl himself in his writings often diverged from his linguistic innovation and speaks just of democracy and non-democracy respectively in different countries. And I believe this is unavoidable. The word 'democracy' is so firmly established that we cannot disregard it. The problem is that it has been subjected to prolonged linguistic 'stretching'; hence the alleged ambiguity of the concept. As I hope later to demonstrate, however, the actual concept – the attribute of democracy – is far more precise than the use of the word in different contexts.

(2) Mention was made above of the relationship between term and concept (the meaning of the term). We shall now turn to another relationship, that between the concept and its reference, that is its equivalent in the world of the senses. Since we are bent on pursuing explanatory empirical studies we obviously want a concept (and therewith a dependent variable) which at least to some extent has an actual reference. Otherwise there would be no variation worth investigating. The question is what degree of linkage with reality do we require? Here I would plead for the moderate (and maybe seemingly self-evident) principle that the form of government we call democratic must be subject to realization among people who are alive today, and should apply to the organizational and infrastructural procedures for collective decision-making of which we have knowledge.[10] The point is that we cannot hold the view that for its realization democracy requires a wholly different breed of people, or that it demands purely speculative organizational and societal conditions of which we can have no knowledge today.[11]

At the same time, we obviously cannot be mere realists. The fact that a form of government can be realized does not entitle it to the epithet 'democratic'. It must also conform to a reasonable extent to the central principles of democracy. Thus we set two requirements: that the form of government be *possible* to realize, and that it appears *desirable* on grounds of principle.

(3) As stated above, our definition will follow from a core formula which incorporates certain essential democratic principles. These can be seen as general objectives which are eventually explicated and finally given an operational significance. We then adopt an essentially deductive approach; we logically derive certain implications from our nuclear criteria. We may thereby encounter problems since the criteria are not crystal clear and, in some cases, there may also be tension between them. Moreover, we must take into account the requirement of realism from which significant consequences ensue. This means that empirical assertions – concerning both facts and the connections between them – are included in the work of definition. The logical inferences are made, we may say, in a context of empirical knowledge. Given our knowledge of how different institutional arrangements function, conclusions can be derived from the core concepts concerning what democracy in actual appearance should be like.

Thus, a problem arises concerning how the definition should be delimited.[12] The overall objective is indeed to specify a concept which can be used in causal analysis, that is to examine the empirical connection between democracy and a number of external features. But already in order to determine what is to be explained (democracy) we must posit several empirical assumptions. And since these are inherent in the concept they are, so to speak, fixed; they cannot be held open for later empirical testing. At the same time we wish, when performing a study, to test as much as possible, which means that we want a minimum of 'locks' at the outset of our work.

Consequently this is the problem: the more we postulate in the definition, the less there is to study. Our ambition should therefore be to incorporate as few firm statements as possible in the specification of the concept.[13] The aim must then be only to include such as can be established with a high degree of confidence, on the basis of our nuclear criteria and with the knowledge we possess. However, in areas of uncertainty – regarding both the desirable and the possible – the question should preferably be left open.

CHAPTER 2

Political democracy

The issue of interest to us is democracy in a specific sphere of society, namely political democracy. And to delimit our subject still further, I would emphasize that we are only concerned with political democracy on the national level. Thus, the focus of interest is the control of the highest organs of state, those which determine the overall public policy, which is primarily pursued via legislation. Political democracy may in this context be formulated as follows:

Public policy is to be governed by the freely expressed will of the people whereby all individuals are to be treated as equals.

This articulates a general principle of popular sovereignty and autonomy; the people are to rule themselves. Their explicit preferences therefore constitute the ultimate ground for the legitimacy of political decision-making. To this is linked a principle of freedom; so far as possible the free, uninhibited will of the people is to be expressed in the political decision-making – and, we may add, no individual preferences shall then be regarded as superior to others. In the latter we find an obvious principle of equality.

Many would surely agree on these principles for democracy as a mode of government. The problems arise when we would go on to say what they may be thought to mean in concrete terms. For the ideas so formulated are only general aims which may allow scope for diverse interpretations. Moreover we may – as realists – not only consider the objectives; these must be confronted with our knowledge of facts, so that the forms of government which are prescribed may to a reasonable extent be adjudged capable of materialization.

Let us begin with the principle of equality. It enjoins that all individuals be treated alike in the political decision-making. This means, firstly, that all will be included and enfranchised, and that, secondly, every individual vote will have the same value.[1] In other

9

words, there may not be any privileges for certain sections of the population. All is fairly clear so far. Yet, it is by no means obvious how the votes cast are to be aggregated, i.e., how they are to be counted together and constitute a decision.

DECISION RULES

Inasmuch as all individuals must be involved and thereby support the decisions once made, unanimity would appear to be the reasonable solution. The advantage of this rule for decisions is its guarantee that every change in public policy is supported by all who may (directly or indirectly) be affected. Its disadvantage is that it is not neutral *vis-à-vis* the various alternative decisions which appear on the agenda; the requirement of only one vote to block a change confers a strong advantage on all proposals which signify preservation of the status quo.[2]

Instead, the majority rule has traditionally been regarded as the most natural for decisions; sometimes it is even represented as an essential characteristic of democracy.[3] Yet the arguments in favour of this method have varied. Giovanni Sartori is here the most pragmatic. He holds that the choice of decision rule should primarily be seen as a technical problem, as a convention which we apply in order to resolve conflicts smoothly. The majority rule then has an advantage purely in terms of efficiency; since it only requires that half the votes plus one of those cast support a proposal it is fairly easy to reach a decision. Consequently, this method offers low decision costs. With this as our sole consideration we could *per se*, as Sartori remarks, make the process even simpler; by applying the plurality method[4] we could reduce the decision costs still further. But other aspects must also be taken into account. Sartori mentions the protection of minority rights. With this in mind we may in certain contexts have reason to apply diverse rules of qualified majority. In any case, according to Sartori, it is hardly a principle of equality which governs (or should govern) our choice of decision rules.[5]

Another, more positive argumentation in favour of the majority criterion is to be found in Douglas Rae and Michael Taylor. They show, very convincingly, that with a presumption of ignorance (in the spirit of Rawls) of the questions which will arise and the attitudes which others will adopt, the majority rule gives the greatest possibility for each to be on the winning side. Thus all have a maximal chance to control public policy and thereby ensure that their political preferences are followed.[6] This argumentation is wholly irreproachable as long as we presume ignorance and that the majority (as regards the individuals involved) may alter from one issue to another. But, as several commentators have remarked, this is by no means always the case.[7] Due to deep divisions, the political life in certain countries is characterized by firmly fixed majority and minority situations (Northern Ireland, Sri Lanka and Zimbabwe may be mentioned as examples). Rae is himself aware of this possible objection to his argumentation. Yet, he points out, there is no reasonable way to solve this problem, i.e., that a united fraction of the population could, via the voting method, invariably gain the upper hand.[8] In this he is, so far as I can see, wholly correct. The conclusion is that the equality – in terms of the same probability of controlling public policy – which according to Rae and Taylor may be achieved under the majority rule, cannot be attained save under special, actual circumstances. In other words, this line of reasoning cannot be said to possess general validity.[9]

Is it perhaps impossible adequately to justify the majority rule on the basis of the principle of equal treatment of the citizens' preferences? If the answer is in the affirmative – and if we find no other method which better fits the principle – we should rather, like Sartori, see the choice of decision rule as a technical issue where for different purposes (other than those here in focus) we can apply the method which seems most practical on discretionary grounds. This then is not a cardinal issue of democracy.

Nevertheless I would maintain that there are strong reasons to stick to the majority rule on the basis of the principle of democratic equality – and this without any assumptions of ignorance or a certain distribution of preferences among the population. The argument is that the majority method alone guarantees that every vote cast has the same relative strength and thereby the same effect on the decisions reached. In a body of (say) 100 individuals, the majority rule requires 51 votes for approval of a proposal to change public policy, and an equal number for its rejection.[10] This means that each vote's relative contribution to the proposal is the same in both cases $(1/51)$.[11] If, instead, a two-thirds majority is applied, 67 votes are required for approval and 34 for rejection, which means that the votes against are worth almost twice as much. With a three-quarters majority their value almost triples, and with a requirement of unanimity (whereby each voter has a veto), the only essential vote against is worth 100 times more than the votes needed for consent.[12]

Thus the majority rule has an obvious correspondence to the principle of democratic equality: the idea that all preferences – as they are manifested in votes cast – should be treated alike. This, as a decision rule alone, guarantees neutrality, i.e., that submitted proposals for decision receive the same treatment.[13]

Consequently the majority method must always be regarded as a central rule of democratic procedure. It means that strong reasons must be adduced when exceptions are made to this rule; these should be reasons which from an internal democratic standpoint appear, at least, just as demanding of consideration (for, as our core formula shows, the equality principle is not the only one which we must take into account). In order to protect the democratic form of decision-making *per se* (including the democratic principles of freedom), it may be reasonable to limit the majority rule. On the other hand, it is not reasonable from an internal democratic standpoint to do so in questions pertaining to the material content of the public policy (such as concern the state's finances, cultural policy, defence policy etc.). There is indeed then always a risk that the majority in different spheres will obtain significant advantages at the expense of the rest of the population. The issue thus consists in the danger of 'the tyranny of the majority' against which the Founding Fathers of the American Constitution, particularly James Madison, strongly warned.[14] Nevertheless we must (albeit with sadness) conclude that a narrow-minded majority rule is not in itself undemocratic. For, as Rae remarked, there is no other, better rule available to avoid the 'risk of tyranny'. The alternative – some form of qualified majority – likewise involves the risk of 'tyranny by the minority' which is hardly to be preferred.

The significance of government by the people

Now for another wide range of problems illuminated by our core formula, namely the principle that *public policy is to be governed by the people* (the idea of popular sovereignty). What exactly does this signify? On reflection we already find that interpretation of the term 'the people' poses serious difficulties. Despite all that has been said and written on the meaning of democracy (paradoxically enough, one might say), surprisingly few thinkers have undertaken precisely to define the 'demos' – the circle of individuals who are to govern.

We have already determined that in principle all are to participate, but who are these 'all'? One way to delimit the circle of individuals is to say that all who are affected by the public policy are to share in the control of its direction.[15] But this definition unfortunately has its shortcomings. Obviously the citizens of a country are affected (although more or less depending on the issue) by the decisions which its national bodies reach. But so also are others who sojourn there for short or long periods (refugees, guest-workers, business people etc.). Furthermore, there is sometimes ground to maintain that decisions made in certain states also in large measure affect individuals in other countries – indeed perhaps a high proportion of the world's population. Then, one may ask, should not all these outsiders – but all the same afflicted – participate in the decision? With this flexible criterion we could finally find ourselves wholly befogged.[16]

The problem is that we cannot create a criterion of delimitation which is much better. In any case, the theory of democracy gives us no such thing. It takes, I think it is fair to say, the circle of individuals for granted by convention (historically and geographically[17]); assuming that there is a people, a limited *demos*, the theory points out what form its self-government will take.

Consequently the difficulty is that the principles of democracy in this case do not give us any clear guidance. At the same time we must (in order later to establish whether or not there is a universal franchise) have a criterion. Under these circumstances there is reason to apply the rule of method which was mentioned above, namely to make a cautious interpretation in the event of uncertainty. What we can then establish beyond doubt is that the citizens of a state should be included in the circle of individuals. In some countries others too who reside there may have the franchise, but the convention here is far from clear and undisputed.[18]

Thus our main rule is to link the circle of individuals to citizenship. Only in cases where this criterion has obviously been manipulated – so as to introduce different kinds of citizenship (whereby certain groups of the population are excluded from the franchise) – can this rule be abandoned.[19]

However, it is far more complicated to investigate what the people are by definition intended to do, namely to control public

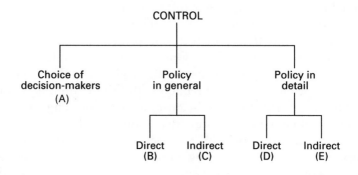

Figure 1. Five kinds of control by the people.

policy. The concrete significance of this clause constitutes the most controversial issue in the debate on the meaning of democracy. As we shall see, several related problems will arise on the agenda. In order to sort out the material there is reason at the outset to distinguish between (I) the object of the control and (II) the form the control takes. Let us begin with the former. Here three options may be roughly differentiated. The most ambitious is case (i) where the people control all public decisions and thereby also the details of policy. In a more limited type of control (ii) the people only give the general guiding lines for the design of public policy but do not pass judgement on the details and the concrete methods. Finally, the least ambitious are the cases (iii) where the control is confined to the appointment of public decision-makers; the people elect their rulers but cannot influence what these later do.

Now for the second aspect; the form of control. Here we distinguish between the direct and the indirect method. The point at issue is (as all should realise) whether the people themselves make the crucial decisions, or whether these are reached by some form of representative. If these two aspects are combined we obtain the control options shown in Fig. 1.

How do these options correspond to the requirements we have reason to set when we speak of political democracy? The most problematic is of course Position A, where the people only elect the decision-makers. Nevertheless, it could be maintained that even this is acceptable so long as the process is open for different kinds of candidates from whom the people can make their choice. Joseph

Schumpeter's formulation of the meaning of democracy contains this very point: we must content ourselves with merely a possibility of appointing our political leadership in open competition but we cannot ask more: 'democracy does not mean and cannot mean that the people actually rule in any obvious sense of the terms "people" and "rule". Democracy means only that people have the opportunity of accepting or refusing the men who are to rule them.'[20]

Schumpeter bases his stance on what he understands as a realistic assessment of facts, that is, of how the democracies he knows actually work.[21] More than he demands is, he thinks, impossible to achieve. This assessment of reality will be examined later. But let us assume for the moment that he is right. The question is then to what extent do the forms of decision-making which he considered deserve to be called democratic in the light of the principles which are to characterize this mode of government. Schumpeter deliberately avoids this question by stating that democracy is only a technique, a method of making decisions. Thus it cannot have any intrinsic value.[22] This is, however, a far too simple evasive manoeuvre. All forms of government in practice consist just in methods and techniques of making decisions. The remaining question is what differentiates the various forms of decision-making. And this cannot reasonably be determined without reference to certain general values which they can be said to realise in at least some measure.[23]

May we then be content with a control which is confined to the choice of decision-makers? If the answer is in the affirmative, we must surely permit ourselves a somewhat qualified interpretation of the democratic principles. It is indeed better for a people to be able to choose their rulers than not. Even if the people give *carte blanche* with reference to the decisions which are to be made, they can still determine what type of persons are to exercise this power. They may therefore be said, albeit weakly, to control public policy; by being able to choose the individuals whom they trust with respect to general judgement, ability to act etc. – and, on the other hand, to dismiss those whom they distrust or dislike – they can at least influence a component in the political decision-making. They control, one could say, the way in which policy is handled but not its substantial content. This is not much, but far better than nothing.

Obviously, from our core formula it would be an advantage if the democratic process could give something more, namely a possibility of controlling also the substantial decision-making. Such is offered, to a varying degree, in the other positions in the figure. At first glance the most attractive option is of course Combination D. Here the people themselves, without intermediaries, make all the decisions, even those on detailed questions of policy. What more could one ask? This is the participatory, populistic (and also anarchistic) ideal democracy. Option C appears in comparison to be a somewhat diluted variant. Here the ultimate decisions are consistently made by elected representatives who, furthermore, possess considerable freedom of action, since the guide-lines they are provided with are generally worded. Nevertheless, it is not certain that even this can be attained. Our former acquaintance, Schumpeter, had, as we saw, no expectations on that point. If he is correct, we must be content with a relatively weak significance of the term 'government by the people'.

The problem which we now face can be divided into two. The first pertains to the people's competence and ability: without a more or less distinct and articulate popular opinion on the factual matters of politics, we can hardly begin to talk of control by the people.[24] Given that such a popular opinion exists, the second question concerns whether it is feasible to aggregate the different views to a collective decision which corresponds in reasonable measure to individual preferences. If not, the process becomes rather futile. Thus we are faced with partly a rationality problem, partly a representation problem.[25]

The question of the citizens' political competence and rationality has been examined in many public opinion polls and election studies. When this research was launched in the 1940s and extended in the following decade a somewhat gloomy picture emerged. The ordinary citizen appeared as largely ignorant of the factual issues of politics and often, indeed, indifferent to the topics which were discussed in connection with the election campaigns. The contrast to the small group of the population which was politically committed (by assignments etc.) thereby was striking. Several of the leading survey researchers concluded that democracy in the sense that the people, the common man, controlled the national policy was not only unrealistic but also, under the circumstances, undesirable. In Schumpeter's spirit, the emphasis instead became the appointment of representatives as the central element of popular rule. Through their greater competence and far wider view these were the guarantees of the long-term survival of the system.[26]

This interpretation of the electorate's ability would not however be the last and final. The political behavioural research of later periods yields, on the whole, a more balanced and, for popular government, more hopeful description of the situation. In a study in the 1960s which attracted much attention, V. O. Key maintained that the voters were not fools. Despite their weak commitment and a lack of knowledge of details, they could in general terms make a rational choice among the main political options. Key's study of those who switch between parties – who tended to be among the most ignorant and ill-informed of the electorate – demonstrated this point; the change was usually prompted by the belief that the party for which the vote was cast better agreed with the elector's own preferences. Thus the act of voting was not fortuitous even for this group. The general judgement is instead that the electorate is 'moved by concern about central and relevant questions of public policy, of governmental performance, and of executive personality'.[27]

As has been confirmed in many later studies, the point at issue is that the people make their choices, in the main, on the basis of wide-ranging attitudes to public policy. In this respect there is a fairly close agreement between people's political views and their voting. At the same time the results indicate considerable ignorance of details. Often only a minority of the population can correctly answer questions even on such topical issues as the level of unemployment and whether the budget deficit has increased or diminished.[28] Consequently, if we impose strict requirements for rationality – which was in large measure the premise for the first 'wave' of electoral polls – we can still today state that the electorate is highly incompetent as a ruling party. The participational ideal, that the people are to be decision-makers in detailed issues of policy, is therefore far from realistic. If, on the other hand, we desire that the citizens provide the guiding lines for the general orientation of public policy, we stand on much firmer ground. The significance of voting seems in reality to be, on the part of the citizenry, to impose a general task as regards political objectives, but to entrust the elected representatives to decide what means (and by the same token what technical solutions) will be the most suitable:

If all that the voters do, through the mechanisms of parties and elections, is to give a general nudge to the ship of state, indicating approval or disapproval of the course it is taking, that is no mean contribution. It may be presumed that citizens know more about what their desires are than about how to attain them; and more about their satisfaction or dissatisfaction with public policy than about how to improve it. If their indication is an unfavorable one, those they elect will be under pressure to find out how to change the situation if they wish to avoid a fate similar to their predecessors.[29]

Thus we may say with a fair degree of certainty that the citizens can function as rational rulers in a wide, general sense. But more than this can hardly be achieved. This conclusion is frequently contradicted by those who advocate participation. They believe that increased participation and a greater responsibility for the design of policy prompts people to become both more interested and more cognizant of various questions of political fact. The process thereby gives rise to a self-strengthening educational effect:

The major function of participation in the theory of participatory democracy is . . . an educative one, educative in the very widest sense, including both the psychological aspect and the gaining of practice in democratic skills and procedures. Thus there is no special problem about the stability of a participatory system; it is self-sustaining through the educative impact of the participatory process. Participation develops and fosters the very qualities necessary for it; the more individuals participate the better able they become to do so.[30]

We seldom if ever see any proof, however, that this effect actually ensues (which is indeed difficult to produce inasmuch as it pertains primarily to a situation in an imaginary future).[31] Thus all we have is a hopeful hypothesis, the validity of which is only conjectural. For instance, the sceptic may point to the fact that in Sweden, with its by international standards very high electoral participation (long around 90 per cent), only one-fourth of the population is aware of whether or not the budget deficit has increased[32] – if the electorate does not even know this, one may ask, is it other than utopian to believe that, with other modes of decision, the people would be so much more familiar with different, far more complex issues on which the participationists feel the people should decide?

Given that the people are capable of actively articulating their opinions on public policy, which in the above (general) sense may be considered feasible, is it then, to turn to the next problem, possible to weigh these individual preferences together in a decision that is representative of the collectivity? The difficulty is that no form of aggregation of preferences is wholly neutral: whatever the method chosen it affects the outcome. With a given number of options (X, Y, Z), and several individual rankings of preferences around them (X > Y > Z, Y > Z > X etc.), different decisions can be reached solely dependent on which method of voting is applied; indeed, in certain cases an option may emerge victorious notwithstanding that several individuals would, in a single-paired comparison, choose otherwise. When applying a certain decision method it is also possible (more or less) to manipulate the result by tactical voting (i.e., at some stage of the voting to support another option than that actually desired). Manipulation of the agenda (by withdrawing options or inserting others) can also affect the outcome.

This implies that no complete, reliable reflection of individual preferences is possible. 'The instrument' to measure the opinion (in a decision-making body or a constituency) always dictates the result to some extent. Thus the rule of the people is beset by a disturbing element of imperfection and fortuitousness. This also allows scope for deliberate manipulation of the decision-making process.[33]

What are the consequences thereof for the theory of democracy? According to William Riker, the said difficulties have a devastating effect on the advocates of the populistic (participative) principles. For if by democracy we mean that what the people want should be public policy – which Riker sees as the essence of populism – we have set up an ideal which (simply because of the aggregation problem) is impossible to attain.[34] What he calls the liberal interpretation of democracy, however, is less afflicted. For its primary purpose is only to achieve a satisfactory control of those who make the decisions. This control is confined not merely to choosing rulers. Insofar as the elections are open, competitive, and regularly held, the representatives are compelled to accede to public opinion in different policy decisions, otherwise they may not be re-elected – this form of indirect control may be called the principle of anticipated reaction.[35] Thus the liberal tradition requires that the people may 'penalize' (vote out of office) disobedient or otherwise unpopular decision-makers. But, even with this objective, problems naturally arise in consequence of imperfection and fortuitousness in the voting procedure. According to the liberal interpretation, however, these do not constitute a major dilemma, in Riker's view. The objective is merely a *possibility* to get rid of unwanted representatives; it is not necessary that this be feasible in every individual case, only that it may be so sometimes.[36]

However, this evaluation of the two models of democracy does not appear convincing. For the basis of the conclusions is that Riker assigns to the populistic view a wholly unqualified perfectionist content: that the will of the people should be reflected simply and fully in public policy. This is opposed to an extremely pragmatic liberal position which, by and large, implies contentment with the imperfect form of control which is possible in reality. That the latter position holds while the former collapses is then hardly remarkable. What Riker failed to do was to provide both standpoints with the best possible interpretation given their purposes.[37] It is indeed true (which could be adduced in Riker's defence) that the adherents of participationism seldom bother to penetrate the aggregation problem and therefore speak light-heartedly of the realization of the will of the people. But this must not prevent us from giving their position a more qualified, reasonable interpretation. Populism too, in my understanding, can be assigned a flexible content inasmuch as its main purpose – an active rule by the people – may be realized as far as this is possible. Thus, conscious of the difficulties inherent in aggregation, we as advocates of this idea could assert that even if our objectives cannot be always and fully attained, we should have an ambition to achieve insofar as is possible, direct popular control of public policy. If we adopt this position, Riker's point obviously vanishes.[38]

Let us now turn to the empirical side of the matter. Is it true that the problems of imperfection which we have seen theoretically illustrated have, in reality, so great an impact that the choices and the decision-making which ensue to a large extent resemble a random process? Representation studies in the few countries where such have been systematically executed give, so far as comparisons can be made, a fairly uniform picture. Parallel studies of the opinions on various political issues held by members of parliament and by the public indicate an average difference of 15 per cent in the distribution of responses[39] (otherwise expressed, the answers show a correlation slightly over 0.30). Thus there seems to be a manifest, if not strong, general connection between the views of the electorate and those of their representatives. As could have been expected, from what was said above, the correspondence is closest for the political issues which have long stood at the centre of the political debate.[40] Thus, if we are not perfectionists with respect to correspondence, we may say that it is possible through the procedure to achieve a decent reflection of the citizens' preferences, at least in certain crucial areas of policy.

The conclusion is that we can hardly consider ourselves obliged to accept Schumpeter's modulated interpretation. Studies of the electoral process in such countries as he himself mentions indicate rather that popular government may have a stronger significance; apart from the choice of decision-makers, it also seems possible essentially to achieve control of the general trend of public policy. In other words, Position C in the figure may be regarded as a feasible option insofar as it fulfils our criterion; to be subject to realization among the people, and with the organizational forms, which we know of today. At the same time this is not to say that it is always possible. All we can assert is that somewhere (indeed in several places) in the world we know it is feasible to achieve the form of popular control of the national policy which is here described.

What then may be said of the other options? Let us begin with the most attractive combination from the participatory viewpoint, Position D, where the people control the public policy without intermediaries in both the general and the particular. As many authors have remarked, such an order is wholly unrealistic in the states which we have today. The obstacles may be summarized in three words: 'size, time and complexity'.[41] The classic democracy, as it was applied particularly in ancient Athens, presumed small territories and a small population which could regularly gather for decision-making in an open popular assembly. But in a state larger than a small town such a mode of government is not practicable (if only for reasons of space and meeting procedures). We could indeed say with Rousseau that the state should be adapted to the ideal form of government, and advocate a division of the giant states of today into micro-units, and thereby accept the costs in other respects which would ensue (in the shape of reduced defence capacity, which was the Greeks' fate, limitations on economy and commerce etc.).[42] But, since this solution presumably appears to the majority as unduly utopian, and probably not even attractive – after all, 'democracy' is not all we want of life – we must adjust the government to the states which *de facto* exist. A democracy in which the people make the decisions 'face to face' is then almost unthinkable. In order to retain as far as possible a strong civic co-operation in the decision-making, we must then either use referenda or a very restrictive representation system, where the elected representatives may only appear as delegates with bound mandates (which is the form best suited to Position E). Referenda (i.e., plebiscites) constitute a method applied in many places[43] and is, of course, a realistic solution, but only to a limited extent. For here the problems of 'time and complexity' enter the picture. We have already referred in passing to these difficulties. They pertain to the citizens' interest and ability to grasp all the political topics at issue and, in addition, to set aside all the time for participation which the decision-making procedure would require. If we disregard all imaginable hypotheses of a happier future, we must curtly say that the people which the model, when fully applied, presupposes[44] are not to be found anywhere in the world we know. This *inter alia* is why referenda, in the states where they are applied, are only used in practice as a very limited supplement to the representative mode of decision-making.[45]

The same argument affects the delegate system (representatives with bound mandates). This also requires, if it is to achieve its purpose, a very active civic involvement in the political issues of the day – otherwise the mandators (the people) cannot bind the representatives whom they elect. There is another difficulty too – that the agenda for decision is always changeable; new issues constantly arise – by reason of external circumstances or in consequence of other actors' behaviour – which the mandators naturally cannot foresee. In complicated contexts (such as modern government life) the model is therefore impossible to apply.[46]

Consequently, none of the purely participative options – the policy-making popular assembly, referenda, the delegate system – seem to be able to function as a primary form of democratic decision-making. By and large, only Position C in Figure 1 remains as a functioning system of substantial control; this involves a representative form and explicit control only in general policy issues; the representatives themselves must decide on methods and details. This may in some measure be supplemented by referenda, particularly in some public policy issues which have attracted much attention.[47] Nevertheless it should be reiterated that what is here described as a possible degree of control may not be attainable in every context nor in all kinds of state. In those countries where the general educational level is low and the infrastructural forms for collective decision-making relatively undeveloped – which is true of large areas of the Third World – there is reason to assume that the control foremost resembles the weaker meaning of the concept that Schumpeter suggests[48] (which, as stated, is not inessential from a democratic viewpoint; the lack of any potential for control is far worse). In brief, the points I would make are, firstly, that a degree of control corresponding to Position C is not, as is sometimes alleged, merely a utopian idea and, secondly, that a more intensive control than this is adjudged hardly practicable. In other words, we have reached a standpoint 'in the middle of the road': it does not relate to a categorical 'minimalism' as regards the possible function of democracy, but nor does it support a committed populistic 'maximalism'.

A NOTE ON THE IDEAL ALTERNATIVE

The point we have now reached of course pertains only to what is practicable (according to our requirement of realism). Nevertheless, one could perhaps consider that the desirable (the ideal) is to be found elsewhere. This argument is presented by many modern participation democrats; faced with all the practical obstacles they (more or less) abandon their 'projects', and accept the ordinary representative system as the chief mode of decision-making at the national level. But they often do so reluctantly. What remains is that a distinctive participatory system is to be preferred from a democratic viewpoint. Indeed, they maintain, only such a system can offer real democracy.[49] Accordingly the government with which the people must live is only a torso, a cryptodemocracy. (Indeed, this idea recurs in Robert Dahl; hence his epithet 'polyarchy' for 'representative democracy as we know it in practice' – the term 'democracy' is instead reserved for a utopian ideal situation which we can never fully attain.)[50]

In order to pacify our democratic conscience (of which we are constantly reminded in the said ways) we must therefore show that the possible system is not distinctly inferior in the light of the guiding principles of political democracy. We do this on the basis of a scrutiny of the ideal alternative, the participatory model, as it would function if it were ever somehow applied.

We begin with the possible practitioners of popular government. The model would require another citizen than those we daily encounter. It presumes a people who tackle all political issues with zeal and knowledge. In short, it requires a 'humanity' which is characterized by a veritable passion for politics. This very thing (or at least a marked development in this direction) is also the explicit objective of many participationists. The idea is that the active participation in the decision-making will change the citizen into a more collectively conscious, solidaristic, and politically responsible individual. This thought is often linked to a vision of a radical change of the society toward communitarianism and socialism.[51]

Whether or not this picture of the future is desirable cannot, however, be determined to any significant extent from the principles of political democracy. The primary point at issue concerns the type of people we want around us and the kind of society in which we wish to live. We frequently hold very different opinions on such matters. And in order to settle the disputes which thereby arise we may apply democracy as a form of decision-making. In this sense democracy is simply a method for the peaceful solution of conflicts; it says nothing *per se* on what substantial decisions we should make as regards the general development of society. There is indeed in principle nothing wrong in asserting that the decision method should be devised to also promote other goals in social life. But then it is primarily these goals which we shall discuss and assess.[52] The participationist vision is hereby only one option among many.

In order to elucidate the argument, it is worth mentioning what political democracy prescribes, i.e., that if a population occupying a territory unites into a state, this state must be governed by the people. Furthermore it declares, more precisely, the form this government should take (some of which has already emerged). But it does not prescribe the composition of the population in spiritual or other respects – only that it, such as it is, should rule. This may, of course, be more or less practicable, but it is then a matter of the purely empirical requisites of democracy – not what democracy *per se* should signify, which we are now considering. Nor does democracy as a political form of government dictate how the people should develop in other respects; this is something which may be determined with democracy as a method. All that we can say in this regard is that an attempt should be made to create the social organization (etc.) which the majority of the citizens want.[53]

Thus the primary issue concerns how the actual decision-making process functions, i.e., how different arrangements create the requisites to enable the majority of the people's preferences (whatever they are) to impinge on public policy. Since this pertains in essence to representation we return to the problems of aggregation. A question left unanswered in our treatment of Riker's argument was whether the two models discussed differ in any other respects from that which he takes as his premise (a difference which primarily consisted because one side was given a locked, perfectionist interpretation). This question will now be raised. Hence, we find that participationism as regards reflection of preferences may offer a manifest advantage. In its simplest, purest form it signifies that the people themselves, without proxies and intermediaries, make the ultimate decisions. The problems are thereby reduced to a single aggregation point. If we have, on the other hand, an indirect system, we have several aggregation stages (we elect representatives, who elect representatives . . . who make decisions). The more intermediate stages there are in a decision-making process, the greater the risk of fortuitousness and manipulation since every phase involves a new aggregation. Advocates of indirect decision-making methods should be fully aware of this state of affairs. And, vice versa, the reduction of this risk to a minimum – and the uncontrolled rule by the elite which in the worst case may therefore be feared – gives participationism (in its pure form) much of its attraction.

Paradoxically enough, such renowned participationists as G. D. H. Cole and C. B. Macpherson seem wholly unaware of the circumstances discussed here. Thus, because they must for practical reasons propose a representative model, they suggest a pyramidal system with an abundance of intermediate stages from the smallest local level to the national (whereby the aggregation problems would be enormous). In Macpherson's case, it is an explicitly Soviet system which is outlined. However, in view of how this system has actually come to function in some quarters, the author immediately encounters difficulties in sorting out how his ideal government by the people could fulfil even elementary requirements of democracy![54]

But let us ignore these misdirected suggestions for application and confine ourselves to the wholly direct (pure) model. As stated, its great advantage is that it offers a minimum of intervening stages and difficulties of aggregation. However, other aspects too must be weighed in the assessment. One problem with the participatory form is its high requirement of activity and interest on the part of the population. As we saw, this is expected to come into being as an effect of the modes of decision-making which are to be applied. Thus the process becomes self-reinforcing. But what happens if 'the cure', once administered, does not work, or does so very slowly? There is here reason to recall that the sometimes much applauded Athenian direct democracy was characterized by an extremely low participation; normally, so far as can be calculated, between five and 10 per cent of the citizens attended the popular assembly and took part in the decision-making[55] – and this notwithstanding that the system was in force for a very long period and under comparatively favourable conditions (the size of the state etc.). In other words, there is a grave danger that the intended 'participatory democracy' involves a very *low* participation (i.e., that we find ourselves in the paradox of utopianism: the inverted result).[56] In consequence of the high activity requirement, the most politically interested part of the population then wields the power. The problem – from the point of view of representativity – is that those who are deeply committed politically are seldom a cross-section of the population in terms of social status or opinion. The individuals who belong to this group are in general better educated and usually occupy extreme positions in different dimensions of opinion (right/left scale etc.).[57] Rule by this group would hardly guarantee a fair reflection of the preferences of the majority of the people.

One advantage of the ordinary representative form (via periodic elections) is that it sets a very low activity threshold, enabling even the moderately interested to make their presence felt. The minority with strong political interest are thereby denied the comparative procedural advantage which they enjoy with the other model.[58]

Finally, a few words about referenda and delegate systems, both of which (by and large) have the aforesaid advantages and disadvantages. The particular point about referenda concerns the setting of the agenda (the formulation of the alternative proposals). Since it is not feasible to take a vote thereon, some person or persons must make the decision, which (as has often been shown in practice) may allow wide scope for tactical manipulation.[59] The method is undoubtedly most suitable in such questions (of great public interest) as allow of a simple dichotomy: yes or no. But in cases where because of the nature of things there is reason to offer several options, e.g., in the form of a scale or a weft of many different components, it is difficult to devise a reasonable ('neutral') agenda and elicit a clear, unambiguous outcome in a plebiscite. In such cases the method is often highly uncertain as a 'tie-breaker'.[60]

The greatest problem with the delegate system is, of course, the tight lock on the representatives' scope for manoeuvre. The aim is to prevent the representatives, once elected, from 'going their own way' and, as decision-makers, diverging from the desires of their principals. The problem consists in the constant changing of the agenda for decision. When new issues arise (or new solutions to old problems) the delegate can do nothing save wait for directives. 'The decision-makers' are thus paralysed for much of their time. This price in the shape of considerable costs of decisions could, however (from a strictly ideal viewpoint), be adjudged well worth the paying for the benefit of popular government. But we would then have a particular notion of the process of democratic government – that the desired correspondence must always precede the fact – before the decision is made. In the usual representative form the elected individual is given a very free assignment. Equipped with certain general guidelines by their principals the representatives may reach decisions according to their own judgement and capacity. If in the eyes of their electors they do a poor job they risk not being re-elected. Instead of detailed control in advance, we here work with a combination of control before and after the fact, which furthermore is very general in both cases. At the same time we incorporate an element of incentive control. In the face of the scrutiny which always awaits, the representative has reason to act in a way which will win the electors' approval.

The role of free representative also confers a manifest advantage; it yields decision-makers who, smoothly and effectively, can enter into compromises and, with reference to the changing priorities of different groups, can carry on political barter – 'if you support me on this I shall support you on other issues'. All such practices require negotiations which for technical reasons of decision-making can only occur between a few actors who meet in person and enter into agreements. Such activities are hardly possible in a large, anonymous assembly of individuals. Indeed this is why so large a proportion of parliamentary decision-making is executed *de facto* by commissions (and at party congresses in different committees); otherwise it would not be possible to reach agreements acceptable to opposing groups.[61] The point is that such 'corridor politics' may be highly expedient regarding the aim to translate as far as possible the electors' preferences into public policy (that is, if we are not total perfectionists concerning the realization of the will of the people – if we were, Rikers's argument would be valid). Whereas the delegate model (and, to some extent, also referenda) has a strong tendency to deadlocked polarization, the free representation form allows wide scope for mutual adjustment. Thus to those who do not have an altogether black/white attitude towards the factual matters of politics (whereby all compromises etc. appear as 'sinful'[62]), the latter form should have considerable merits. The strength of the freer mandate and the general control before and afterwards is that it gives us, as electors, a greater probability of having our wishes fulfilled in public policy, at least in some measure. It is for this reason that when appointing our representatives we do not invariably elect those whose opinions coincide most closely with our own. We also take account of whether the candidate in question has the judgement and the skill in politics required to achieve some of our objectives. For democracy cannot only be a mode of maximal articulation and representation of the citizens' views – if it is so, then it is merely a therapeutic process.[63] It also requires a kind of internal effectiveness: that the views penetrate as far as possible into concrete public policy.

Accordingly, it seems difficult to prove that the idea of participation in its different forms is preferable on the basis of the principles of political democracy. It undoubtedly has certain advantages but also some major drawbacks. In an overall judgement, the latter outweigh the former in my opinion. Thus acceptance of representative democracy should not cause anyone pangs of conscience. On the other hand, we should of course, be aware of the problems inherent in this mode of decision-making.

RIGHTS AND THEIR PROTECTION

As I have tried to demonstrate, we have good reason to regard representative elections as a primary indicator of political democracy. Hence, it remains to explain what characterizes a democratic election process, and the framework of political rights of which it should be part. The general aim, according to our core formulation, is that the government should function as a channel for the 'freely expressed will of the people'. This imposes fixed requirements for how the system should function in other respects.

In order to fulfil their purpose, the elections which are held must be open, honest and, of course, also effective in the sense that the organs to which representatives are elected have full right of decision over the design of public policy. Thus the elections must pertain to organs which are fully competent – and which are wholly composed of elected members – and the execution of the process must be correct and regular throughout. In order to function as a channel of a free, popular opinion, all manner of views and of candidates must be able to emerge and offer alternatives to the electorate. No-one may be prevented by prohibitions, reprisals or threats from standing for election or otherwise, as individuals or as organizations, propagating their political opinions. And these rights, of course, must not exist only in the immediate context of the elections. In order to exercise control over, and scrutinize the activities of the regime in office – and to establish effective alternatives to its policy – a wide spectrum of political freedoms and rights must be continually maintained, all to guarantee an open, uninhibited exposure of the people's preferences.[64]

Establishment of these regulations means that democracy curtails its own sphere of decision-making; such a government refrains from making certain decisions – e.g., on restrictions in freedom of expression – which would undermine the rule of the people *per se*. In other words, in order to safeguard the principle of democratic freedom, the principle of popular sovereignty is waived. This trade-off between different principles however, it should be pointed out, is somewhat controversial. In the tradition of Rousseau (which is advocated by, among others, Jacobins, Marxists and some modern participationists), the idea of popular sovereignty has been the leitmotiv so that little or no importance was attached to the need for limitations to defend the principles of freedom. Indeed, it is alleged, the people can hardly need to protect themselves against themselves.[65] The premise, then, is that the people and their government constitute an indivisible whole, whereby diverse conflicts (in any case what is regarded as legitimate conflicts) are more or less defined out of existence. Thus problems of freedom are faded out as well. But democracy in practice is fraught with conflict and constantly subject to erosion. There is a risk that the majority will use its decision-making authority to restrict the political rights of the minority, whereby the principle of the equal opportunity for all to express their preferences is set aside. Moreover, there is a constant vertical field of tension between the people and their elected leaders. In consequence of aggregation problems the citizens (the electorate) invariably face difficulties in fully controlling the actions of the political leadership; with the government in their hands, and with the use of the manipulative methods which the democratic procedure always offers, a political elite can remain immune to the popular opinion and limit, or wholly abolish, the instruments of democratic control. To give the political leadership unlimited powers is therefore beset with manifest danger (we should recall Lord Acton's dictum: 'All power tends to corrupt and absolute power corrupts absolutely').

Thus, what is required are limitations to safeguard minority rights together with regulation and restriction of the government's – and thereby the political leaders' – competence to make decisions. On second thoughts this cannot be adjudged a limitation of popular sovereignty; on the contrary, a defence of the principles of political freedoms constitutes a protection for the meaningful exercise thereof. If the people as a whole is to be able to exercise self-government, each individual must be guaranteed autonomy – for his opinions, and to work for their propagation and execution. A popular government without liberties is only a sham democracy.[66]

So far, we can feel secure in our stance; the question whether democracy for its existence requires certain limitations can reasonably be given a single answer. It is also clear that these rules and rights must bear a universalist, judicial stamp implying they are equally valid for all; no privileges or exceptions for certain individuals or groups may exist. Thus in this respect democracy is in its design closely connected with the principle of the *Rechtsstaat*[67] which, when applied to the different spheres of social life, possesses precisely this universalist, legal content ('states should be built on law).

With reference to government life this is usually called constitutionalism. Nevertheless this term is somewhat obscure, since in this context it is wont to be used on two (interrelated) levels; to (i) denote an institutional rule system equivalent to the idea of a *Rechtsstaat* (or more precisely a special case thereof); or (ii) to signify the legal methods which may be employed to enforce the said institutional rules. Accordingly, in the latter case it is a question of constitutional 'meta-rules', applied for the purpose of maintaining the regulations which protect the democratic procedure.[68] Constitutionalism in this respect usually refers to such arrangements which make it difficult to change the rules of democratic procedure. These may take several forms, e.g., requirement of a qualified majority, rules for delayed decision-making, or insistence on a legal inquiry before a constitutional court.[69]

The question is whether democracy requires constitutionalism in the latter, far more specific sense. In this case it is not merely a matter of whether the rules of procedure should be legally binding (which seems more or less self-evident) but that they should also be so framed as to have a far more specific character than conventional legislation. The Founding Fathers of the American Constitution answered this question firmly in the affirmative; as is well known, the life of the US Government has from the outset been characterized by a carefully planned (although not immutable) system of constitutional checks and balances. The underlying purpose, articulated primarily by Madison, has naturally been to root the fundamental rules so solidly that they can hardly be abrogated. Another effect thereby ensues: since the procedural order appears as given, these issues are depoliticised to such an extent that the general conflict level in the society is muted. Thus, the stable continuance of democracy is further promoted.[70]

These ideas are contradicted by a line of argumentation with a populistic bent, in which Paine and Jefferson are the prominent historical figures, and which is today frequently adduced by the adherents of participatory democracy. Here we see a contrast between democracy and constitutionalism (in the last-mentioned sense). The main objection is that an introduction of constitutional blocks allows those individuals who stipulate the constitutional framework to impose it on those who succeed them. One generation, it is alleged, cannot be entitled to bind its posterity; this is an obvious limitation of the principle of democratic sovereignty (the idea of the people's – that is all living peoples – self-government).[71]

It is, of course, entirely true that popular sovereignty is curtailed (which is also the desired effect), but this is not to say that this is unfair. As we have already mentioned, safeguarding the democratic principles of liberty may very well justify various limitations and (by the same token) even including constitutional blocks. This is not the crux. The doubt instead concerns whether the proposed arrangements actually yield the intended effect. Even Madison was obliged in his discussion of different limitations to admit that there is no really secure, watertight system. He gives examples from various American states of hair-raising violations of valid provisions of the Constitution. He therefore concludes that legal arrangements *per se* do not suffice to ensure compliance with the regulations; positive support from the surrounding civilian society is also required (he makes particular mention of the need for social and organizational pluralism).[72] Madison is here engaged in a discussion of various possible empirical requisites for democracy which we will not pursue in this context; such issues should be left open for later investigation. As we shall see, there are many different theories on how the foundations of democracy are sustained in reality. Thus the rigorous constitutionalist thesis – that democracy requires certain legally imposed obstacles (organs of supervision, 'delaying devices' etc.) – is, strictly speaking, only one hypothesis among many.[73]

Accordingly, we may state that popular democracy in its elementary sense requires legally enforceable rules to protect both its procedures and the essential civil liberties. These requisites should be incorporated in the very definition of political democracy. On the other hand, we cannot say for sure how the said rules in their turn are to be protected and maintained – that is for future empirical research to settle. In other words, constitutionalism in what we called the second sense must not be included in the concept of democracy.

ANOTHER KIND OF DEMOCRACY?

The attributes here described are the general characteristics of democracy as a mode of decision-making. I have maintained that political democracy can only have *one* reasonable content; it postulates universal and equal franchise combined with the majority rule, and is exercised chiefly in the representative form, enclosed by legally valid rules of limitation to safeguard both the electoral process and the political liberties. To counterbalance this we have in several contexts tested the populistic, participatory model which, however, did not prove to be a meaningful alternative; it is impossible to realize this model in practice nor, in an eventual application, does it appear more desirable in terms of democratic principles.[74]

Accordingly, political democracy is defined as a form of decision-making, as a mode of government, in which the people is both the object and the subject of government: 'democracy is the power of people over the people'.[75] The citizens control the state and are in their turn controlled by it. It is this double relationship which generates the need for both channels for the input of preferences (via the holding of elections in association with political liberties) and of various restrictive institutions (to protect these rights). Only in this way can the people themselves decide on the public policy to which they are subjected. Independent of its structure in general, every functioning state coerces its citizens; the uniqueness of democracy is that the citizens determine how this power is to be exercised.

Consequently, the primary characteristic of a democracy is a government *by* and *from* the people. But, as we all know, there has also been another interpretation: democracy as a government *for* the people. In this case, the chief criterion of democracy is that the citizens are favoured somehow by the public sector. On the other hand it makes little (or no) difference if the citizens, the object, participated in the decision on its direction. Thus the substantial content of policy is the cardinal issue – not the mode of the decision-making. This is the leitmotiv of the mode of government known as people's democracy, which bears Lenin's signature on its theoretical substructure; it is in the states which he and his successors established that the principles of a people's democracy find practical application.[76]

Thus two doctrines of government stand opposed. Should not both then be called democratic, albeit different in type?[77] With maintained sharp distinctions we could speak of X- and Y-democracy, and thereby dispense with all terminological disputes. Nevertheless, this would make too great a concession to linguistic convenience. The problem is that the people's democracy variant cannot be reasonably derived from democratic tenets. Despite its pretensions it is not an option within the democratic tradition – but an alternative *to* (and specifically distinct from) democracy.

Much could be said on this score[78] but in order to support this assertion I would briefly offer the following: to speak of a government for the people is an empty, unverifiable statement if no mention is made of how it could be proved. In the course of history many despots have maintained that they rule for the good of their subjects, and that they are best capable of doing this without the peoples' participation in the decision-making process. The idea of a people's democracy is only a variant of this age-old theme.[79]

In a democracy, the test of whether the policy pursued is in the interests of the people consists in free formation of opinion and elections – according to the simple belief that only the people themselves can pass judgement on this issue. The holding of open elections is, in fact, nothing but a gigantic opinion poll concerning the direction of the public sector.[80] We do not know of a safer method of examining what policy best serves the citizens. In this respect, the people's democracy has nothing to offer; it does not provide any method at all. It postulates that a government for the people's benefit can exist without any such checks.

The premise of a people's democracy requires that the people (or in our case, its great majority) have a uniform will, and that this can be discerned and given force without consultation of and co-operation by the citizens – these tasks are best executed by a superior, autonomous, decision-making elite. Only under these conditions is the doctrine logically possible to maintain. Thus, if there are no conflicts among the people or between the people and the political leadership, there is no need for control devices; politics is then *de facto* depoliticized and can be played as pure administration (in this perspective, Lenin's profound contempt for the parliamentary process – with its deceptive talk and eternal debates[81] – is understandable).

Essentially, this argument involves a number of assertions about reality: concerning the preference structure within the population, and how it can best be discerned and represented. However, the assertions which are made are dubious to say the least. That the citizens should agree on both goals and means in all the spheres of politics (concerning taxes, the environment, industrial, defence and regional policy, social care, culture, housing etc.) – and how the different desires should be weighed against each other – of course defies belief. Furthermore, irrespective of what preferences the people have, it is hardly likely that these are best interpreted from outside, by distant observers (i.e., by the avant-garde who constitute the decision-making elite). The usual objection is encapsulated in the simple 'shoe pinching' analogy – the wearer of the shoe is probably in the best position to know where it pinches.[82] And no more need to be said. The Leninistic idea is based on the belief that the decision-making elite has wholly superior – and moreover infallible – knowledge of the people's good. Thus it becomes a theory for total political paternalism. In democracies, minors (children and mentally retarded individuals) are usually excluded from political influence – in a people's democracy, the entire population would be likewise treated. What is offered consists of government from above where the people are only the object. This is the opposite of democracy: autocracy.[83] To declare otherwise is only to play with words. And this is no innocent, immaterial game: 'Once it is asserted that it is not necessary to pay attention to people's declared wishes in arriving at a judgement about their real wants, then one has started on – indeed one is half-way down – a slippery slope to the justi-fication of pernicious forms of tyranny.'[84]

Consequently, we can hold on to, and strengthen, our earlier viewpoint. Democracy as a mode of decision-making has in the main *one* reasonable meaning; moreover it only makes sense to speak of democracy as a mode of decision-making. Hence, it naturally follows that political democracy must mean the same thing irrespec-tive of the state or part of the world where it is examined. East, West, North, South – economically developed or less developed country – it makes no difference to how the *concept* (and thereby our dependent variable) is to be defined. On the other hand, here and there on the map the *requisites* for the application of democracy may be different. But that is another matter which should not be confused with the definition of the concept.[85]

BASIC AND OPTIMAL CRITERIA

Finally it should be emphasized that the general idea here outlined is a kind of basic definition of democracy.[86] The points made provide the criteria which constitute the elementary characteristics of this form of government. It would be another matter to give the optimal criteria of democracy – according to which we could determine whether the states which fulfil the elementary criteria are more or less democratic than each other. We shall not yet undertake this task but – I would point out – if we did, we should encounter far greater diffi-culty in reaching firm conclusions.[87] For here political democracy's own principles would give far less certain guidance (and to involve external objectives – pertinent to the society's development in general – would still be to speak of something else).

Thus, the eventual result of an optimum assessment is left open. Yet it must be said that possible optimum values may not be opposed to the basic criteria so that the former are attained at the latter's expense. It is self-evident that a 'deepening' of democracy may not signify that the elementary characteristic of this form of government is curtailed, or indeed comes to an end.[88] Insofar as we can speak of two levels of democracy, these must be seen as complementary, so that the optimal criteria serve as a superstructure on the basic criteria.

In other words, if one wants to study the empirical requisites of democracy, it seems natural to focus on the fundamental character-istics of government according to the aforesaid basic criteria.

CHAPTER 3

An index of democracy

What we on the concrete level call political democracy comprises various means, in the shape of institutional arrangements, which enable the citizens to control public policy. They pertain to the holding of elections, under certain forms, to the central, national decision-making organs, and to the maintenance of certain fundamental political liberties. These instruments of popular control must be in the nature of rights, and thereby apply equally to all. We shall now try to define what these rights signify in detail and, when they exist to varying extents, how they are to be graded and weighed.

The objective is to establish a number of empirical criteria for the evaluation of the level of democracy in the 132 countries which are the object of the study. These criteria are to result in a scale where the countries' different performances, the relative level of democracy, can be read. This scale, our index of democracy, is constructed on the basis of the following considerations.

(1) The measurements to be applied are divided into two main groups: elections and political liberties. The selection of attributes in the respective categories was governed by the ambition to heed as far as possible the conditions which appear essential *vis-à-vis* the basic criteria of democracy. This implies, as was stated above, a limitation with regard to the factors which are relevant in the context. The requisite according to the basic criteria is the actual existence of a number of political rights:[1] to be allowed to vote and thereby make a meaningful choice between different candidates and different policies, to be able to form parties and organizations, to be permitted to arrange demonstrations and strikes, to be able publicly (in speeches and various media) to criticize the policy pursued, etc. The issue throughout then is 'to be allowed', 'to be able' to do certain things. In other words there may be no prohibitions or equivalent obstacles which prevent the citizens from exercising these

rights. It is not thereby proscribed that, for example parties and organizations be formed or that strikes, demonstrations and criticism of the government occur to some extent. Democracy, in its basic meaning, can exist in principle even when there are no parties, and indeed even when, with reference to debates and opposition, there is a high degree of political consensus.[2] The important point is that such phenomena should not result from prohibitions, coercion and reprisals.

Naturally there are, on the other hand, cases where the political rights may be restricted quite legally. Groups which seek to impose their political will by acts of violence and by menace cannot be permitted freedom of action in a democracy. It must be feasible for the government to intervene in self-defence against such phenomena.[3] Democracy means rule by the people on the basis of peaceful procedures for solution of conflicts. It sets a limit for the type of methods which can be tolerated. Yet, it is worth noting, for those who abide by democratic methods there is no reason to impose restrictions as regards political bent. A group which advocates separatist standpoints signifying that a certain part of a country should secede from the state is in a democratic perspective entitled to do so as long as it obeys the given rules of the game. By the same token, it must even be considered legitimate to work for a change of government in democracy's disfavour. In other words the principles of political democracy are very tolerant in one respect; they impose no restrictions concerning *what* citizens may work for, only *how* they work. They establish a number of guidelines – and fairly fixed ones – for the forms of political activity.[4]

(2) Concerning elections I shall consider a number of attributes pertinent to the franchise and the validity of elections in terms of democracy. This involves elections to both the leading executive organ and some body of representation (parliament, popular assembly, etc.). In the latter case, however, for operative reasons, there is a limitation in that only election to the lower chamber, where there are several, will be included. It goes without saying that this is a source of uncertainty. Nevertheless, as far as I can judge, a major error of classification is hardly likely. Where a senate, an upper house, or the like exists, its members are frequently elected according to essentially the same principles – in terms of democracy – as apply to the lower chamber. And when this is not the case, the organ often has a purely advisory or symbolic function.

As regards the executive power, it may sometimes be difficult to determine where this rests – and what elections (if any) should thereby be considered. The problem arises when there is both a prime minister (or equivalent) and a head of state who are appointed in democratically different ways. The criterion applied is who appoints and dismisses the members of the cabinet and, when a parliamentary order is applied, who is responsible to the popular assembly for the government's existence or non-existence.

(3) The object of classification of individual attributes is primarily to include and plausibly rank the factors which appear relevant in the context. At the same time, it goes without saying that the empirical material available sets its own limits. Indeed, the requisite must be that the classifications are based on fairly accurate data on the subject for the countries investigated. With these two viewpoints in mind (the theoretically desirable and the empirically possible), categorization of diverse attributes varies. Most precise and comprehensive is our determination of the degree of suffrage and its pertinent aspects. Here we may – albeit in some cases with only an approximation – arrive at a percentage for all the states. As regards other attributes relevant to elections and political liberties respectively, a rougher order of precedence is applied which nevertheless (from the aforesaid premises) is more refined concerning the latter subject.

This varied classification must, however, not steer the relative importance, in the form of grading, attached to the diverse attributes; the latter should be subjected to independent assessment.[5] In my opinion, it is reasonable to regard the incidence of elections and political freedoms, the two main components of the study, as equally important when we evaluate the degree of democracy in different countries. Thus the starting point for the grading is that these components are assigned the same weight.

(4) The situation to be discussed comprises the circumstances which prevailed in 1988. Since, however, changes pertinent to democracy (in both its favour and its disfavour[6]) occurred in certain countries during this year, it is necessary to take a narrower temporal objective, which is the end of 1988. Indeed, as regards elections, we must often go several years back in time to the latest election to be held. Nevertheless, here too the situation as it existed at the end of 1988 is described, that is, how the popular assembly or executive then in office was elected.[7]

(5) The empirical material is taken from several sources.[8] The following periodicals were used throughout for all continents: *Keesing's Record of World Events, Chronicle of Parliamentary Elections and Development* (published by the International Centre for Parliamentary Documentation), *Amnesty International: Year Book* (together with special reports on individual countries), *Country Report on Human Rights Practices* (Report submitted to Congress by US State Department), *Political Parties of the World* (published by Alan J. Day), *Index of Censorship, IPI Report: World Press Freedom Review* (published by the International Press Institute), *Constitutions of the Countries of the World, Freedom of the World. Political and Civil Liberties* (published by Raymond D. Gastil), *Democracy. A Worldwide Survey* (ed. Robert Wesson), *The Europa World Year Book* and *Economic Intelligence Unit* (published by *The Economist*).[9]

Concerning several continents and countries we also compiled information from articles in journals and newspapers, among which the following are chiefly worthy of mention: *Electoral Studies, South, Le Monde, The Financial Times, Dagens Nyheter*, and *Svenska Dagbladet*.[10]

In addition regular use was made of a number of publications on specific areas: *Caribbean Insight, Latin American and Caribbean Contemporary Record, Latin American Monitor, Latin American Weekly Report, NACLA: Reports on the Americas, Nyheter från Latinamerika, Africa Confidential, Africa Report, The African Review, East Africa, Journal of Modern African Studies, The Indian Ocean Newsletter, Area Handbook* (articles on the Middle East and North Africa), *Middle East Contemporary Survey, Asian Yearbook, Asian Survey, Far East and Australasia* and *Far Eastern Economic Review*.[11]

ELECTIONS

Universal suffrage

Universal, equal suffrage is one of the primary characteristics of political democracy and should, naturally, be included among our empirical indicators.[12] We must take into account whether certain citizens are excluded from the franchise by reason of such attributes as race, sex, financial and social status or literacy.[13] As stated above, the franchise will be associated with citizenship. When, however, the authorities, as in South Africa, have made a large proportion of the population citizens of cryptostates (so-called homelands[14]), this must be seen as a restriction of the franchise.

In general it may be said that the most usual shortcoming in this context is the total lack of elections. This situation prevails in thirty-two countries concerning the executive power, and in eighteen with respect to the parliament (which consequently does not exist). Where, however, there are elections in any case, such discriminatory restrictions as those mentioned above are very unusual; limitations of democracy nowadays tend to assume other forms. The best known exception is South Africa, where 73 per cent of the population, the Blacks, are not allowed to vote. Extensive restrictions also apply in Western Samoa. Here only the head of a family has the vote; these, so far as I could judge, constitute some 20 per cent of the population.[15] As late as twenty years ago literacy requirements were imposed in several countries, not least in Latin America. These are now almost wholly rescinded, and in the few cases where they remain they have no significance worthy of mention.[16]

Furthermore, we must take the periodicity of the elections into account. It is required that they be held at legally prescribed intervals. Yet, since it is constitutionally possible in some countries to prolong the mandate of elected representatives,[17] we require a further time limit which is here set at twelve years. When this is exceeded, elected politicians can no longer be adjudged to have democratic support. This criterion affects *inter alia* Lebanon, where the Parliament was last elected in 1972, and Taiwan, where the great majority of the MPs, and of the assembly, which appoints the President, hold mandates from the 1940s (representing Mainland China). Thus at the last election in Taiwan, only 24 and 9 per cent of the seats respectively were filled through the vote.

A corresponding requirement is that the members of the relevant organs may not be chosen in any other way than by public elections. Thus, corporative arrangements, where certain groups are assigned a special quota of the seats, must be seen as a limitation of democracy; they violate the principle of an equal franchise.[18] Similarly, we must consider the fact that in certain countries a number of the parliamentary seats are filled by the executive power, which in its turn has less democratic status.[19] This is the case in Tanzania, for example, where 18 per cent of the members must therefore be considered as not elected.

Participation in elections has been used in a good number of studies as an indicator of the level of democracy.[20] Yet its use, at first, engenders serious problems of measurement. In all probability, the information provided on polling is frequently unreliable. In countries where the actual purpose of holding elections seems primarily to be to show the populations' unanimous support for the regime, and where there is no insight into the procedure, there is reason to assume that the published figures for participation are essentially fabricated.[21] Even in the cases where there are grounds for trusting the reports, there are also problems of comparability insofar as voting is compulsory in many states, which usually increases the turnout.[22]

Yet the fundamentally more important objection is that the percentage who vote in the elections is hardly a measurement to be included among the democratic basic criteria. As stated above, the citizens must enjoy certain political rights – in this case the right to fill all the seats in the central national decision-making organs by voting in periodic elections. But just as we cannot require a certain level as regards other activities which must be permitted – e.g., demonstrations, strikes and party politics – nor can we with respect to democracy *sensu stricto* prescribe a higher or lower percentage of voting in the elections. Desires for a widespread participation in elections belong to the discussion of the optimal criteria of democracy (where indeed this as a value is by no means undisputed).[23] Thus it is only to be considered in the cases where the fundamental requirements for democratic procedures are to a great extent satisfied. Otherwise the issue becomes a comparison of 'apples and pears'. In countries where the elections are controlled from above in all essentials, an abstention from participation (if indeed this is possible) can hardly be seen in any perspective as a democratic shortcoming – which, on the other hand, it may very well be in the states where the elections offer a fair opportunity for the citizens to control public policy.

Thus, we infer that two factors must be considered with regards to franchise: its extent in the population, and the number of seats in the relevant organs which are filled by public elections (with reference to constitutional requirements of periodicity and a time limit of twelve years). The value for each state is expressed as a percentage which is so reckoned that the proportion who have the franchise is multiplied by the proportion of seats to be filled by public elections.

If, for instance, 20 per cent of the citizens have the right to vote and these fill 90 of 100 seats in the organ to which the election is held, the result is as follows:

$$0.20 \times 0.90 = 0.18$$

Accordingly, the outcome as regards the franchise – for parliament and the executive power respectively – may vary between 0 – the cases where no elections are held – and 1 – where no limitations such as those mentioned here are imposed.

Meaningful elections

With reference to the overriding purpose of democracy – to give expression and effect to the people's political preferences – we must consider not only the incidence of the franchise but also the circumstances under which elections are held and what influence they really exert over the exercise of the national policy. The requirements which may be imposed here are divided into three categories: (1) open elections; (2) correct elections; and (3) effective elections. Together these conditions constitute the distinguishing mark of what we collectively call 'meaningful elections'.

Open elections

By an open election we mean an election where several options are on offer, and the outcome is thus not fixed in advance. This signifies that it must be possible for several candidates to run for each seat or post to be filled, and there should be no limitation of the right of nomination. Indeed, the aim of democratic elections is that the electorate may pass judgement on various – and in the event of disagreement, the most diverse – options concerning the trend of public policy.

It makes little difference how this unlimited right to propose candidates is manifested: the important point is that it exists *de facto*. Consequently, an election between a number of independent individuals who, furthermore, have only slightly divergent political platforms, could satisfy our requirement of an open electoral process – provided, of course, that the lack of organization and major differences of opinion do not result from their prohibition.[24] Many surely recognize this type of uncomplicated democracy from club activities and similar 'minor' contexts. And such, in large measure, is also the political process at the national level in several of the small island states in Oceania.[25] But this is, of course, exceptional. Elections – irrespective of whether they are more or less open – are usually held in some kind of party form. Thus, it is natural to speak, as we shall here to a great extent, of electoral limitations (or openness) in terms of what restrictions (if any) are imposed on candidates belonging to different parties (in practice, this is usually the way restrictions to run are applied). The general criterion, however, pertains to the extent to which candidates representing different political options (irrespective of whether or not these are organized) are allowed to compete in the elections.[26]

The measurement of open (and sometimes even of correct) elections is in some studies derived from the proportion of votes (or seats in parliament) won by the victorious party. The limit of 70 per cent usually serves as a demarcation criterion; if the victor obtains more the election is adjudged irregular.[27] Yet this is an unsatisfactory measurement. There are examples from several countries where the opposition party obtained more than 30 per cent, and that despite major limitations and inadequacies in the electoral procedure as a whole (the latest elections in Turkey and Liberia may be mentioned as illustrative cases).[28] Similarly there are countries where the opposition failed to reach the said limit, notwithstanding that the elections were otherwise open and even essentially fair (such has long been the case in Botswana for instance).[29]

Apart from the fact that this measurement gives rise to many a misjudgement it also, when used as the chief yardstick, yields too crude a classification.[30] Among the many one-party states which, naturally enough, fall below 'the line', there is a significant variation in the openness of the elections, which is worth considering. In barely half of these states (in the Third World), elections are held according to the pure one-list model; in other words, there is only one candidate standing for each seat. Accordingly, in these countries the electorate is not offered much of a choice. In other one-party states, however, elections are held with several candidates for each mandate. Thus competition and options for the electorate exist here, but are very limited in terms of policy.[31] Moreover there are a few countries, both non-party and one-party states, which apply a pyramidal form of representation where alternative candidates are offered at the base, the local level. Finally, it should be mentioned that even in countries where opposition parties are allowed to contest the elections – and may receive a large percentage of the votes and a number of seats in the Parliament (even over 30 per cent) – there may be essential differences regarding the openness of the elections.[32]

Our classification of the degree of openness in the elections is based on a five-point scale ranging from zero to four. The elections in which there is only one candidate for each of the posts to be filled are assigned to Category I, which carries o points. It should be emphasized that this classification is only applicable when rival candidates are prevented – by explicit prohibitions or other discriminatory measures – from running for office. The situation in different countries in this regard is usually fairly obvious. Yet there is one problem of drawing the line which is worth illustrating. I refer to those cases where opposition candidates may stand, but refuse to do so, with the result that there is no competition for the majority of the parliamentary seats. The elections in Jamaica (1984) and Tunisia (1986) may be mentioned here as distinctive examples. In the former case the election was boycotted by the large (and only important) opposition party because of discontent concerning its date; it was alleged that the government had broken an unofficial agreement to hold it later. Yet notice was given of the election according to constitutional regulations.[33] In Tunisia all the opposition parties abstained, since they did not accept the conditions under which they were permitted to take part. The previous election had been gravely marred by ballot rigging, which was now widely believed to be repeated. Furthermore, the opposition parties were subjected on this occasion to clear discrimination, since a large number of their leading candidates could not be nominated. In this case, the boycott must be interpreted as a consequence of unacceptable conditions; hence the election must be assigned to Category I. In contrast this is not true for Jamaica; here it cannot be maintained that the opposition was prevented in any real sense from taking part.[34]

The states which hold elections corresponding to Category I – most of them one-party regimes – are, as we see, assigned no points, which means that they have the same outcome as the countries where no national elections whatever occur (as in pure military regimes such as Chad and Ghana, or traditional monarchies such as Saudi Arabia and Brunei). Then – it could be objected – should the fact that elections are nevertheless held not be reckoned as a difference, and a plus with respect to democracy? We must also bear in mind that several earlier scholars who pursued empirical studies in the field attached considerable importance to just this dividing line: whether elections, of any kind, are held or not.[35] Yet with such a classification more attention is paid to the appearance (the outward form) than the actual content of the procedure. Elections where the outcome is foregone from start to finish function only as a façade – they have no value in democratic terms.[36]

The states which apply indirect elections with several intermediate stages and with, however politically narrow, scope for alternative candidates in the first phase, on the local level, are assigned to Category II (1 point).[37] This pyramidal model gives, as compared with direct elections (which is the case in Category III) greater scope for manipulation and control at the 'halts' on the way up to the national level, and must therefore be considered to have less democratic value.[38] Elections of this type are customary in a few countries. Some of these are non-party, under military rule (Libya and Niger), others are one-party states (China, Cuba and Mozambique).

Where competitive national elections are held for most of the seats – but within a uniform, politically or organizationally defined framework – the assignment is to Category III (2 points). These comprise one-party states where there are several candidates from whom to choose, such as Kenya, Tanzania and North Yemen, and certain non-party states such as Iran and Nepal. The same classification also applies to those countries where, side by side with the party of government, the possibility exists for one or more subaltern parties (who possess no real autonomy) to put candidates up for election – as happens, for example, in Indonesia, Iraq and Vietnam.

Category IV (3 points) is applicable in the cases where candidates representing mutually independent parties and political programmes may take part in elections, but restrictions are simultaneously in force against certain organizations of political trends. These include Egypt (where, among others, Marxists and religious fundamentalists are excluded), Turkey (where, apart from the said trends, also regional and fascist groupings are prohibited) and Singapore (where Communists are forbidden to stand for election).

Assignment to the highest Category, V (4 points), requires that no such restrictions exist. Here we find a large number of countries with multiparty systems the world over, and also the states in Oceania, where no parties have emerged but where the elections must nevertheless be regarded as wholly open.

Correct elections

The next point to consider pertains to how the election campaign and the voting procedure are organized. The requisite is naturally that these be correct, with no elements of cheating or other irregularities. But such is not always the case. There are many ways to 'rig' an election. The secrecy of the ballot can be set aside with the effect that people dare not vote according to their convictions. It is possible to manipulate the electoral roll in order to omit certain voters – e.g., those who come from areas with a known political colour – or make sure that reliable individuals can vote several times. Certain groups can be prevented from voting by threats and menaces, and it is also possible to arrange for the absence of voting papers for certain candidates and parties, or for the closure of voting stations in certain places. Moreover, the distribution of constituencies and seats can be so arranged that certain parties or sections of the population are systematically favoured (so-called gerrymandering). Furthermore, the party in power can interfere in various ways with the oppositions' campaign or use government resources, e.g., national media, unilaterally to disseminate its own manifesto. In addition, it is feasible to achieve the desired outcome of the election by losing or adding votes at the count, or simply presenting the result which suits.[39]

It goes without saying that all such practices must be regarded as irregularities. But there are some possibly doubtful borderline cases which are worthy of note. I refer to vote buying and so-called client voting. The former case signifies that an individual in return for immediate payment (in cash or in kind) votes for a certain candidate. The practice known as client voting has a similar 'commercial' quality insofar as the voting is prompted primarily by the promise of certain material advantages to (most commonly) a group if the candidate in question is elected.[40] Despite the said similarity, there is an essential difference between these two modes of voting.[41] The client case (provided no other irregularities are simultaneously present) is only a matter of people voting according to a narrow, and perhaps short-term, self-interest which nevertheless must be judged 'the traveller's own business'. As was said earlier, the principles of democracy do not say that certain preferences are worth more than others. They stipulate only that the people's political desires, such as they are, must influence the public decision-making process.[42] The purchase of votes, on the other hand, must be regarded as an unacceptable practice. This is *de facto* tantamount to selling the franchise, which is incompatible with the principle of democratic equality.[43]

Correct elections require, among other things, that there be institutions for control of the procedure.[44] How these are to work in practice may, as far as we are concerned at this juncture, be seen as an open question. The important thing is that they are neutral. Thus it may not, as has long been the case in Paraguay and Mexico, be the party in power which, in practice, uncontrolled conducts the holding and supervision of elections. In addition these organs must also be effective in the sense that possible irregularities are actually brought to light and that their decisions on controversial issues are obeyed.[45]

Naturally it is by no means easy to obtain a clear idea of diverse irregularities in the elections. Indeed, certain measures are undertaken more or less in secret. Often we have only rough estimates of the extent of such activities and their influence on the election results. Furthermore, in some countries it is almost a ritual of the political game that the loser accuses the victor of cheating (and of winning chiefly for this reason). More or less loose rumours of electoral irregularities can easily be spread. This calls for caution in our judgement. Only when independent observers assert that certain improprieties have occurred do we consider the information reliable. Vague, unconfirmed rumours, however (which are repeated now and then in the sources we use), are assigned no evidentiary value. The risk is, of course, that we thereby underestimate the extent of the problem. The usual scholarly requirements for certain documentation – as certain as it can be in this context – must nevertheless be considered to carry the greatest weight.

Our assessment of the correctness of the elections is reached according to a five-degree scale, where the two extremes and the middle are the starting points for the classification as follows:

I   (0 points):   Very grave irregularities which in all probability greatly influenced the result.

II   (1 point):

III (2 points):   Serious irregularities which probably influenced the result.

IV   (3 points):

V   (5 points):   The elections were wholly or essentially correct.

Let us begin with the positions which were explicitly defined. The most serious cases, where the outcome of the elections was highly dependent on extensive ballot rigging, are assigned to Category I. As typical examples I can name Liberia – where the military President in office won the election held in 1985 by a bare margin, a result which independent observers characterized as wholly fabricated – and Paraguay, where the elections held during General Stroessner's long reign (from 1954 until early 1989) were well nigh farcical.[46]

In the countries placed in the middle Category (III) the irregularities, however numerous, are minor in type and extent. Here I may mention Senegal, where there were problems with ballot papers (for certain parties), in conjunction with a remarkably disordered control of the electoral rolls (which, for example may have enabled double voting). Another typical example in this category is Nicaragua (1984). The irregularities which occurred here consisted primarily in that the regime adopted various measures to obstruct the opposition's opportunities for campaigning.[47] Yet, in none of these cases was the election result seriously affected by the said defects in the procedure.

It is hardly necessary to explain what Category V represents. On the other hand, it remains to examine the significance of Categories II and IV. These were used to label the countries which fall between the first three stated positions. For clarity's sake I may mention Mexico. Here, for many decades, elections were held which resembled those of Paraguay, led to the same predetermined result, and used similar methods. At the latest election, however, a generally acknowledged improvement occurred. Nevertheless, many of the old problems remain; namely the lack of insight into the work of the electoral committee, which is under government control. Since the deficiencies, taken together, appear more serious than the cases placed in Category III, Mexico is assigned to Category II. If, on the other hand, the irregularities which occur are more moderate, as compared with Category III, then Category IV is considered. Hither are assigned such cases where the regime obviously used the public resources for its own advantage during the election (Bahamas and The Gambia), and where opposition groups prevented the other side's voters from voting by acts of violence (El Salvador and Jamaica).

Effective elections

Side by side with the requirements for openness and correctness in elections we must also expect those elected really to have a say in the design of the public policy.[48] Thus the point at issue is the actual competence of the elected officials, which may vary considerably from country to country. However, it should be remarked immediately that we are not here concerned with the question of the distribution of power between the popular assembly and the executive organ in a democracy. We have no reason to take account of whether there is a strong executive arm – as is often the case in presidential systems with direct elections (such is the pattern in particular in Latin America) – or if a parliamentary form prevails, e.g., of the Westminster type. In a constitutional issue of this kind the principles of democracy can hardly give us any guidance; other considerations enter the picture.[49]

The crux in our context concerns whether elected organs are limited in their decision-making by instances which, for their part, have no democratic support – by a monarch (as in, for example, Morocco and Nepal), by the military power (as in South Korea and Turkey), by a governing party whose position is not subject to elections (which is the situation in many countries, particularly in Africa), or by a theocratic elite (as in Iran).

Popularly elected organs in the countries examined will be classified according to the following scale on the basis of the aforementioned views:

I   (0 points):   No competence.
II   (1 point):   Some competence, very serious restrictions.
III (2 points):   Substantial competence, major restrictions.
IV   (3 points):   Considerable competence, minor restrictions.
V   (4 points):   Full competence.

To Category I are assigned the type of popular assemblies of an essentially ceremonial nature which are to be found in several states, particularly those under one-party rule. As an example, I may mention the Parliament in Ethiopia, which meets several days each year and then invariably ratifies the decisions which the executive power (controlled by the Party) has submitted and, moreover, occasionally already enforced. It is true of all the cases which are assigned to this category that the elected organs are totally non-essential with respect to the design of the national policy. In contrast, they are not completely so in Category II. This includes the countries where popularly elected organs have a real right but are very limited in initiating and making decisions. The Kenyan Popular Assembly illustrates this case. Its members often raise and pursue different local issues (pertinent to problems in the constituencies they represent). On the other hand, they have no say in matters of a more overriding national or essential nature; there they are expected to follow the President and the Party line. This rule was clearly illustrated in 1988, when the President submitted a most controversial proposal, as it would turn out, concerning changes in the Election Act (for the worse in a democratic perspective). It was unanimously approved after a short debate by the Assembly.[50]

More competence is required for placement in Category III. Iran may be cited as a typical example. Here, there is an active Popular Assembly which, often during lively debates, makes decisions on many important economic and social questions. The President, who is appointed in a competitive election, also has considerable powers. But above these organs stands the religious elite and, in particular, its foremost representative, Khomeiny,[51] whose stance in various spheres could not be questioned during the lifetime of the regime – thus the official line on certain issues was established.

Another example is Nepal, which also has a vigorous parliament but, at the same time, has a king who traditionally has a strong position. In order to become law, decisions must be approved by the King – and this approval is not then, as in more eroded monarchies, merely a matter of form.

In the cases under Category IV the organs in question have considerable competence – with the exception of certain special spheres. The countries assigned hither are consistently such where the military have surrendered political power for the benefit of rule by the people. Nevertheless, they have not wholly relaxed their grip. In the countries in question (such as Brazil, Turkey and Pakistan), the military retain considerable autonomy in 'their own' affairs and thereby usually also in matters pertinent to the maintenance of the internal order.

When no restrictions such as those described here exist – or at least not to any palpable, obvious extent – Category V is applicable.[52]

We have thereby stated the measurements which were used in the study of the attributes which fall into the main category of elections – the franchise and meaningful elections, which in their turn consist of two and three subsections respectively. The count is executed in such a way that the figure (in percentage) which emerges concerning the franchise is multiplied by the total value of the points for meaningful elections. These latter values (from 0–4) are then added. Nevertheless, certain provisos are applied inasmuch as the attributes which compose the characteristics of meaningful elections must be considered to be interrelated. It would not be reasonable to award points for the absence of ballot rigging if the elections were not relatively open. For it is only then, so to speak, that irregularities become really necessary; when only candidates for one party (or the equivalent) may stand, the regime's position as such cannot be threatened in the elections. The conclusion is that only elections which in terms of openness correspond to at least Category IV receive points, because they were more or less correctly executed. In addition, the general rule applies that if a state receives 0 points for one of the three attributes, it will also obtain 0 points as a total value for meaningful elections.[53] The logic behind this is that the electoral process must be seen as a continuous chain; if one link is missing, the procedure becomes meaningless. Thus, for example, elections to an assembly without any competence whatsoever must be considered wholly nonessential from the democratic viewpoint (however open they were); similarly the competence of an organ becomes of little interest if its members are selected in completely closed elections or via extensive ballot rigging.

In this way a state receives at most 12 points – $1(4 + 4 + 4)$ – for elections to the popular assembly and the executive body respectively. Consequently, the total award can be 24 points at best.

POLITICAL FREEDOMS

When evaluating the degree of democracy we must also take into account the existence of a number of political freedoms. They pertain to the actual right of all citizens to express their opinions openly, in speech, in writing and in various media, to organize parties and other associations and to engage without hindrance in political activities in the form of meetings, demonstrations, strikes, etc. At the same time we must consider the incidence of political violence and harsh reprisals. These phenomena can, when they are systematically applied, have the result that political freedoms are *de facto* curtailed. But they also shed light on how severe the consequences are. If political dissidents risk incurring very severe penalties (loss of life, torture, or long terms of imprisonment under harsh conditions) the curtailment of liberties will naturally exert a stronger effect than in the cases where the sanctions are milder (e.g., in the form of house arrest or moderate fines). Given the same kinds of restrictions of political freedoms in two states, the conditions may for these reasons be regarded as far worse in one compared to the other.

It must be emphasized that the point at issue concerns only *political* freedoms. In previous measurements of democracy this demarcation has not always been strictly maintained. Thus in certain cases various social rights have been included;[54] in others the incidence of diverse economic freedoms (the right of private ownership, a market economy, etc.) has been taken into account.[55] On the basis of the definition strategy which was declared earlier, these are attributes which must be excluded from the concept of democracy. Otherwise we could not study the connection between political democracy and its social and economic conditions – which with reference to the scholarly debate concerning the requisites of democracy is (as we shall see) very interesting.[56]

Our measurement of political freedoms will be based on three scales, the values of which are later weighed together. The first pertains to organizational freedoms, the second to freedom of opinion, and the third to the incidence of political violence and repression.

Organizational freedoms
In general, two kinds of rights are here at issue; on the one hand, the right to form and maintain political associations and, on the other, the right to engage in such extrovert activities, in the form of meetings, demonstrations, etc., as these organizations are wont to practice – but which may, of course, also occur *ad hoc* and more spontaneously. Political associations denote, for a start, parties. Where the right of free organization is offered, the formation of parties is normally the primary form for collective popular influence on the direction of public policy.[57] A similar task, but with a specific

narrower scope, is also performed by diverse non-profit and interest organizations. Here, the whole range of such associations is, of course, worthy of consideration. Yet, we must by reason of incomplete information confine ourselves merely to trade unions. It should be added that we are concerned throughout with associations which are autonomous *vis-à-vis* the regime in question, which means that they elect their own leaders and decide on the content of their policies themselves.

Accordingly, the right to form parties is included among the political freedoms. This appears as self-evident. Nevertheless, the scrupulous reader may possibly wonder whether a kind of double book-keeping is here involved, since the existence of several parties also entered the picture during the measurement of the elections' degree of openness. Notwithstanding, we should then, firstly, bear in mind that this was not the fundamental criterion in that context (but whether candidates representing different political tendencies could participate). Furthermore, it is by no means certain that the incidence of parties signifies that these may take part in the elections which are held. The presidential plebiscite in Chile in 1988 may be mentioned as an example. Active parties were present but these were not permitted to put up any rival candidate to the President in office. Moreover, we may also cite Burma, where parties could emerge in 1988, in contrast to the case at the previous election, and Lesotho, which has a not inconsiderable party system but no elections (after a military coup in 1986). And the reverse situation may prevail so that there was freedom for various parties to operate and different opinions to be expressed at the last election, but the agenda was subsequently restricted. Zimbabwe is an illustrative case in this respect. In addition there are all the one-party regimes (or the like) which allow a modicum of competition in diverse forms in the elections (such as Kenya, Libya and Vietnam) but which do not permit any free, autonomous formation of parties.

Political democracy is, we must generally recall, a multi-dimensional concept. Notwithstanding that the occurrence of elections (i.e., meaningful elections) is among the fundamental features of government by the people, we must also take account of the political context in general. To allow several parties to operate signifies that elections, when they are held, will be more open, and that the possibilities of political influence (via the submission of demands and the exercise of control over the regime's activities) between the elections will be far greater. And even where no elections at all are held, the same condition must be adjudged valid.

In our grading or organizational freedoms, the right to maintain political associations, parties and trade unions will be seen as the most important. In this context, such fixed, institutionalized forms for political work must be regarded as the most significant instruments for civic influence. Freedoms of action (the right to hold meetings, to strike, etc.) assume their value foremost when this right already exists.

Since we are here, and in what follows, concerned with weighing on a scale a fairly complex set of attributes (with a wide range of variation) there is reason to use a refined classification. Thus, we shall apply a scale with nine values, as follows:

I	(0 points):	No freedoms.
Ib	(1 point):	
II	(2 points):	Certain freedoms, very great restrictions.
IIb	(3 points):	
III	(4 points):	Considerable freedoms, great restrictions.
IIIb	(5 points):	
IV	(6 points):	Most freedoms, certain restrictions.
IVb	(7 points):	
V	(8 points):	All freedoms.

In Category V, we find a large number of states which impose no restrictions on the freedoms which are here at issue. On the other hand, in the cases where these freedoms are wholly lacking the placement is in Category I. This applies to such countries as Cuba, Zaire, Saudi Arabia, Iran and North Korea, where all collective political activity (insofar as such exists) is strictly subject to, and controlled by the regime.

If autonomous trade unions (but not parties) may exist, and if, furthermore, there is the right to strike throughout most of the labour market, Category II is applicable. A country such as Zambia may be mentioned as a typical example. When the trade-union autonomy or the right to strike is defective or generally vague – as is the case in Kenya, Kuwait and Indonesia for example – the placement is lowered one step, to Category Ib.

At the subsequent levels of the classification it is presumed that autonomous parties are allowed to exist. When such is the case, but where at the same time considerable restrictions are imposed – so that certain groups are excluded – then Category II is relevant. I may mention Chile and Madagascar as typical cases. In the former country Communists, who have traditionally occupied a strong political position, are forbidden to pursue party activities. In Madagascar discrimination of the reversed ideological significance is practiced. Here several parties (with a wide political range) are allowed to operate within the framework of a loose national 'front' with a socialistic bent. Parties which do not comply with the front's, however vague, basic principles may not exist. The same placement is also used for several countries, such as Uganda, which allow greater freedom of party formation but have very extensive restrictions as regards these parties' outward activities.

The intermediate Category, IIb, is used for similar cases where, however, the autonomy of the parties or the trade-union freedoms are infringed. For illustration, I may mention Morocco, where the regime (King Hassan) exercises some control over the recruitment of the leaders of the existing opposition parties.

In Category IV, we find those cases where the limitations on the formation of parties are of minor significance, and those where no restrictions exist in this respect, but where freedom of action is severely curtailed. Singapore and Taiwan may be cited as examples of the former. In both these countries Communist parties are prohibited, which nevertheless is not (at least nowadays) considered to be an essential limitation in the political life. Sri Lanka can serve to illustrate the second kind of restrictions which justify placement in this category. In this country, despite the very tense political situation, there are no restrictions on the formation of parties or on their activities. Yet, by reason of the state of emergency, the rights to strike and to demonstrate are curtailed.

As to the rest, the next category, this time IIIb, is used for the cases where the conditions are similar, but worse. Liberia and Fiji may serve as examples. In Liberia, opposition parties are allowed to arrange meetings more or less at will, at least in the larger towns, but they are at the same time prevented from making joint public manifestations. Moreover, the trade unions are not permitted to strike. In Fiji, the military coup which occurred in 1987 did not result in the dissolution of the previously existing parties. Nevertheless, their possibilities to meet, to demonstrate, etc. were drastically curtailed, as were the trade-union activities.

Finally Category IVb, which also represents an intermediate

position, in this case just below the best placement. It is used for the
states where only moderate limitations of freedom of action can be
assigned to the debit side. One example is Senegal, where the
opposition parties in certain regions, particularly outside the big
cities, have difficulty in arranging meetings; another is Mauritius,
where the right to strike, which by law should exist, in reality is
essentially curtailed by an almost impenetrable, officially enjoined
procedure for negotiations.

Freedom of opinion
The concept of freedom of opinion covers freedom of expression and
of the press, by which we mean all kinds of media, including radio,
TV and also the publication of books. One question which has been
raised in this context concerns the extent to which the spread of
ownership of newspapers or state monopolies (which is most
common in the realm of TV) should be considered.[58] As I see it, the
circumstances in these respects are not the primary ones. As regards
the broadcasting media a national monopoly may very well provide
a reasonable degree of freedom of opinion (countries such as Botswana, Mauritius and Papua New Guinea may be offered as confir-
mation); the crux is whether the state upholds the necessary requirements for impartiality and neutrality in the programmes offered.
Essentially the same can be said about the press in general. The
cardinal point is not the ownership conditions, but the actual right
to carry on a many-sided, uninhibited mediation of ideas and news.
Thus it may be worth remarking that in several countries where the
press, *sensu lato*, is largely privately owned – as in Paraguay, Iran
and Indonesia – there is extensive control of what is said and written
in the media.

What we are to scrutinize are the incidence of prohibitions,
threats, coercions, etc. which prevent publicists and journalists –
and, for that matter, also the person in the street – from articulating
and disseminating opinions and actual information concerning the
situation in the country (and elsewhere). There are many methods to
this end. The more obvious ways of controlling the media include
explicit censorship (advance examination) of what is to be printed or
transmitted, authority for the regime to decide which newspapers,
journals, etc. may be issued, or which individuals shall hold the
leading posts (chief editors and the like). But there are also a number
of more covert measures which may have an equivalent effect,

causing journalists and others to practise a more or less comprehensive self-censorship. This can take the form that those who are incautious in what they write or say are imprisoned, subjected to threats, lose their jobs, are excluded from studies, etc. Control can also be exercised by financial pressure, e.g., to the extent that the media are dependent for their survival on national grants or income from advertisements (which the regime exploits) or in consequence of the state's ownership of the printing industry, or due to limits on the import of essential components, e.g., printer's ink.

In our scrutiny of the status of freedom of opinion, we apply the same classification (I to V with the intermediate positions) and grading as in the case of the organizational freedoms, so that the scale need not be repeated.[59] In Category I, where no freedoms exist, all the expressions of opinion which may be deemed as criticism of the regime are prohibited, as is all independent reporting of news; violations of this rule – even in private life – are closely supervised. Such totalitarian conditions (North Korea may be adduced as one of the more extreme cases) are usually maintained via a fine network of secret police combined with an extensive system of informers.

Category II contains those countries where very limited criticism and news services may exist – and then only in certain areas and against those in power at a low level. Thus, for instance, it is possible in Tanzania and Cape Verde to draw attention to certain financial irregularities (corruption etc.) in the administration and the state-owned companies, whereby the officials responsible, e.g., company managers, may be subjected to explicit criticism. On the other hand, there can be no talk of calling into question the government and the policy it pursues in the relevant spheres.

Category III is applicable when it is permitted to air and pass judgement in the regime's political tendency – but with significant exceptions. To illustrate this point I may mention Liberia, where the press may be fairly candid about the conditions in the country, and thereby also about the Government's doings. But it is not feasible directly to attack the Head of State and the leading Cabinet Ministers. When the tolerance is clearly greater than this – but where there are nevertheless certain definite reservations – Category IV is relevant. South Korea may be cited as a typical case. Here the media may, by and large without constraint, illuminate and critically scrutinize the doings (or the absence thereof) of the

Government and high officials. But at the same time certain questions are taboo, namely those pertaining to the sensitive relationship
with North Korea.

The intervenient Categories (Ib, IIb etc.) are used to take
account of the extent of possible surveillance of the citizens,[60] and to
cover those cases where various media receive different treatment –
e.g., the press is relatively free while radio and TV are more
controlled. The highest intermediate position, VIb, is applied also
for the countries where restrictions on freedom of thought and
expression are in general very few.

Political violence and oppression
Insofar as attention was paid in previous studies of democracy to the
incidence of political violence and diverse reprisals, the measures
taken by the regime in power were usually the focus of interest.[61]
This may seem natural. With the police and the military at its
disposal a government as a rule has by far the greatest potential for
the adoption of sanctions against undesirable elements. Moreover, it
is undoubtedly true that oppression under state control is the most
common, and its effect on the whole the most paralysing for political
life in the countries we study. But there are exceptions. In some
countries, political violence engineered by units wholly or partly
independent of the government constitutes the most serious threat to
the exercise of political freedoms. It may be members of the police or
the armed forces who on their own authority practise oppression
against certain groups; such is the case in several countries in Latin
America, for example. Similar actions (in the form of political
murders, kidnappings, etc.) may also be performed by purely
private organizations; by guerrilla groups, gangster syndicates, or
parts of the 'ordinary' party system. The latter was the case for long
periods in Colombia's history; a country which is nowadays best
known for the extensive political violence practised by drug syndicates, and moreover partly in conjunction with some guerrilla
groups of long standing. Yet the most conspicuous example of an
uncontrolled 'private war' is, of course, Lebanon. Very extensive
political violence by diverse independent political groups also occurs
in Sri Lanka.

In my view, the source of the outrages makes little difference in
democratic terms. The crux is not the question of responsibility but
the actual effect, namely that citizens are thereby hindered in the

exercise of their political rights. Thus we cannot only take account of oppression which is undoubtedly instigated by a government. The similar, more systematic activities which are perpetrated by various 'paramilitary' bodies or groups wholly independent of the regime should also be considered when we assess the status of political rights in different countries.[62]

In this case, too, a scale from I to V with intermediate positions is used. I should say from the outset that the latter are here employed, with regard to those countries which appear as doubtful (border-line) cases in the classification presented below:

I   (0 points):   Very extensive incidences.
Ib   (1 point):
II   (2 points):   Extensive incidences.
IIb   (3 points):
III   (4 points):   Substantial, but limited, incidences.
IIIb (5 points:
IV   (6 points):   Minor incidences.
IVb   (7 points):
V   (8 points):   No incidences.

Category I contains the most serious cases. It includes such countries as Iran and Somalia where political murders, torture, disappearances and arbitrary imprisonment occur on a large, systematic scale. At the same time the judiciary lacks autonomy (or is circumvented) and consequently fails to provide any protection for the citizens. When outrages of this type are less serious, Category II is used. Sudan and Nicaragua may serve as examples, two countries which are beset by a long-standing civil war and concomitant widespread acts of violence. Nevertheless, the war, violence, etc. are chiefly confined to certain regions of the countries; in other areas, the situation is much better.

Placement in Category III requires that the incidences of political violence and oppression are fairly limited. Political murders, disappearances, torture or political prisoners should here be rare occurrences. In this assessment, the size of the population must of course be taken into account. What may be considered a 'slight' incidence of torture is not (in absolute figures) the same in India and Togo, both of which have been assigned to Category III.[63]

In order to qualify for placement in Category IV, a country may not have any political murders, disappearances, or torture. But there may be a certain potential for arbitrary arrest. Moreover, the autonomy of the judiciary may be incomplete. Sierra Leone and Swaziland are examples of this. The state of emergency which prevailed in 1988 in Sierra Leone allowed the brief imprisonment of hundreds of people. Yet the purpose of these measures was merely to combat widespread economic crime. As far as we know, there are no political prisoners in the country. The judiciary is largely autonomous but there are instances of political interference in certain cases; furthermore, corruption occurs in the procedures, particularly in the lower courts. In Swaziland, on the other hand, the courts are wholly autonomous and function justly. Nevertheless, political imprisonment (mild in degree and minor in extent) may occur now and then.[64]

We have thereby three scales for determining the position of the political freedoms. The aggregated value is derived from addition of the points (from 0 to 8) obtained in each case. But a restriction is applied. In order to receive points for absence of political violence and oppression, a country must be able to show at least some achievement in the realms of organizational freedoms or freedom of thought and expression. Otherwise we should find that a state such as Saudi Arabia, where these freedoms are conspicuous by their absence, obtained points simply because the level of political sanctions is moderate. A wholly autocratic government does not become more democratic, so to speak, just because it can be sustained with a minor degree of oppression. Thus we have the rule that to obtain points in this respect, a state must accumulate at least two points (of 16 possible) relating to organizational freedoms and freedom of opinion.

The outcome of the evaluation of political freedoms may thereby vary from 0 to 24 points. When these are combined with the points relating to elections (also 0 to 24) we have a scale which extends from 0 to 48. In order to arrive at an overview we have converted these values to an index from 0 to 10.[65] This is shown in Table 1. The classifications 'en route' are illustrated in Tables 2–10.

The accuracy of this index can be discussed from several viewpoints. There are, as stated, certain reservations as regards validity. With respect to elections we take into account only the parliament's lower chamber if there are several and, concerning organizational freedoms, only trade unions are considered besides parties. With better information and thereby a more complete picture in these respects the grading could have been more precise. But, on the whole, as far as I can judge, the outcome would have remained approximately the same.[66]

Given the measurements used, it is feasible to question the rules applied for the combination into an index. The cardinal issues here seem to be whether attributes which are herded into a single dimension (political democracy) are internally correlated to a reasonable extent, and whether the outcome for the different states would change with another distribution of points between the attributes – the latter pertains in other words to how robust the index turns out to be. The former, which concerns the homogeneity of our index, has been examined via correlation of the two main components,

Table 1. *Index of level of democracy in 132 countries in 1988*

Latin America and the Caribbean			
Argentina	9·6	Guyana	3·8
Bolivia	8·5	Haiti	2·7
Brazil	8·1	Jamaica	9·0
Chile	2·1	St Kitts-Nevis	9·8
Colombia	8·3	St Lucia	9·8
Equador	9·2	St Vincent and Grenadiens	10·0
Paraguay	2·1	Suriname	8·5
Peru	7·9	Trinidad and Tobago	9·8
Uruguay	9·4	*Africa south of the Sahara*	
Venezuela	9·2	Angola	0·0
		Benin	1·0
Belize	9·8	Botswana	9·6
Costa Rica	9·8	Burkina Faso	1·0
El Salvador	6·3	Burundi	0·4
Guatemala	7·5	Cameroon	0·8
Honduras	8·3	Cape Verde	1·7
Mexico	7·3	Central African Rep.	0·8
Nicaragua	4·8	Chad	1·0
Panama	1·9	Comoros	2·7
		Congo	1·3
Antigua and Barbuda	9·6	Cote D'Ivoire	2·7
Bahamas	9·0	Djibouti	2·1
Barbados	10·0	Equatorial Guinea	0·0
Cuba	0·8	Ethiopia	0·0
Dominica	10·0	Gabon	1·9
Dominican Republic	9·0	Gambia	8·7
Grenada	9·6		

Table 1. (*Cont.*)

Ghana	1·5	Qatar	0·0
Guinea	1·7	Saudi Arabia	0·0
Guinea-Bissau	1·3	Syria	0·6
Kenya	2·2	Tunisia	2·9
Lesotho	3·5	Turkey	6·7
Liberia	3·1	United Arab Emirates	0·2
Madagascar	7·3	Yemen (N)	2·5
Malawi	1·3	Yemen (S)	0·0
Mali	2·1		
Mauritania	1·3	*Far East and the Pacific*	
Mauritius	9·6	Afghanistan	0·0
Mozambique	1·0	Bangladesh	3·5
Niger	1·5	Bhutan	2·5
Nigeria	2·3	Brunei	1·7
Rwanda	2·5	Burma (Myanmar)	0·6
Sao Tome and Principe	0·0	China	1·9
Senegal	8·3	India	9·0
Seychelles	2·0	Indonesia	1·8
Sierra Leone	3·2	Korea (N)	0·0
Somalia	0·0	Korea (S)	7·5
South Africa	2·9	Laos	0·0
Sudan	6·8	Maldives	4·0
Swaziland	2·6	Malaysia	6·9
Tanzania	2·0	Nepal	3·2
Togo	1·3	Pakistan	8·3
Uganda	2·3	Philippines	8·1
Zaire	1·3	Singapore	7·3
Zambia	3·3	Sri Lanka	7·3
Zimbabwe	5·8	Taiwan	3·7
		Thailand	7·1
Near East and North Africa		Vietnam	1·5
Algeria	2·1		
Bahrain	1·3	Fiji	3·1
Cyprus	10·0	Kiribati	9·9
Egypt	5·8	Marshall Islands	10·0
Iran	2·1	Micronesia, Fed. States of	10·0
Iraq	0·6	Nauru	9·6
Israel	9·0	Papua New Guinea	8·8
Jordan	2·1	Solomon Islands	9·6
Kuwait	1·9	Tonga	5·4
Lebanon	1·5	Tuvalu	10·0
Libya	0·6	Vanuatu	8·8
Morocco	3·4	Western Samoa	6·0
Oman	1·7		

Table 2. *No elections*

	Parliament	Executive
Afghanistan (one-party)		x
Bahrain (monarchy)	x	x
Bhutan (monarchy)		x
Brunei (monarchy)	x	x
Burkina Faso (mil.)	x	x
Burma (one-party)		x
Burundi (mil.)	x	x
Chad (mil.)	x	x
Chile (mil.)	x	
Congo (one-party)		x
Ethiopia (one-party)		x
Fiji (mil.)	x	x
Ghana (mil.)	x	x
Guinea (mil.)	x	x
Haiti (mil.)	x	x
Iraq (one-party)		x
Jordan (monarchy)	x	x
Kuwait (monarchy)	x	x
Lesotho (mil.)	x	x
Libya (mil.)		x
Mauritania (mil.)	x	x
Morocco (monarchy)		x
Mozambique (one-party)		x
Nepal (monarchy)		x
Niger (mil.)		x
Nigeria (mil.)	x	x
Oman (monarchy)	x	x
Qatar (monarchy)	x	x
Saudi Arabia (monarchy)	x	x
Swaziland (monarchy)		x
Tonga (monarchy)		x
Tunisia (multiparty)		x
Uganda (mil.)	x	x
United Arab Emirates (monarchy)	x	x
No election within twelve years		
Laos (latest election: 1975, one-party)	x	x
Lebanon (latest election: 1973, multiparty)	x	x
Malawi (latest election: 1970 one-party)[69]		x

Table 3. *The franchise – restrictions*

South Africa (multiparty: 73·3 per cent excluded from the franchise

Western Samoa (multiparty): About 80 per cent excluded from franchise

Table 4. *Percentage elected – restrictions*

Bhutan (monarchy):
> *Parl.*: 106 of 151 members are elected by the people in national elections, the remainder (30 per cent) are appointed by religious bodies (10 members), industry (1) or the King (24).

Gabon: (one-party):
> *Parl.*: 9 of 111 members (8 percent) are appointed by the President.

Gambia (multiparty):
> *Parl.*: 5 of 42 seats (12 per cent) are reserved for 'Chief's representatives'

Indonesia (one-party):
> *Parl.*: 100 of 500 members (20 per cent) are appointed by the President (military representation).
>
> *Exec.*: Half of the electoral assembly is chosen by Parliament and half by various political organizations and regional assemblies – the selection is made centrally by the Party (0.5 × 0.8 = 0.4).

Kenya (one-party):
> *Parl.*: 12 of 102 seats (12 per cent) filled by Presidential appointees.

Kiribati (non-party):
> *Parl. and Exec.*: 1 of 39 members (3 per cent) appointed by Banabas Island Council of Leaders (whereby general elections are not prescribed).

Malawi (one-party):
> *Parl.*: 11 of 123 seats (9 per cent) filled by Presidential appointees.

Morocco: (monarchy):
> *Parl.*: 60 of 305 members (13 per cent) are appointed by professional organizations and trade unions.

Nepal (monarchy):
> *Parl.*: 28 of 140 members (20 per cent) are appointed by the King.

Seychelles (one-party):
> *Parl.*: 2 of 25 members (8 per cent) appointed by the President.

Sierra Leone (one-party):
> *Parl.*: 22 of 127 seats (17 per cent) appointed by Paramount Chiefs (12) and the President (10).

Sudan (multiparty):
> *Parl. and Exec.*: 28 of 301 members (9 per cent) elected by 'graduate constituencies'. Elections in certain regions for 41 seats (14 per cent) could not be held.

Swaziland (non-party):
> *Parl.*: 10 of 50 members (20 per cent) appointed by the King.

Taiwan (multiparty):
> *Parl.*: 229 of 302 members (76 per cent) have not been elected within 12 years.
>
> *Exec.*: 812 of 896 members (91 per cent) of this Assembly, which elects the President, have not been elected within 12 years.

Tanzania (one-party):
> *Parl.*: Of 244 members 25 are appointed by the President, and 5 by Zanzibar's House of Representatives (which is not elected in competitive elections). Furthermore, 25 members sit *ex officio* (appointed by the President). Total: 45 (18 per cent).

Tonga (monarchy):
> *Parl.*: Of 29 members, 9 are elected by the people in national elections, while the remainder (69 per cent) are chosen by 33 aristocrats (9) or the King (11).

Zambia (one-party):
> *Parl.*: 10 of 136 members (7 per cent) are appointed by the President.

Table 5. *Open elections*

I (0 p.)

Parl. and Exec.: Angola, Benin, Burma, Cape Verde, Djibouti, Equatorial Guinea, Gabon, Guinea-Bissau, Korea(N), Mali, Sao Tome and Principe, Somalia, Yemen (S)

Parl.: Afghanistan, Congo, Tunisia

Exec.: Algeria, Cameroon, Central African Republic, Chile, Comoros, Côte d'Ivoire, Ethiopia, Kenya, Rwanda, Seychelles, Sierra Leone, Syria, Tanzania, Togo (Zaire), Zambia

II (1 p.)

Parl. and Exec.: China, Cuba

Parl.: Libya, Mozambique (Niger), Swaziland

III (2 p.)

Parl. and Exec.: Indonesia, Iran, Maldives, Vietnam, Yemen(N)

Parl.: Algeria, Bhutan, Cameroon, Central African Republic, Comoros, Côte d'Ivoire (Ethiopia), Iraq, Kenya (Malawi), Nepal, Rwanda, Seychelles, Sierra Leone, Syria, Tanzania (Togo) (Zaire), Zambia

IV (3 p.)

Parl. and Exec.: Egypt, El Salvador, Korea(s), Madagascar, Malaysia, Nicaragua (Paraguay), Singapore, South Africa, Taiwan, Thailand, Turkey, Uruguay

Parl.: Morocco

V (4 p.)

Parl. and Exec.: Antigua and Barbuda, Argentina, Bahamas (Bangladesh), Barbados, Belize, Bolivia, Botswana, Brazil, Colombia, Costa Rica, Cyprus, Dominica, Dominican Republic, Equador, Fed. States of Micronesia, Gambia, Grenada, Guatemala (Guyana), Honduras, India, Israel, Jamaica, Kiribati (Liberia), Marshall Islands, Mauritius, Mexico, Nauru, Pakistan (Panama), Papua N. Guinea, Peru, Philippines, Senegal, Solomon Islands, Sri Lanka, St Kitts-Nevis, St Lucia, St Vincent and Grenadiens, Sudan, Suriname, Trinidad and Tobago, Tuvalu, Vanuatu, Venezuela, Western Samoa, Zimbabwe

Parl.: Tonga

Note: The countries in parentheses were not awarded any points since they have 0 points for Correct Elections or Effective Elections.

Table 6. *Correct elections*

I (o p.)
Parl. and Exec.: Bangladesh, Guyana, Liberia, Panama, Paraguay
II (1 p.)
Parl. and Exec.: Mexico, Papua N. Guinea
III (2 p.)
Parl. and Exec.: Egypt, Malaysia, Nicaragua, Senegal, Singapore, Thailand
Parl.: Morocco
IV (3 p.)
Parl. and Exec.: Bahamas, Bolivia, El Salvador, Gambia, Jamaica, Taiwan
Exec.: Korea(S), Philippines, Sri Lanka
V (4 p.)
Parl. and Exec.: Antigua and Barbuda, Argentina, Barbados, Belize, Botswana, Brazil,
Colombia, Costa Rica, Cyprus, Dominica, Dominican Republic, Equador, Fed.
States of Micronesia, Grenada, Guatemala, Honduras, India, Israel, Kiribati,
Madagascar, Marshall Islands, Mauritius, Nauru, Pakistan, Peru, Solomon
Islands, South Africa, St Kitts-Nevis, St Lucia, St Vincent and Grenadiens, Sudan,
Suriname, Taiwan, Trinidad and Tobago, Tuvalu, Turkey, Uruguay, Vanuatu,
Venezuela, Western Samoa, Zimbabwe
Parl.: Korea(S), Philippines, Sri Lanka, Tonga

Note: Refers only to those which obtained ≥ 3 points for Open Elections.

Table 7. *Effective elections*

I (o p.)
Parl.: Ethiopia, Malawi, Niger, Togo, Zaire
II (1 p.)
Parl. and Exec.: China, Cuba, Indonesia, Vietnam, Yemen(N)
Parl.: Algeria, Bhutan, Cameroon, Central African Republic, Côte d'Ivoire, Iraq,
Kenya, Libya, Morocco, Mozambique, Rwanda, Sierra Leone, Seychelles, Swazi-
land, Syria, Tanzania, Tonga
III (2 p.)
Parl. and Exec.: Egypt, Guatemala, Iran, Nicaragua, Taiwan, Zimbabwe
Parl.: Nepal, Zambia
IV (3 p.)
Parl. and Exec.: Brazil, El Salvador, Honduras, Korea(S), Madagascar, Pakistan,
Philippines, Suriname, Thailand, Turkey
V (4 p.)
Parl. and Exec.: Antigua and Barbuda, Argentina, Bahamas, Barbados, Belize, Bolivia,
Botswana, Colombia, Costa Rica, Cyprus, Dominica, Dominican Republic,
Equador, Fed. States of Micronesia, Gambia, Grenada, India, Israel, Jamaica,
Kiribati, Malaysia, Maldives, Marshall Islands, Mauritius, Mexico, Nauru, Papua
N. Guinea, Peru, Singapore, Senegal, Solomon Islands, South Africa, Sri Lanka, St
Kitts-Nevis, St Lucia, St Vincent and Grenadiens, Sudan, Trinidad and Tobago,
Tuvalu, Uruguay, Vanuatu, Venezuela, Western Samoa

Note: Refers only to those which obtained ≥ 1 point for Open Elections and Correct
Elections.

Table 8. *Organizational freedoms*

I (o p.)

Afghanistan, Algeria, Angola, Bahrain, Benin, Burundi, Cameroon, Cape Verde, Central African Republic, Chad, Congo, Cuba, Equatorial Guinea, Ethiopia, Guinea-Bissau, Iran, Iraq, Korea(N), Laos, Libya, Malawi, Maldives, Mauritania, Mozambique, Oman, Quatar, Rwanda, Sao Tome and Principe, Saudi Arabia, Seychelles, Somalia, Syria, Tanzania, Togo, United Arab Emirates, Vietnam, Yemen(N), Yemen(S), Zaire

I b (1 p.)

Bhutan, Burkina Faso, China, Côte d'Ivoire, Djibouti, Gabon, Guinea, Indonesia, Kenya, Kuwait, Mali, Niger, Nigeria

II (2 p.)

Brunei, Ghana, Sierra Leone, Swaziland, Zambia, Zimbabwe

II b (3 p.)

Burma, Egypt, Jordan, Lebanon, Lesotho, Morocco, Paraguay, South Africa, Tunisia

III (4 p.)

Chile, Comoros, Madagascar, Nepal, Nicaragua, Turkey, Uganda

III b (5 p.)

Fiji, Haiti, Korea(S)

IV (6 p.)

El Salvador, Guyana, Haiti, Liberia, Malaysia, Nauru, Pakistan, Peru, Singapore, Sri Lanka, Taiwan, Thailand

IV b (7 p.)

Bolivia, Dominican Republic, Equador, Mauritius, Mexico, Senegal, Sudan, Suriname, Vanuatu

V (8 p.)

Antigua and Barbuda, Argentina, Bahamas, Bangladesh, Barbados, Belize, Botswana, Brazil, Colombia, Costa Rica, Cyprus, Dominica, Fed. States of Micronesia, Gambia, Grenada, Guatemala, Honduras, India, Israel, Jamaica, Kiribati, Marshall Islands, Papua N. Guinea, Philippines, Solomon Islands, St Kitts-Nevis, St Lucia, St Vincent and Grenadiens, Tonga, Trinidad and Tobago, Tuvalu, Venezuela, Western Samoa, Uruguay

Table 9. *Freedom of opinion*

I (o p.)
Afghanistan, Angola, Burma, Cuba, Equatorial Guinea, Ethiopia, Iraq, Korea (N), Laos, Quatar, Sao Tome and Principe, Saudi Arabia, Somalia, Syria, Yemen(S)

I b (1 p.)
Bhutan, Brunei, Burkina Faso, Cameroon, Central African Republic, Libya, United Arab Emirates, Vietnam

II (2 p.)
Bahrain, Benin, Burundi, Cape Verde, Chad, China, Congo, Ghana, Guinea-Bissau, Indonesia, Iran, Malawi, Mauritania, Mozambique, Niger, Oman, Panama, Seychelles, Tanzania, Togo, Yemen(N), Zaire

II b (3 p.)
Comoros, Côte d'Ivoire, Djibouti, Gabon, Guinea, Jordan, Kenya, Kuwait, Mali, Nicaragua, Paraguay, Rwanda, South Africa, Swaziland, Zimbabwe

III (4 p.)
Algeria, Chile, Fiji, Lebanon, Liberia, Malaysia, Nepal, Vanuatu

III b (5 p.)
Bangladesh, El Salvador, Haiti, Madagascar, Morocco, Nigeria, Sierra Leone, Singapore, Sri Lanka, Taiwan, Tunisia, Turkey, Uganda, Zambia

IV (6 p.)
Antigua and Barbuda, Bahamas, Bolivia, Brazil, Colombia, Dominican Republic, Egypt, Gambia, Grenada, Guatemala, Guyana, Israel, Korea(S), Mexico, Pakistan, Peru, Senegal, Solomon Islands, Sudan, Suriname, Thailand, Venezuela

IV b (7 p.)
Botswana, Honduras, India, Jamaica, Lesotho, Mauritius, Philippines, St Kitts-Nevis, St Lucia, Tonga, Trinidad and Tobago, Uruguay

V (8 p.)
Argentina, Barbados, Belize, Costa Rica, Cyprus, Dominica, Equador, Fed. States of Micronesia, Kiribati, Marshall Islands, Nauru, Papua N. Guinea, St Vincent and Grenadiens, Tuvalu, Western Samoa

Table 10. *Political violence and oppression*

I (o p.)
: Afghanistan, Burma, Burundi, Ethiopia, Iran, Iraq, Korea(N), Lebanon, Somalia

I b (1 p.)
: (Angola), El Salvador (Laos), Mozambique, Sri Lanka, Sudan

II (2 p.)
: Chile, China, Colombia, Guatemala, Indonesia, Nicaragua, Peru, South Africa, Syria, Uganda, Vietnam (Yemen(S))

II b (3 p.)
: Algeria, Benin, Brazil, Burkina Faso, Chad (Cuba), Ghana, Haiti, Honduras (Libya), Morocco, Philippines (Saudi Arabia), Turkey

III (4 p.)
: Bahrain, Bangladesh, Cameroon, Central African Republic, Comoros, Congo (Equatorial Guinea), Guinea, Guinea-Bissau, India, Jordan, Kenya, Malawi, Mauritania, Mexico, Nepal, Niger, Panama, Paraguay (Quatar), Taiwan, Togo (United Arab Emirates), Yemen(N), Zaire

III b (5 p.)
: Brunei, Egypt, Equador, Gabon, Israel, Kuwait, Liberia, Malaysia, Maldives, Nigeria (Sao Tome and Principe), Seychelles, Tanzania, Zambia, Zimbabwe

IV (6 p.)
: Argentina, Bolivia, Cape Verde, Côte d'Ivoire, Djibouti, Dominican Republic, Fiji, Guyana, Jamaica, Korea(S), Madagascar, Mali, Oman, Pakistan, Rwanda, Sierra Leone, Singapore, Suriname, Swaziland, Thailand, Tunisia, Venezuela

IV b (7 p.)
: Bahamas, Belize, Botswana, Costa Rica, Gambia, Lesotho, Senegal, Vanuatu

V (8 p.)
: Antigua and Barbuda, Barbados, Bhutan, Cyprus, Dominica, Fed. States of Micronesia, Grenada, Kiribati, Marshall Islands, Mauritius, Nauru, Papua N. Guinea, Solomon Islands, St Kitts-Nevis, St Lucia, St Vincent and Grenadiens, Tonga, Trinidad and Tobago, Tuvalu, Uruguay, Western Samoa

Note: The countries in parentheses were awarded no points since they do not have a minimum total of two points for Organizational Freedoms or Freedom of Opinion.

election and political freedoms.[67] The coefficient becomes 0.79, which must be considered as a satisfactory level. The robustness of the index has been tested by several recalculations with a different distribution of points between the attributes under consideration. Thus we have in one case raised the values for elections by 50 per cent (as a result the original record was multiplied by the factor 1.5) and in another we similarly treated those for the political freedoms. Despite these alterations in the weight of the points the correlation between these scales and our index lies on the 0.99 level. Moreover, we have examined the effect of the threshold values which are applied in certain cases. We proceeded by taking different steps to reduce the points awarded for these attributes. These manipulations made very little difference, however; the scales which emerge closely resemble the original.[68] In other words, the robustness of our index is highly satisfactory.

Finally, we come to the question of the reliability of the classification concerning the attributes which have been discussed. There are, primarily, two difficulties here. The first concerns the quality of the factual base at our disposal. The difference between countries and kinds of attribute may be substantial in this regard. Occasionally we must be content with meagre, and perhaps also somewhat vague, data (e.g., on the number of political prisoners which, for natural reasons, may be difficult to elicit exactly). With more copious, and more detailed, information the classification may well have been somewhat different in several cases. Secondly, even with the best factual basis, it may be difficult to arrive at a fair internal grading inasmuch as the conditions relating to one aspect (e.g., concerning organizational freedoms) may be so different between the states. An unsatisfactory situation in one country must often be compared with different kinds of defect in another, which may naturally give rise to many a problem in drawing the line. The final result which is presented must therefore be interpreted with caution. In all probability minor differences, in the magnitude of $+/-$ 0.2, are invariably within the margin of error. If one state received the value 2.5 and another 2.7 (or 2.3) the difference is of no significance; it may ensue from a lack of data. Then there is the other kind of uncertainty: whether we could give the individual cases a reliable grading, given the information we had and the categories we used. Reclassifications which I myself undertook suggest that the outcome (with the summary procedure adopted) may in several cases swing

0.2 per cent up or down – on rare occasions twice as much: 0.4 per cent. In general we may say that if a state is assigned 3.0 points this means its 'real' value is presumably between 2.4 and 3.6. For differences outside this range of uncertainty (+/− 0.6), however, there is reason to assume that the degree of democracy actually does vary between countries.

Without greater hesitation, we may thereby assert that the levels of democracy in the countries of the Third World are strikingly uneven. The spread of the scale is, we may say, U-shaped (which is the opposite of a so-called normal distribution): the great majority of the cases fall into the lowest or the highest third with very few in between. Thus, the main pattern is that the states are democratic to a great or a slight extent. To occupy the position 'semi-democratic' is obviously difficult.

It should be pointed out that this result diverges considerably from the pattern which emerged in some earlier studies in the field. Above all, it strongly contradicts the (mutually variable) spread on the scale which was reported by Philip Coulter, Kenneth Bollen, Robert Jackman and Tatu Vanhanen. A comparison of the different outcomes – which is naturally of great significance for the understanding and explanation of the varying levels of democracy – is given in Appendix A.

PART TWO

Explaining the level of democracy

CHAPTER 4

Introduction

In this section we shall explore a number of theories on the requisites of democracy. These are grouped into three categories, each of which is the subject of a chapter: socio-economic conditions (Chapt. 5), demographic and cultural conditions (Chapt. 6) and institutional conditions (Chapt. 7). It should be remarked that this is a somewhat rough division; naturally it is impossible to draw hard and fast lines between the various explanations. This division merely attempts to elucidate what in each theory constitutes the principal problem as far as democracy is concerned, that is, where a change (if such is possible) should preferably occur if democracy is to be promoted.

The layout is throughout such that I first present the general statements of the respective theory, its basic tenets and empirical assertions. The aim here is to offer, according to my ability, the best possible interpretation of the ideas in question, which means that I sometimes also 'stretch' the theory with further arguments which seem to fit the picture and strengthen its position.[1] Then follows an empirical examination based on the index of the level of democracy which was presented earlier. The objective is to test the extent to which the emergent differences between the countries in terms of democratic performances can be explained by the theories and related hypotheses which are discussed.

The inquiry employs statistical procedures, chiefly by application of regression analyses. For each type of explanation which is subjected to scrutiny a test is first made in the form of a simple (bivariate) regression. We can then see whether each of the variables at issue is associated (positively or negatively) with democracy. We then proceed to multiple regression which allows simultaneous testing of different variables. We can thereby discern (i) how much the factors in question together explain, which is expressed in percentage explained variance and (ii) how strong they are *vis-à-vis* each other, which is manifested in the magnitudes of the regression coefficients.[2] In this way, new theories are examined step by step; these are operationalized into testable variables, which are first examined separately and then together with the attributes that previously proved to have statistically significant connections with the level of democracy.

The results are summarised in a concluding chapter. In addition, we here complicate the picture by raising *inter alia* the following questions: (a) Whether it makes any difference if the requirements for statistical certainty are lowered, and if all the interesting explanatory variables are tested simultaneously and not in the order (according to category) which was previously applied. (b) The extent to which the demonstrated connections between democracy and other attributes are global, or regionally contingent. (c) Explanatory factors of a structural vs. an actor-oriented nature, including the significance of political leadership. (d) What causes what: do the attributes X, Y and Z have an effect on the level of democracy, or could it be the other way around?

The whole matter is concluded with a discussion of how this type of inquiry is related to another possible approach, namely case studies. Some views are then expressed on how continued research into the requisites of democracy may be pursued.

CHAPTER 5

Socio-economic conditions

MODERNIZATION

The hitherto greatest (in terms of adherents and research pursued) and most dominant theory of the prerequisites of democracy is the modernization theory (sometimes also called the development theory). It was launched in the late 1950s and had its heyday in the early and mid-1960s. In purely scientific terms, it coincided with the politico-sociological-cum-functionalistic vogue, which was characterized by a strong emphasis on the significance of the value and norm systems for the explanation of political behaviour, and which, with regard to method, often involved quantitative studies, i.e., collection of mass data which are subjected to statistical analysis.

Temporally speaking, it also coincided with a very hopeful period for the spread of democracy: in the years around 1960 a good many colonies in Africa gained their independence with the introduction of democratic forms of government, and several countries in Latin America too then abandoned military government in favour of rule by the people. Democracy seemed generally to be in progress. This state of affairs should to some extent explain the optimistic view which frequently characterized the analyses of the modernization school.

Its basic tenet is that a general economic development – measured in GNP/capita, the degree of industrialization, urbanization, etc. – should bring about an overall transformation of the society which, in turn, gives rise to a political change in democracy's favour. It is expected that a general social mobilization will ensue which Karl Deutsch, one of the leading advocates of the modernization school, defined as 'the process in which major clusters of old social, economic and psychological commitments are eroded or broken and people become available for new patterns of socialization and

77

behaviour'. This pertained to a development 'away *from* a life of local isolation, traditionalism and political apathy, and ... *into* a different life of broader and deeper involvement in the vast complexities of modern life, including potential and actual involvement in mass politics'.[1]

In concrete terms, the belief was that economic and social development would result in greater literacy and a generally higher educational level among the masses of the population, which would promote openness and a deeper insight into political issues. A similar effect was expected to ensue from increased media exposure: by reading newspapers, listening to radio and watching TV, the people would acquire a broader outlook and deeper tolerance by reason of a richer, more varied flow of information. In the same way, the citizens would become more interested in, and familiar with political issues, which would contribute to increased participation; in terms of both electoral turnout and deeper commitment to party and organizational work. Thus, the modernization theory may be seen in large measure as a dynamic theory concerning the beneficient effect of education and mass communications on political life. The idea was first formulated in detail in Daniel Lerner's book *The Passing of Traditional Society*, 1958, and summarized somewhat later by the man who would be the school's most renowned exponent, Seymour Lipset: the said process 'broadens men's outlook, enables them to understand the needs for norms of tolerance, restrains them from adhering to extremist doctrines, and increases their capacity to make rational electoral choices'.[2]

Furthermore, the economic and social development was expected to have other positive effects. Through industrialization and a generally increased prosperity, formerly oppressed and underprivileged groups would obtain improved political resources, and thereby greater possibilities to hold their own in public life: an educated, organized working class would emerge, and, equally important, a growing middle class would subject the traditional elite of landowners, the military and officials to an even harder competition for political power. As a result of economic progress – and with that an increasing 'cake' – it should also be less difficult to satisfy different groups' demands on the public sector. The problems inherent in the distribution of income in the society were expected thereby to become easier to resolve, which in turn should promote a generally greater tolerance and spirit of co-operation in politics.

Similar effects were postulated to result from urbanization and the internal migration of people which the economic modernization would involve. People could thereby break free of their formerly closed, traditional environments, often pervaded by authoritarianism and, by increased mingling and interaction with other population groups, develop more open, 'democratic' attitudes.[3]

Thus, the modernization would bring about a series of changes at the mass level which, according to the postulated scenario, could further a democratic development. Previously excluded groups could, through increased competence and organization, acquire reinforced political resources. Moreover, via economic growth, mass communications, and an increasing social and geographical mobility, the antagonisms in the society could be modulated and possibilities created for the peaceful mode of conflict-solving that democracy implies.

The exponents of the modernization school, however, did not merely display images of reality; they could also present abundant empirical support for their theses. By collecting data from some 50 states, Lerner demonstrated high statistical correlations between, on the one hand, level of education, degree of urbanization, and mass communications and, on the other, democracy measured in terms of political participation.[4] And, from similarly broad-based studies, first Lipset and later also Philip Cutright could document a strong connection between degree of economic development and different measures of democracy.[5] Among the many scholars who presented similar results, James Coleman and Bruce Russet may also be mentioned. The former examined a number of states in Africa, Asia and Latin America, which were classified on a scale from 'competitive' to 'semicompetitive' and 'authoritarian'. For the whole population, as for each continent, a clear connection emerged between the countries' economic standing and the type of government applied.[6] Using the same classification, and a selection of twice as many countries (89), Russet reached a similar result. It was, he concluded, 'good evidence that a reasonably high level of economic development makes the success of democracy more likely'.[7]

Thus, it is in no way surprising that the modernization school very soon gained a prominent academic position. It presented 'hard' data, which could be incorporated in a generally worded theory of political change which in turn – this was a further strength – could be linked to a wider economic theory for development in the countries of the Third World. According to this wider viewpoint, development, practically all along the line, could be launched via a general process of learning and diffusion. With assistance and through good examples (by, for instance, establishment of foreign companies), and as a result of the grafting of new ('rational') systems of norms and behaviour, the development could gain momentum. The developing countries were expected thereby to move in the same direction – economically, socially and politically – as Western Europe and the USA.[8]

From the point of view of the countries giving aid – such projects were at this time initiated on a larger scale – this was undoubtedly an attractive theory. It offered bright prospects, and moreover its practical content was fairly simple. All its objectives, both material and political, would ensue from economic development which would soon, it was hoped, gain impetus.[9]

But the optimism would only too soon be crushed. Despite diverse major aid efforts, no general 'take-off' occurred. The economies of the developing countries proved in many cases to stand still – if not retrogress.[10] And, from the viewpoint of democracy, the picture did not improve, but rather deteriorated. In many of the countries in Africa which at independence adopted a democratic order (enjoined by the colonial power), diverse modes of authoritarian government (military juntas, one-party regimes, or a more personal dictatorship) were eventually introduced, and in Latin America military power again broadly occupied the halls of government in the mid-1960s.

Furthermore, it was now not only reality which resisted. The theses and general tenets of the modernization theory were subjected to, eventually, ever more intensive, intellectual and political criticism. It was accused of ethnocentrism (that is, a manifestation of narrow Western values), and an increasing number of researchers also began to challenge the explanatory model on which the theory was based.[11]

The first scholar emphatically to question the central theses of the modernization school was Samuel Huntington. In his grand work *Political Order in Changing Societies*, 1968, he figuratively overturned one of the basic tenets of the modernists, i.e., that economic and social change would give rise to a political culture more favourable to social peace. In reality, Huntington asserts, rather the opposite occurs; the conflicts in society and in political life do not diminish through modernization – but are usually sorely aggravated. When the traditional, ingrained conditions suddenly start to change this often leads to an exacerbation of the diverse rifts in the population. It is in this phase that religious fundamentalism is wont to erupt, with serious political clashes as a result. In the same way, ethnic and other divisions are strengthened, which in traditional societies seldom caused major problems (pre-Colonial Africa is cited as an example). Huntington's explanation is that the demands for change – often imposed from above or from outside – result in a greater uncertainty, or are indeed regarded as a threat. This accentuates the needs for group identity and the desire to protect traditional values and patterns of life. Thus, the emergent social transformation does not give rise to the politically favourable social 'spiral' which the adherents of the modernization school envisaged.[12]

Nor was it difficult to find striking deviations from the pattern predicted by the theory. It was feasible *inter alia* to point to India, which had long been characterized, in several respects, by a low degree of socio-economic development, and simultaneously good democratic achievement. Moreover, there were several countries where the inverse conditions prevailed, e.g., in the rich oil states of the Arab world.[13] The theory seemed to limp also in an historical perspective. Thus Robert Dahl recalled that the USA, at the time (1830s) when Tocqueville wrote his famous work *De La Democratie en Amerique*, had a very low degree of development measured in GNP per capita. Furthermore, he demonstrates, the degree of urbanization was minimal. Well-nigh the entire population was rural. Agriculture predominated as a means of livelihood, and the country lacked most of the means of mass communication which characterize a modern society. After this presentation of the facts Dahl reaches the following conclusion:

A social scientist armed only with the data examined so far – and the theories often used to explain these data – might justifiably conclude that in the early nineteenth century there was scarcely a chance for the development of democracy in America, yet I suspect that most of us continue to find Tocqueville's interpretation more convincing.[14]

Perhaps then, were the connections which Coleman *et al.* had reported not reliable? Let us see what the subsequent research could prove. The conditions at the beginning of the 1960s have been subjected to a good many investigations; with regard to comparative studies of democracy this is by far the most penetrated period. The study most quoted, and for good reason, is that executed by Kenneth Bollen. Starting from far more precise definitions of concepts than his predecessors, and applying more sophisticated statistical techniques, he could evince essential relationships between the degree of economic development and the variation in the level of democracy between countries.[15] Indeed, similar results have emerged in other investigations, also for other periods.[16] In other words, the theses of the modernization school have not been directly refuted. At the same time, it is clear that there is no simple, total connection between different dimensions of modernization and the way in which the mode of government is designed; this issue could be illustrated for every period by several examples divergent from the theory. The question is how these deviations should be understood.

One approach to the problem is to assume that the connection is not linear (which implies that not every increase of the one variable involves a corresponding increase of the other). Deutsch himself already thought in these terms. The social mobilization which provided the impetus for the transformation process would have an impact, as he postulated, only when the different indications of development – urbanization, literacy, media exposure, income per capita etc. – passed certain threshold values. Only then could they work in a distinct, convergent direction.[17] Yet, Deutsch did not submit any empirical evidence for his hypothesis. On the other hand, Deane Neubauer could in an investigation demonstrate threshold effects – but of an opposite nature. While Deutsch thought that the relationship was limited downward (as a floor) Neubauer's results indicated that it was limited upward (as a roof); up to a certain level different dimensions of socio-economic development influenced the degree of democracy – after that they had hardly any effect at all.[18] This observation that the connection is broken, almost curvilinear in character, was confirmed by subsequent studies.[19]

Another way of explaining the deviant cases is to pay regard to the mutual coherence of the socio-economic factors. According to the 'ideal' model, development in the form of urbanization, industrialization, increased popular education, etc., is thought to proceed in parallel, or is at least integrated in the same direction. But, of course, it is not certain that this is the case – Lerner's early study already showed that. In the countries which he investigated, major discrepancies emerged between different measurements of development, particularly between urbanization and literacy, with the effect that progress was far greater in the former than the latter respect. According to the author, such imbalances tended 'to become circular and to accelerate social disorganization' both politically and economically.[20] Similar ideas were expressed by Huntington, who for his part emphasized the problems which may arise when demographical and educational changes are not accompanied by a corresponding economic development. When individuals migrate from rural to urban environments, and when the educational level, literacy, and exposure to media increase, their demands and expectations in social and economic respects also grow. If, by reason of a low or stagnant rate of economic growth, these cannot be satisfied, this will result in alienation and strong tensions in society. It is in these situations, says Huntington, that political and religious extremism have their best breeding ground, and such atmospheres hardly promote the growth of the models of political decision-making which democracy involves.[21]

So much for the debate hitherto concerning the theses of the modernization school. Let us now turn to what our own study has to say on these issues. As basis for the analysis we have compiled various data on the countries investigated. The degree of economic development is measured, as is customary, in terms of GNP and energy consumption per capita, the percentages employed in different sectors (agriculture, industry and service), and the size of industrial production in relation to GNP. As a sign of the actual standard of living, we have information on the consumption of calories and infant mortality in the population. Moreover, we have measurements of the degree of urbanization, literacy, the percentage of the population who attended education at different stages of the school system (primary, secondary and higher), and on the level of media exposure and mass communications, that is, the distribution through the population of daily newspapers, telephones, and radio and TV sets.[22]

Before presenting the findings, I would insert a comment pertinent to the selection of countries. The great majority of studies of democracy based on data from several countries cover a number of states not only from the Third World but also from the First (Western Europe and North America).[23] Hence, the general connections between democracy and degree of socio-economic development are probably strengthened, since this link has long been manifest in the First World. In other words, the picture may change when we, as here, only consider the conditions in the Third World and, furthermore, which has not previously been done, include all the independent states there.

Now for the point. The different measurements of development may be expected to have significant internal connections. To a great extent, this proves to be the case. A high GNP and energy consumption per capita go hand in hand with a far advanced industrialization and urbanization, few employed in agriculture and a comparatively high standard of living for the population – and vice versa.[24] Moreover, literacy, education at various levels, and the different measurements of media exposure and mass communications are, without exception, strongly correlated with each other.[25] A factor analysis, which allows an overall test of the connections between a number of variables, reveals an equivalent pattern: the latter attributes cluster together while the purely economic variables form a separate group.[26] In other words, when we speak of socio-economic development in the part of the world which we are studying, we must be aware that it is not a wholly uniform phenomenon. It is rather a state of affairs that is divided into two dimensions; one which pertains to the degree of economic development in different respects, and one which relates to the level of popular education and mass communications.[27] At the same time it should be remarked that these dimensions, like several of the attributes included on each 'side', are essentially correlated. Thus, the level of literacy has a manifest connection (in an easily understood direction) with the degree of urbanization and the percentage employed outside the agricultural sector, and it is also, albeit more moderately, correlated with the GNP level and the extent of industrialization.[28] Other measurements of popular education and mass communications also exhibit coherence with the economic attributes, although these are generally weaker.

When we consider the association with democracy the picture, as illustrated in Table 11, varies somewhat. Particularly as regards the percentage employed outside the agricultural sector and the infant mortality in the population – but also concerning literacy – a linear association with the level of democracy emerges. With respect to GNP per capita, urbanization and calorie consumption we find another tendency; the degree of democracy rises from a low to somewhat higher levels of development only to flatten out or decline thereafter. Here we may, although more or less explicitly, establish

Table 11. *Average level of democracy by different measurements of socio-economic development, in intervals.*

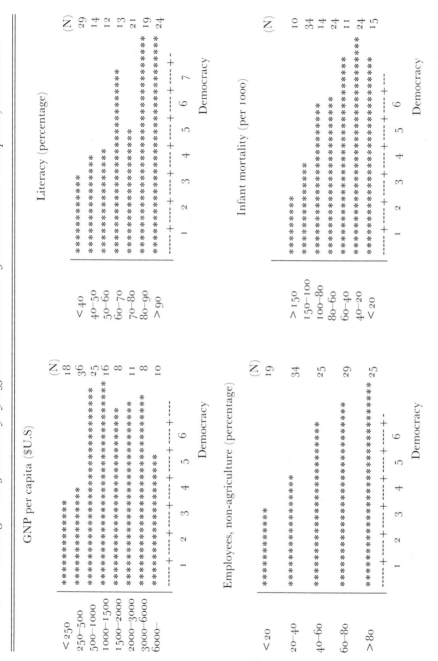

Table 11 (*Cont.*)

Urbanization (percentage)

	(N)
<15	14
15–30	33
30–45	33
45–60	26
60–75	13
>75	13

```
< 15    **************
15-30   ******************
30-45   ********************
45-60   **************************
60-75   ****************
> 75    ***********************

        +----+----+----+----+----
        1    2    3    4    5
                Democracy
```

Calorie consumption per capita

	(N)
<2000	19
2000–2200	22
2200–2400	28
2400–2600	20
2600–2800	13
2800–3000	14
>3000	16

```
< 2000      ****************
2000-2200   ****************
2200-2400   ********************
2400-2600   ***********************
2600-2800   ***********************
2800-3000   ****************
> 3000      ***************

            +----+----+----+----+----+
            1    2    3    4    5    6
                    Democracy
```

Table 12. *Included measurements of socio-economic development and level of democracy. Simple regression.*

	Standardized regression coefficient	Explained variance (percentage)	
GNP-level (Log)	0.24**	5.8	(N:132)
Energy consumption (Log)	0.24**	5.7	(N:129)
Employed in agriculture	0.29**	8.7	(N:129)
Employed in industry (Log)	0.19*	3.5	(N:129)
Employed in service	0.35**	12.3	(N:129)
Industrial production	0.05	0.3	(N:127)
Urbanization (Log)	0.17	2.8	(N:131)
Calorie consumption	0.13	1.8	(N:124)
Infant mortality	−0.44**	19.7	(N:132)
Education, primary	0.35**	12.7	(N:132)
Education, secondary (Log)	0.33**	10.8	(N:132)
Education, higher	0.29**	10.7	(N:121)
Literacy	0.46**	21.4	(N:132)
Radio sets	0.27**	7.3	(N:122)
TV sets	0.03	0.1	(N:123)
Telephones	0.35**	12.3	(N:131)
Daily newspapers	0.30**	8.8	(N: 98)

* significance at the 0.05 level
** significance at the 0.01 level
Note: Here, and henceforth, a two-tailed test of significance is applied.

such threshold effects, as Neubauer (with a far different selection of countries)[29] reported. Yet, as we saw, this is not a general pattern for the usual measurements of socio-economic development.

In a simple regression against the level of democracy, several variables have – as is shown in Table 12 – connections which are statistically certain (significant) at the level of 0.05 or better.[30] Table 13 presents three multiple regressions, from which we may infer the relative strength of the different attributes, both in the form of mutual controls and how much they jointly explain. Here a selection has obviously occurred. Firstly, only those measurements which previously exhibited statistical significance are considered. Secondly, by reason of, in some cases, strong mutual connections between the variables which would render the regression analysis uncertain, a limitation must be applied. Thus, the GNP level and the energy consumption are very strongly correlated ($r = 0.90$)[31], as

Table 13. *A selection of measurements of socio-economic development and level of democracy. Three multiple regressions.*

	Standardized regression coefficients	Explained variance (percentage)
(A)		
GNP-level (Log)	−0.08	
Employed in service	0.41**	
		12.6
(B)		
Education, primary	0.07	
Education, secondary	0.04	
Education, higher	0.05	
Literacy	0.29*	
Radio sets	0.01	
Telephones	0.17	
		24.9
(C)		
Employed in service	0.11	
Literacy	0.40**	
		22.1

* significance at the 0.05 level
** significance at the 0.01 level

are the percentages employed in agriculture, industry and service (r = 0.85–0.95) and literacy and infant mortality (r = 0.85). In consequence, only one of the variables in each case could be included.[32] Finally, in order to avoid too fragile a basis, I have excluded the distribution of daily newspapers, since it was not possible to obtain useful data for over 30 of the countries.

We see the results. In the rivalry between the two economic attributes, GNP and the proportion employed in service, the latter wholly dominates the picture. Thus, the situation regarding the labour market and production appears more important for democracy than how rich the countries are. The following regression includes several variables which relate to popular education and mass communications. As is evident, one of these takes precedence over the others, namely literacy. When we move on to the 'final round' – where the two attributes which were previously the strongest combined – we find a very striking outcome. When literacy and the percentage employed in the service sector are opposed, the connection between the latter variable and democracy is reduced to insignificance. Thus, the proportion of the population who can read is clearly the most decisive of the different measurements of the degree of socio-economic development which are included here. Its strength also emerges from a comparison of the explanatory variance in the tables presented: it is little raised from the cases (see Table 12) where literacy appears alone and those where other measurements are also included. All in all, it seems that the association between the other attributes and democracy consists largely of a reflection of the influence of literacy; indeed, the more they are internally correlated with literacy, the stronger is their individual connection with democracy.

In the debate on modernization, the thought has sometimes been expressed that its components may be more or less interchangeable. Thus, it has been mentioned that low literacy could be recompensed by a relatively strong expansion of the broadcasting media. Even if people are incapable of benefiting by what is written in newspapers etc. they can still, it is maintained, obtain information and a broader outlook by listening to the radio, for example.[33] In order to test this we included, in a regression, literacy and the distribution through the population of radio and television sets. The results indicate, however, that no substantial compensatory effect of these broadcasting media exists.[34]

Another idea, which would apply more generally with regard to modernization, is that the level of development valid on every occasion is not the most essential element, but rather the actual rate of the process of change.[35] Bearing in mind that we could here only check on a few measurements of change over time – that is, GNP level, calorie consumption and infant mortality – we did not find any proof of this hypothesis. Each of these indicators of change in the degree of development has rather moderate or weak associations with democracy,[36] which also fade away when they are matched against literacy.[37]

As we saw earlier, imbalance between certain components of development is believed to create problems in this context. Lerner referred to the relation between urbanization and literacy, while for his part Huntington voiced doubts chiefly with respect to the imbalance between, on the one hand, education, literacy and urbanization and, on the other economic development. However, neither of these authors (or anyone thereafter) has empirically tested the extent to which these assumptions are justified.

In order to test these ideas, we have established a number of measurements which for each country states the mutual balance in terms of relative degree of development between different modernization variables: for the degree of urbanization in relation to literacy, and for several indicators of degree of economic development related to the level of education, literacy and urbanization. We have thereby obtained some 40 measurements in all.[38] On the whole, these do not give rise to any directly disturbing observations. As could be expected from the results already reported, an 'uneven' development in favour of the degree of education – e.g., high values for schooling and literacy are not balanced by a similar relative level in economic respects – is no problem as far as democracy is concerned. On the contrary, such imbalances usually involve a higher degree of democracy.[39] The relationship between urbanization and certain measurements of economic development are among the few exceptions worth mentioning. If the level as regards the former clearly surpasses the latter, this has a negative effect on the degree of democracy. Moreover, in one case – concerning the balance between urbanization and the percentage employed in the service sector – this connection is significant even when literacy is included in the regression.[40] Thus, we here find support for one of the arguments expressed by Huntington. But as is clear, this is an isolated example. The reverse situation usually prevails or, which is the most common, there is no connection whatever between an asymmetrical degree of development and democracy.

When it was formulated, the modernization theory derived its inspiration from the largely unanimous development – economically, socially and politically – which occurred in the Western world.[41] The same process, it was thought, would ensue in the developing countries (as they came to be called). In the study of these states, as it proceeded here, we find that this belief does not lack justification. Yet, it is not primarily the economic factors – which have loomed large in recent research in this field[42] – which are interesting in this context. The crucial point for a political change in the said direction chiefly comprises those attributes which pertain to popular education. Here in turn one component rises above the mass, namely the proportion of literates among the population. With reference to the development of democracy, this seems to be the central factor in the modernization process.

DEPENDENCY

It is a characteristic feature of the modernization school, as of its like-minded critics (such as Huntington), to assign the problems – the obstacles to development – internally in the countries concerned. This approach is in stark contrast to the so-called dependency school which emerged in the late 1960s and assumed a strong position in the debate. Intellectually, it derives inspiration from the Marxist theory of imperialism; with reference to the conditions in the Third World it may be said to constitute a more concrete, modern application of this analytical model.[43] The principal idea is that the difficulties of the developing countries are caused chiefly by their external economic relations: they represent the 'underdog' in an uneven, exploitive, international system. In the words of one of the school's prominent figures, André Gunder Frank, they occupy positions as satellites, which are economically and therefore also politically inferior to the capitalistic metropoles of the Western world (other common epithets are 'peripheral states' and 'core states'). The solution of these countries' dilemma then cannot reasonably be that prescribed by the modernists, namely an increased interaction – in terms of trade policy, culture and politics – with the Western world. On the contrary, these bonds, characterized by an uneven exchange, should be cut loose. Only through independence and self-confidence can the countries of the Third World obtain the possibility of development and progress.[44]

With these theoretical tenets it is by no means surprising that the political systems in the Third World are often fragile and beset by authoritarian rule. This indeed is a consequence of dependency: they are controlled by the great economic powers which intervene – directly or by proxy – when their status seems to be threatened in various ways. The usually rapidly changing internal groups which hold the power to rule occupy a very weak position. And this is not only true *vis-à-vis* the external metropoles; they also frequently have very slender roots in domestic policy.

The idea is that the penetration of external capital requires a loyal political support group in the countries concerned. A kind of coalition is therefore created between local land-owners, the merchant class and traditional elite groups (not least the military), on the one hand, and the governments of the metropolitan countries and the multinational companies on the other; all for the purpose of keeping the yield on the investments up and the labour costs and consumption down – which calls for tough political methods. Hence the emergent middle class does not play the role favourable to democracy assumed by the modernization school, nor do the workers, who are oppressed and excluded from political influence.[45]

The dependency theory may be seen chiefly as a theory of unevenly divided resources; whole nations, nay even continents, find themselves as clients of the financial centres of the Western world. In such a position of structural inferiority, a democratic development can hardly gain momentum: firstly, because the domestic actors simply are not masters of their own house but act as instruments of the far too strong external forces. Secondly, the dependence situation involves severe internal conflicts in the countries concerned. An increasingly dual society takes shape; a distinct separation emerges between a few, modern, capitalistically penetrated centres and a large, generally stagnant, traditional sector. At the same time, growing social divisions are created between a prosperous elite and the poverty-stricken majority of the population.

In other words, the dependency school could offer a very general, well-nigh all-embracing, interpretation of the problems of the Third World; both its poverty and its unstable, often undemocratic, modes of government. Furthermore, it was highly coherent in theoretical terms – and at the same time cogently simple in its content: the different shifts in political life could essentially be seen as a reflection of the prevalent capitalist relationships in the world economy. Thus, it also gave clear indications on how the countries in question could escape from 'the trap of underdevelopment' in which they were caught. It was needful to break the bonds with the exploitative international market system. This could be achieved by broad popular mobilization, nationalization of foreign companies, and a general transition to socialist-oriented forms of production. The development of Cuba (after Castro's take-over of power) particularly – and to some extent also, such countries as Tanzania and the former Portuguese colonies in Africa – was held up as an example to be followed.[46]

Nevertheless, the theory would be afflicted soon after its heyday by about the same kind of difficulties as prevented the further propagation of the modernization school. The imminent reality did not offer exactly the prospects envisaged. Many of the states which concentrated on independence encountered major economic problems (on the other hand development gathered momentum in those countries – such as South Korea – which sought a purged 'dependence policy' *vis-à-vis* the international capitalist system);[47] nor were the explicit programmes for a broad popular mobilization crowned with success.[48] Soon enough, the scientific criticism too ensued. The theory was accused of being far too axiomatic and closed, and in its concrete content obsessed with the developing countries' external trade relationships, with the effect that the analyses of the internal conditions were subject to a rigid and stereotyped interpretation.[49]

The empirical tests which were performed on the dependency theory chiefly concerned its predictions in the economic sphere.[50] This is understandable *per se*: basically it is a theory about obstacles to economic growth and how these can be overcome.[51] Nevertheless, some tests of the predicted political consequences have been executed. Thus, Robert Kaufman and his colleagues carried out a study of the connection between economic dependence and several political variables (participation in elections, trade-union membership, constitutional stability and militarism) in Latin America. The results were, in the words of the authors, 'rather mixed'. In some cases the relationships flowed as expected (signifying that economic dependence had a negative effect in the said respects), while in others they were weak or directly opposite. Moreover, scrutiny for other attributes – degree of economic development and literacy – indicated that these had in general greater explanatory power.[52] Kenneth Bollen too should be mentioned, who in a wide-ranging study demonstrated a predicated negative and significant connection between the degree of democracy and the countries' peripheral position.[53] This result, however, has been strongly questioned. When another researcher later repeated the study, with a somewhat different methodological layout, the connection disappeared, as also occurred when alternative measurements of the attributes in question were tested.[54] It may also be remarked that Bollen himself in a subsequent study, with a different set of control variables, reported results pointing in the same direction, implying that dependency has little or no relevance in this context.[55]

Several measurements have been used for the study of dependency, the following four being the most common: (1) trade dependency, i.e. a country's total trade, imports plus exports, in relation to its GNP (or GDP); (2) partner dependency: how great a share of the imports or exports come from or go to a certain country;[56] (3) commodity dependency; that is, how high a percentage the largest export item (or the two largest) represents of the total exports, and (4) investment dependency: the proportion of direct foreign investments in a country in relation to its GNP (or GDP).[57] The overall logic is, of course, that countries which in these respects are markedly dependent are, to the same extent, sensitive and vulnerable to pressures from outside – e.g., by embargoes or blockades – which severely restrict their scope for action, and thereby both hamper their economic development and curtail the opportunities for popular participation in political decision-making.

Partly in reaction to the generally poor outcome of the theory (not least as regards its economic predictions), an alternative mode of measuring dependency was suggested by David Snyder and Edward Kick. The idea is to give a total measurement for the interaction in several senses between states, and then not merely in terms of trade but also concerning military interventions, diplomatic relations and treaties. A number of networks or blocs comprising groups of states thereby crystallize. On this basis, the countries in turn may be divided into a hierarchy with reference to their 'World System Position' (core, semiperiphery and periphery).[58] With this reformulation, however, Snyder and Kick have, as other researchers remarked, dissociated themselves from the original premises of the dependency theory: they include (with equal weight) many, mutually disparate attributes in their bloc model.[59]

In this inquiry, we shall use the traditional measurements of dependency which were mentioned above together with a fairly simple indicator or a bloc-relationship, namely the proportion of trade a country has with the EC, with the USA, with the Soviet Union and Eastern Europe, and with the other countries in the world.[60] According to the premises of the dependency theory, the first two kinds of relationship (particularly that with the USA) should have an adverse effect, while an extensive economic interaction with the Soviet bloc, as with the group of 'Other countries', may be expected to be advantageous, since it involves a greater independence from the international centres of the capitalist world.[61]

On the whole, it may be said that the indicators of dependency

Table 14. *Included measurements of dependency and level of democracy.*
Simple regression.

	Standardized regression coefficient	Explained variance (percentage)	
Total trade (Log)	0.19[*]	3.5	(N:132)
Partner concentration, imp.	0.09	0.7	(N:129)
Partner concentration, exp.	0.00	0.0	(N:128)
Commodity concentration	−0.42[**]	17.7	(N:120)
Direct investments	0.26[**]	6.7	(N:127)
Trade, EC, imp.	−0.40[**]	15.9	(N:126)
Trade, EC, exp.	−0.14	2.1	(N:126)
Trade, USA, imp.	0.53[**]	28.1	(N:127)
Trade, USA, exp.	0.37[**]	13.4	(N:126)
Trade, Soviet bloc, imp.	−0.26[**]	6.9	(N:118)
Trade, Soviet, exp.	−0.22[*]	4.7	(N:117)
Trade, others, imp.	0.19[*]	3.7	(N:128)
Trade, others, exp.	−0.03	0.1	(N:127)

[*] significance at the 0.05 level
[**] significance at the 0.01 level

mentioned here have a fairly moderate internal coherence. In general, the correlation between the attributes is weak,[62] and factor analysis reveals a strikingly splintered pattern.[63] Thus, there is reason to question the frequent references to dependency as a kind of uniform, coherent phenomenon. Given the measurements used, it is rather a matter of a number of fairly disparate attributes (whether this derives from the primary assumptions of the theory or the current ways of applying it would seem to be open to discussion).

Table 14 illustrates the association between level of democracy and measurements of dependency. The outcome obviously varies considerably. The variation between the countries with regard to partner dependence in trade has no effect on democracy.[64] On the other hand, we find that trade dependency and investment dependency − against the theory's predictions − exhibit clear positive relationships, while the commodity concentration gives − in accordance with the theory − a markedly negative outcome.[65] Regarding trade with different blocs, the results indicate that dealings with the USA have a highly favourable effect on the degree of democracy, which is undoubtedly in stark contrast to current notions in the

Table 15. *A selection of measurements of dependency and level of democracy. Two multiple regressions.*

	Standardized regression coefficients	Explained variance (percentage)
(A)		
Total trade (Log)	0.00	
Commodity concentration	-0.27^{**}	
Direct investments	0.23^{**}	
Trade, EC, imp.	-0.25^{**}	
Trade, USA, imp.	0.33^{**}	
Trade, Soviet bloc, imp.	-0.18^{*}	
		49.4
(B)		
Total trade (Log)	-0.04	
Commodity concentration	-0.26^{**}	
Direct investments	0.22^{**}	
Trade, EC	-0.18^{*}	
Trade, USA,	0.26^{**}	
Trade, Soviet bloc, imp.	-0.21^{*}	
Literacy	0.23^{*}	
		53.4

* significance at the 0.05 level
** significance at the 0.01 level

writings of the dependency school. This is also the case (although not as strikingly) concerning trade relations with the Soviet Union and Eastern Europe, which display negative connections. Yet we see that trade with the EC, particularly regarding imports, yield an outcome which supports the assumptions of the theory. To some extent the same can be said about trade with the rest of the world. It is otherwise worth noting that, irrespective of the direction of the connection, import dependency affects most strongly the degree of democracy in the countries under study.

In order to check on the mutual links, two multiple regressions are presented in Table 15. The first comprises a selection of the just-scrutinized dependence variables,[66] while the second also includes literacy; as we found previously, the strongest modernization variable. Matched against other measurements, trade dependence demonstrably loses its significance in the context. The other indicators of dependence, however, stand firm, although the coefficients now, naturally, become lower. Moreover, a glance at the explained variance – which lies at around 50 percent tells us that the included measurements of economic dependence together have a strong effect on the level of democracy in the countries under study (albeit as we already observed, sometimes in an unexpected direction). It may be added that among these, trade with different blocs yields the strongest effect.[67]

Then when literacy is included in the regression, no major changes ensue. This emphasizes the fact that the external economic relations 'in their own right' have a considerable influence on the design of government in the Third World.

Beside the ordinary commercial links, aid is an important factor for many of the countries we study. Thereby, one could assert, a state of dependency is also created which (according to the same logic as before) limits the autonomy of the recipient countries.[68] In our study, two measurements of this kind of dependency were included, namely the total amount of aid in relation to GNP and the proportion of assistance from the largest and the second largest donor respectively. These attributes are, it would appear, only weakly intercorrelated[69] and they also have, in general, a moderate connection with the indicators of dependence which are discussed above.[70]

With regard to the level of democracy, the extent of aid in relation to the GNP has no effect at all.[71] On the one hand, concentration on the donor side gives a result worthy of note. Counted on the percentage for the two largest donors a positive, significant relationship emerges.[72] Accordingly, concentration in this respect appears favourably to democracy. Yet it should be remarked that the relationship is weakened (and becomes insignificant) when the commercial relations are included.[73] In other words, side by side with other measurements of dependency, aid dependence has little influence in the context.

In contrast to earlier studies, we could here demonstrate a very pronounced support for the idea that the mode of government in the Third World is influenced by the countries' external economic relations. But the dependency school's interpretations of the relationships have not thereby been confirmed overall. An expected outcome could indeed be recorded as regards the concentration of commodities and trade with the EC countries. On the other hand, from the theories' viewpoint it must appear problematic that an extensive trade with the USA (and , on the other hand, little such with the Soviet bloc), together with a high proportion of foreign direct investments, seems to have a positive effect on the development of democracy in the Third World.

DISTRIBUTION OF INCOME AND PROPERTY

The thought that the mode of government is a reflection of the economic distribution in society was formulated already by Aristotle, who maintained that the best government could be achieved only in those states where the wealth was more or less evenly divided among the citizens. When, on the other hand, the economic resources were strongly concentrated in the hands of a few, only oligarchy,, tyranny, or an extreme form of majority rule would ensure. We find similar observations in Alexis de Tocqueville's classic work on democracy in America. The feature which he regarded as an essential requisite for democracy in USA was the – in contrast to contemporary Europe – very even distribution of land ownership, that is, an agricultural economy dominated by smallholders.[74]

In modern research into democracy, the idea of the significance of the economic distribution has been emphasized chiefly by Robert Dahl and Roland Pennock. In their eyes, as in those of earlier advocates of this line of reasoning, the main problem is that economic resources are easily transformed into political resources, which results in a structural imbalance concerning the ability of different social groups to protect their interests. Furthermore, economic and political power in conjunction are wont to promote a mutually reinforcing process which contributes to an ever stronger concentration of resources – what Dahl called a 'runaway cycle of ever-increasing inequalities: a small minority with superior resources develops and maintains a hegemonic political system (often headed by a single dominant ruler) through which it can also enforce its domination over the social order and hence strengthen the initial inequalities even more'.[75] Such a cumulative process has often left its mark on traditional agrarian societies:

Because in an agrarian society the possession of land or a right to the produce of the land is the main source of status, income and wealth, inequality in land is equivalent to inequality in the distribution of political resources. To put it differently, in an agrarian society inequalities will be cumulative, not dispersed, and (as Harrington, the seventeenth-century English philosopher argued) power will be highly correlated with landed property.[76]

The advent of industrial society thereby resulted in a radical change. The subsequent location of resources can indeed be very uneven *per se* but at the same time it is more mobile, dispersed and, in the main, more difficult to concentrate. Pennock summarizes the differences between the two types of society as follows:

In a landed economy where ownership is highly concentrated, wealth carries with it knowledge, status, and political power. In an industrial society, political resources, such as education, organizational skills, access to leaders, and the like tend to be much more widely distributed. In addition, it is perhaps of equal importance that in a landed society those at the top of the pyramid have interests in common and little to divide them. In a complex industrial society, on the contrary, interests are highly diversified. The extractors, processors, and fabricators of aluminium may have much more in common with their employees than they do with their competitors in the steel industry. Importers tend to be at odds with manufacturers, cotton farmers and processors with the makers of synthetic fibres and fabrics, and so on and so forth. An important political consequence, then, of the situation just described is that a given degree of economic inequality does not produce the same sharp political alignment of haves and have-nots in an industrialized society that it does in a society where land is the chief form of wealth. To this should be added the fact that industrialized societies tend to have less inequality than agrarian societies, and also greater class mobility.[77]

This thesis – that the concentration of political resources is dependent on the forms of production – may also be expanded to embrace earlier epochs. Thus it has been demonstrated in historical and anthropological research that pre-agrarian societies (hunter-gatherer peoples and nomads) are usually characterized by a striking equality as regards the distribution of property and other standards of economic value – the simple fact is that there is little to accumulate. At the same time, the social and political stratification is fairly weak and relatively mobile to boot. These societies are therefore often described as primitive democracies: they are characterized by substantial elements of what (with a slightly anachronistic terminology) we could call participation in the political (i.e., collective) decision-making.[78]

The fixed agrarian production form (the so-called Neolithic revolution) is generally considered to give rise to a consistently stricter hierarchy: a surplus is here created which can be accumulated and, moreover, the availability of cultivable land is often very limited, which results in a distinct stratification between those who own property and those who do not. Furthermore, certain types of production require a substantial societal infrastructure – such as an irrigation system – which necessitates centralized modes of organization and also essentially greater defence measures to protect what has been built up from external threats.[79] Thus a self-reinforcing process is frequently set in motion; this results in the strong concentration of economic and political resources which Dahl and Pennock describe, and which in its most extensive form gives rise to the wholly closed hierarchies that Karl Wittfogel, in his famous work of the same title, called oriental despotism.[80]

On the whole, and with many simplifications, we could thereby, in association with Dahl's arguments, speak of a major historical pendulation from the egalitarian 'primaeval societies' to the agrarian, often strongly concentrated social structures, and then partly back again – in the industrial stage – to a wider dispersion of economic and political resources.

A part of the thesis (in a somewhat expanded form) can be so interpreted. And what is said seems obvious; it is a matter of an economically founded difference in power resources between the citizens. In addition, Dahl highlights another aspect; serious inequality generates frustration and tensions in the society, which also hamper a democratic development.[81]

As could be seen, this train of thought may be given an attractive historical framework. But does it go any further than this? Is there any detailed empirical evidence of the actual existence of the aforesaid crucial association between economic distribution and democracy? A comprehensive study (with data from 47 countries) was executed in the 1960s by Bruce Russett. A fairly clear pattern here emerged. In the countries where the inequality of the distribution of wealth (measured in ownership of land) was below the mean value, somewhat over half (13 of 23) were democratic, while the other category, characterized by greater inequality, contained only a few democracies (4 of 24).[82] Corresponding studies have been presented in recent times by Tatu Vanhanen, who included far more cases than did Russett. Furthermore, Vanhanen's study incorporates an historical dimension which allows comparison over a very long period. Side by side with other socio-economic variables (e.g., degree of urbanization and level of education), he examines the association between the percentage of family farms (as a measure of concentration of wealth) and the degree of democracy in the period 1850–1979 (covering 119 states). This attribute gives quite substantial connections for the early stages (in the expected direction), but these eventually wane; for the period 1950–79, it is the weakest of the relationships studied.[83] A later inquiry, based on data from the 1980s, yielded well-nigh the same result, which thus indicates that the distribution of wealth in the agrarian sector in our time has very little significance in the context.[84]

So much for the distribution of wealth as a measure of the degree of economic equality. Another is the distribution of income. Its association with democracy has been tested in several studies based on comparative data. Notwithstanding that the picture is not entirely uniform, the main impression is nevertheless clear: the relationships have been weak or nonexistent.[85]

Let us now see what our investigation can show. As regards the distribution of wealth we must, as in earlier studies, confine ourselves to the agrarian sector – unfortunately, no data are available concerning the conditions in other respects, e.g., within the industrial sector, which for many countries would be more relevant nowadays. The material also imposes limits with regard to the distribution of income. We did obtain more or less reliable information on the proportion which accrues to the 10 per cent of the population who earn most and the 20 per cent who earn least respectively. Yet, we have no data at all for the majority of countries: at best, concerning the 20 per cent with the lowest income, we have data for 65 states.[86] Nonetheless, the selection may be wide enough to serve as a clear indication of whether the level of democracy is related to the income distribution in the countries. It should be remarked that the sample was no larger in previous studies of the subject.

Table 16 presents a test of the said variables. As we should expect, a relatively high income share for the group which earns least and an extensive dispersion of the ownership in agriculture (measured in the percentage of family farms) will favour democracy, which in both cases should be defined in positive regression coefficients. But, as is clear, our measurements of income distribution show a perceptible negative relationship. However, it is not statistically significant.[87] A similar pattern, but still weaker, emerges for the percentage of family farms.

Table 16. *Distribution of income and property and level of democracy.*
Simple regression.

	Standardized regression coefficient	Explained variance (percentage)	
Income share for the lowest group (20 percent)	−0.18	3.0	(N: 65)
Percentages of family farms	−0.09	0.1	(N:111)

Now we could imagine that the result would change once other attributes – chiefly such as pertain to the countries' production orientation – are taken into consideration. As we have seen, theoreticians in this field are wont to believe that an uneven economic distribution among the citizens will have particularly strong social and political effects in those societies which are dominated by agrarian production. Furthermore, for the simple reason that concerning wealth distribution, we only have data from the agricultural sector, it seems relevant to test whether the variation with respect to the forms of production affects the outcome.

For this reason, we have executed a series of regressions where the size of the industrial production, and the percentage employed in different sectors (agriculture, industry and service) are included as control variables. Thereby, however, the picture is not essentially changed. For our measurement of income distribution a weak relationship in the 'wrong' direction remains. Concerning the percentage of family farms, there is indeed an occasional veer in the sign (from negative to positive), but the magnitude of association is still low.[88]

The idea that the mode of government is closely linked to the material, economic distribution in society – the so-called class stratification – has deep roots in politico-sociological thought. Grandiose, historically sweeping theories have been constructed with this idea as the main empirical premise. Nevertheless, it has proved difficult to document this assumption via ordinary tests against data, particularly regarding the distribution of income. In several studies its putative association with democracy (in a number of respects) has been conspicuous by its absence. Thus our investigation is only one more negative result among many. As regards distribution of wealth, there is the problem that only the situation in the agrarian sector could be illuminated. Notwithstanding, the certainty of our conclusions is increased by the possibility of control for the forms of production. As we saw, variation therein makes no difference: the insignificant connection between the level of democracy and the distribution of wealth in the said respects persists.[89]

These results in their turn give reason to cast doubt on the alleged historical linkage between mode of government and production conditions, whereby the economic and social stratification is presented as the intervenient, decisive variable (the idea that the agrarian societies are politically more authoritarian than the pre-agrarian and the industrial). If this does not prove valid today – when, however, a wide variation exists between the countries concerning production – it seems in any case probable that exaggerated importance has been attached to the connection also for past ages. Then, as now, presumably other things better explain the variegated modes of government.

ECONOMIC SYSTEM

According to a good many scholars, democracy is closely associated with a certain form of economic organization, namely with capitalism. Reference is then frequently made to an historical parallelism: capitalism and democracy burgeoned at about the same time. Furthermore, one may, as Charles Lindblom did, remark on the fact that all the countries which in our day are the most democratic contain substantial elements of market economy and private ownership.[90]

As a contrast to the specifications of the thesis which will follow, it is worth mentioning that the idea of capitalism's positive impact on democracy has been vigorously questioned. Authors such as Laski, Cole and Tawney for their part postulated the existence of a conflict between capitalism and democracy. The arguments adduced tend to follow two lines: firstly, it is claimed that the economic hierarchy created by the market and private ownership stand in direct logical contrast to the principles of popular self-government which democracy represents. Furthermore, an empirical objection is put forward. There is in capitalistic society a wide, ever-growing gap between rich and poor – 'the haves and the have nots' – which promotes increasing inequality in political resources and which, finally, unless the economic system is radically changed, can generate a conflict with such strong outbreaks as to lead to the collapse of political democracy. (The argument is obviously a variant of the idea of the impact of socio-economic inequality, linked in this case with the form of economic organization).[91]

At the logical level, these critics of capitalism undoubtedly have a strong case. The mode of decision-making in the market economy – the rule of contract – is obviously different from that of democracy. In a democracy all are assigned the same influence (according to the principle of one person one vote), but in the market economic strength decides the matter. On this fact there is little room for disagreement.[92]

On the other hand, the latter empirical statement, which is of course of most interest to us, can certainly be called into question. In the context of the said criticism – and often in direct polemic against it – authors such as Hayek, Schumpeter and Tingsten have held a diametrically opposed view, namely that a development away from capitalism, and toward a planned economy and extensive public ownership, would constitute a serious threat to the survival of democracy.

One of the cardinal beliefs of these authors is that by reason of its strong elements of contemplation and individual autonomy, capitalism promotes a dispersion of power in society which creates a favourable basis for political democracy. Thus Joseph Schumpeter has this to say:

> The bourgeois scheme of things limits the sphere of politics by limiting the sphere of public authority; its solution is in the idea of the parsimonious state that exists primarily in order to guarantee bourgeois legality and to provide a firm frame for autonomous individual endeavor in all fields.[93]

The factor which is chiefly emphasized is the need for a limitation of the external competence of the government. In particular, Friedrich von Hayek has therefore strongly warned against a transition to a comprehensive planned economy. Such a system would require a very far-reaching delegation of initiative and real authority to the executive organs, and especially to the actual planning bureaucracy. The channel of popular influence, the parliament, would soon lose control in consequence of this structural imbalance. The executive, and the planners, would wholly dominate the scene, and democracy be degraded to a mere formal procedure.[94] We find a similar analysis, with direct reference to Hayek, in Herbert Tingsten. In his view, a planned economy at the market's expense would generate a cumulative process of power concentration which would ultimately afflict the political freedoms essential for democracy – e.g., freedom of the press and the right to strike. For, says Tingsten, the logic of the planned economy implies that the powers which could counteract a consistent attainment of the plan's objectives must be suppressed. A strongly concentrated, organizationally coherent economic and political power in its turn breeds passivity and fear among both the citizens and potential opposition parties. None dares seriously to resist the political leaders who control his livelihood.[95]

The association between capitalism and democracy via a limited government and a general 'diffusion of power and influence' is also emphasized by Lindblom.[96] Moreover, we find a broadly similar analysis in authors of a Marxist bent, such as Barrington Moore and Göran Therborn. According to Moore, the historical contribution of capitalism to modern democracy chiefly consist in its dissolution of the closed local power monopolies which characterized the older, feudal agricultural economy. The transition to commercial agriculture and the emergence of a numerous merchant class in the towns created a far more splintered and mobile power structure which, in due time, enabled also peasants and workers to acquire political influence.[97] The crux for the development of democracy therefore consists, firstly, in success in breaking the political hegemony of the land-owning upper class and, secondly, the rise of a politically influential class of town-dwellers:

Without going into the evidence further or discussing the Asian materials that point in the same direction, we may simply register strong agreement with the Marxist thesis that a vigorous and independent class of town-dwellers has been an indispensable element, in the growth of parliamentary democracy. No bourgeois, no democracy.[98]

According to Therborn's interpretation, the historical connection at issue is understandable in view of the impersonal market competition of capitalism and its lack of a single power centre:

Capitalist relations of production tend to create an *internally competing, peacefully disunited ruling class*. In its development, capital is divided into several fractions: mercantile, banking, industrial, agrarian, small and big. Except in a situation of grave crisis or acute threat from an enemy (whether feudal, proletarian or a rival national state) bourgeois class relations contain no unifying element comparable to the dynastic kingship legitimacy and fixed hierarchy of feudalism.[99]

In addition, Therborn emphasizes another factor important for the dispersion of power and political resources; capitalism lays the foundation for a working class with a solidarity and an organizational effectiveness which the lower classes in earlier modes of production could not achieve. This movement – built up in the form of parties and trade unions – has often taken up the cudgels in the struggle for political democracy.[100]

Another merit of capitalism to attract comment is its purely economic efficiency. This system, says Dan Usher, has enabled an enormous material increase which has benefited not least the common people. Assuredly, it is characterized by hierarchy, privileges and substantial class differences. But the gap between rich and poor is nevertheless moderate compared with most other types of society. What is more, the barriers to social mobility are, in relative terms, very low. Capitalism can therefore contribute to a mitigation of the general conflict level in society. Instead of an increased polarization, it could through an (at least in absolute figures) higher living standard for large groups, and a general economic and social modernization, create the conditions for increased harmony in political life.[101]

When we now proceed to test the validity of the ideas presented here it is important to effect a delimitation of what we mean by 'capitalism'. In common parlance, and sometimes also in scholarly debate, this term is used in a rather diffuse and broad sense. It is not uncommon to include such matters as pertain to the size and direction of the public sector as criteria of capitalism – or its opposite (socialism). A policy which by various means seeks a substantial redistribution in society, or major public so-called welfare measures – state schools, hospitals, etc. – can thus be taken as signs of an order divergent from capitalism. The total volume of the public services too can serve as a measure thereof.[102] It is worth mentioning that in the few studies which have empirically tested the link between capitalism and democracy, just this criterion is used.[103]

Notwithstanding, like Peter Berger, I would advocate a narrow delimitation of the concept of capitalism, namely to denote only certain organizational conditions in the production life (which also closely follows Marx's and even Weber's definitions of the subject).[104]

Thus the concept relates to an economic system where the means of production are privately owned, and where the activities are carried on for the purposes of profit according to the terms of the market. These criteria, I would assert, are the essential character-istics of the concept. This is not to say that when speaking of capitalism (or not), other conditions may not be included (e.g., such as were mentioned earlier). As is known, there are no patent rights in the field of terminology! The problem is only that we then obtain a multidimensional concept which implies that we *de facto* postulate empirical connections which may not manifestly exist. For scientific purposes, it is therefore reasonable to separate things as far as possible. As Berger has pointed out, capitalism in the narrower, economic sense can in reality be combined with diverse conditions as regards public welfare policy and the like. Countries which apply a capitalistic order need not necessarily have a nightwatchman state.[105]

It becomes even more unreasonable if, as has happened in research into democracy, only the size of the public sector serves as a measure of capitalism. For example, I can mention that Tanzania then appears as more capitalistic than its neighbour Kenya – a classification which undoubtedly inverts the standard concepts. And, I would add, this is far from the only odd outcome of an application of this criterion. In other words, such matters as pertain to the direction and size of the public sector will not be considered in this context. These issues will instead be raised in a special order (see Chapt. 7, Institutional conditions).

The problem is to find useful data for ranking the countries with respect to their degree of capitalism as we have now defined it. In my view, it is possible to use a classification presented by Raymond Gastil.[106] The advantage of the division he makes is its primary concern with the organization of the economic system. Nevertheless it also includes, as supplements, other attributes. Thus, for every category a division is made with reference to the said economic system's 'inclusiveness', that is, the extent to which it has displaced more traditional forms of production. Since this chiefly relates to the degree of general economic development (modernization), this classification is excluded (with the consequence that we confine ourselves to the main categories). Among the countries char-acterized by a considerable (but at the same time limited) govern-ment involvement in the life of production, Gastil makes a further distinction between two kinds of system: 'Capitalist-Statist' and 'Mixed Capitalist', the latter being marked by extensive measures of welfare policy. For reasons already reported, however, this distinction is dispensable. These categories are instead combined.

With this adjustment of Gastil's scale we obtain an, as I think, fairly reasonable division of the countries into the following classes:

1 Socialist
2 Mixed Socialist
3 Mixed Capitalist
4 Capitalist.[107]

It is worth mentioning that this measurement of the degree of capitalism has a positive connection – but on a very modest level – with the size of the public sector.[108]

When we consider the world, using the above classification, we find on the one hand obvious support for the thesis of the economic system's association with democracy. All the states which apply markedly socialistic forms of production have low values for democracy (none are above 2.5 on our index), while every country with high values (above 7) is at the other end of the scale (Capitalist or Mixed Capitalist). On the other hand, there are among the more or less capitalistic countries at least as many which exhibit low achievement with respect to democracy (Haiti, Chile, Cameroon, Brunei, Saudi Arabia etc.). And even in the Mixed Socialist group there is a wide dispersal in this regard (Madagascar, Guyana, Syria and Burma may be mentioned as examples).

In other words, it is not a matter of a total connection (if such was expected). Nonetheless we can – as Table 17 shows – on an aggregate level point to a comparatively strong linkage between the attributes we are now discussing. This result undoubtedly provides support for the ideas which Schumpeter *et al.* proffered.

The question is whether it is also possible to ascertain more closely

Table 17. *Economic system and level of democracy. Simple regression.*

	Standardized regression coefficient	Explained variance (percentage)	
Capitalism	0.49[**]	24.1	(N:130)

** significance at the 0.01 level

Table 18. *Economic system and various components of democracy. Simple regression.*

	Standardized regression coefficients	Explained variance (percentage)
Elections	0.37[**]	14.1
Political freedoms	0.58[**]	33.8
Organizational freedoms	0.53[**]	27.9
Freedoms of opinion	0.56[**]	30.9
Political violence and oppression	0.47[**]	22.1

[**] significance at the 0.01 level

the nature of this relationship. One idea was, as we said, that through its better economic efficiency, capitalism generates generally higher prosperity which moderates the antagonism between different social groups. It thereby becomes easier to apply the democratic mode of settling conflicts. The way in which production is organized is in fact connected with the economic standard and the growth of the GNP in the expected direction – but on a fairly low level.[109] Yet, since these attributes for their part have only a minor impact on the level of democracy, this can hardly be the explanatory link.[110]

The most widely fostered interpretation of the nature of the connection pertains to the higher degree of social pluralism which allegedly ensues from capitalism. In that case, if we distinguish the different components that are parts of our measurement of democracy, there should be – firstly – a closer relationship as regards economic system and political freedoms than with respect to elections. Secondly, among the political freedoms, a strong connection should in particular emerge concerning organizational freedoms and freedom of opinion.

As we see from Table 18, the first hypothesis receives considerable support. Democratic achievements which relate to elections are demonstrably less strongly associated with the design of the economic system than the political freedoms. The outcome is more diffuse as regards the second hypothesis. The absence of political violence and oppression indeed shows a weaker association than the other two components – thus far it is right. But the difference is so slight that it should not be taken as justification for any firm conclusions. On the other hand, the manifest difference with regard to elections and political freedoms is worthy of note. It provides support for the interpretation that asserts that the link with democracy is primarily due to the fact that capitalism as an economic system gives a higher degree of civil autonomy – both individually and organizationally – which 'overflows' into more extensive political liberties.

Anyhow, what we have observed so far is a simple (bivariate) association. It remains to be seen whether this holds when other attributes are controlled. As enlightenment en route I can mention that the economic organizational form is moderately correlated with the indicators of modernization which were discussed above (signifying that countries which apply socialism are on the whole somewhat less developed).[111] The link with the trade variables is in general stronger. Most marked is the relationship concerning trade with the Soviet bloc, with which the socialist countries, as could be expected, have a fairly extensive exchange, and the capitalist lands very little. We find a reverse pattern, though less distinct, concerning trade with the USA. It may also be mentioned that countries with a capitalistic bent are more open for direct investments and have a lower commodity concentration in their exports.[112]

Table 19 presents a multiple regression where the variable of interest at present is matched against the measurement of modernization and dependence respectively which previously exhibited

Table 19. *Economic system and level of democracy. Multiple regression.*

	Standardized regression coefficients	Explained variance (percentage)
Capitalism	0.18[*]	
Literacy	0.22[*]	
Commodity concentration	−0.22[**]	
Direct investments	0.18[**]	
Trade EC, imp.	−0.14	
Trade USA, imp.	0.26[**]	
Trade Soviet bloc, imp.	0.10	
		55.1

[*] significance at the 0.05 level
[**] significance at the 0.01 level

considerable connections with democracy. The result is that a substantial link persists – but at a much reduced level. Moreover, it is
clear that the economic system is not the most prominent attribute
in the context.

Thus, we have found that the design of the economic system is
clearly related to the level of democracy. Our scrutiny has also
indicated that, as many theorists on the subject have asserted, there
is in particular a close association between capitalism and political
freedoms. Yet, we can establish that variation in terms of socialism/
capitalism appears as less decisive for democracy's part than the
socio-economic conditions which we formerly dwelt upon.

CHAPTER 6

Demographic and cultural conditions

CLEAVAGES

If conflict is to be managed effectively, opposing camps must be willing to *compromise*. This implies not simple recognition of the opposition's right to hold its views and campaign for them, but also some degree of moderation in political positions and partisan identifications. Extremist viewpoints and intense attachments obstruct the accommodation and bargaining necessary for effective conflict management.[1]

This quotation – which refers just to the democratic mode of conflict solving – expresses an opinion which is shared by many. In order to grow and to survive, it is alleged, the free government of the people must be safeguarded by a political culture which is pervaded by an elementary consent regarding the general rules of behaviour. In paradoxical terms, there must be agreement on the establishment of a system which is distinguished by dissonance and often strongly opposed wills. Despite actual conflicts, it is essential to protect even the opponents' full right to promote their standpoints.[2] This 'balance between unity and division, between co-operation and conflict' – as Herbert Tingsten says – is difficult to attain.[3] When applied, popular government has often been prone to cause division rather than promote fellowship.[4]

According to Dankwart Rustow, it is against this background that one condition in particular must be fulfilled: democracy requires a national unity, a sense of affinity between the citizens which surpasses other loyalties.[5] The problem is that this is frequently lacking. Many states are instead divided by deep cleavages between different population groups.[6] These gaps – which are usually ethnic, religious or socio-economic in character – have the result, in the most serious cases, that people feel loyalty and confidence only within their own group and, in recompense, hostility and distrust toward outsiders.

Nevertheless, all cleavages are not regarded as being equally difficult to handle. The most troublesome are generally adjudged to be the ethnic and the religious, since these are characterized by more of a dichotomy (that is, a kind of either/or) and, in addition, have a profound emotional significance for the groups concerned. On the other hand, in the event of economic disputes – e.g., pertinent to salaries, taxes and social welfare benefits – it is often easier to formulate compromises which suit both sides, partly because the issues here are more obviously divisible, partly because the values involved are more instrumental in nature.[7]

Several observers have therefore voiced deep pessimism concerning the possibilities of democracy in societies characterized by religious and (in particular) ethnic differences. Under such circumstances, Alvin Rabushka and Kennet Shepsle maintain, it is very difficult to effect a reduction of the level of conflict. Politicization of ethnic gaps and organization of parties along such lines instead creates an increasingly intransigent political culture where compromises and coalitions between groups are well-nigh impossible to attain. This often results in a war waged by all against all of the kind Hobbes describes in his state of nature. The authors therefore conclude that 'the resolution of intense but conflicting preferences (is not) manageable in a democratic framework'.[8]

There is much evidence in support of such a view. In Northern Ireland democracy has been rendered impossible by relentless feuds between the religious factions among the population. In Cyprus fragile co-operation between Greeks and Turks was ruptured in the mid-1970s; in consequence the state is now *de facto* partitioned. And at the same time the still current chaotic civil strife which broke out in Lebanon put an end to the relatively democratic government (though with very specific elements) which had been in force by and large since the 1940s. Serious, and at times violent, ethnic conflicts are also a feature of political life in both Malaysia and Sri Lanka. In these cases, however, a pluralistic mode of civilian government could be maintained – although essentially limited, primarily as regards the political freedoms. In Fiji, however, the strong tensions between the two equally matched groups of the population (Melanesians and Indians) prompted the military in 1987 to take power, which they have since retained.

As Donald Horowitz remarked, the ethnic issue is in general a major problem – latent or overt – in most Asian countries, and this is the case also in many places in the Caribbean.[9] Yet the difficulties

are greatest on the African continent (south of the Sahara). This is
in large measure a consequence of the types of state which were
created by the colonial powers:

Almost every state in sub-Saharan Africa is multi-ethnic in social composition. They are arbitrary political units in geographical shape and size,
population membership, political identity, and socio-economic reality.
Their boundaries were drawn by European empire-builders, who paid
little regard to the borders of traditional societies. Most African states are
composed of many different peoples who are ethnically distinct in terms of
race, colour, language, customs, geographical residence, and so forth – or
some combination of these factors.[10]

South Africa is *the* country on the Continent where the ethnic
divisions exert the strongest influence over the conditions: as is well
known, the country is governed along explicit, racist principles. In
Nigeria and Uganda, where pluralistic forms (multi-party systems
and open elections) have been tried on occasions, the government
has repeatedly collapsed by reason of tribalistic and religious conflicts, with civil war and serious outbreaks of violence as a result.
Similar conditions have prevailed in the Sudan (for this reason, a
military coup occurred in 1989). Mention may also be made of
Ethiopia and Angola, which have long been plagued by civil war
(which derived largely from ethnic antagonisms) and Zimbabwe,
where the transition from a fairly pluralistic state of affairs to
one-party government (of a still obscure nature) which began in
1987 was partly due to the ethnic tensions which prevailed between
the two main parties (ZANU and ZAPU).

The significance of the ethnic factor has also been emphasized in
several comparative inquiries. In a study of political changes in 90
countries during the post-war period (1950–75), Michael Hannan
and Glenn Carroll found that 'ethnic diversity destabilizes politics,
especially competitive politics'.[11] A similar result emerges in Tatu
Vanhanen's previously mentioned study with data from the 1980s:
'nearly all ethnically extremely plural countries ... are Non-
democracies'.[12] In addition, Bingham Powell found that a lack of
homogeneity in the population contributes to increased political
violence (measured in the number killed in political conflicts) in the
countries he investigated.[13]

In order to test how various cleavages relate to the level of
democracy we obtained data on the ethnic, linguistic and religious
composition of the populations in the countries under study. In

other words, we distinguish three types of division which, it must be remarked, are not the norm. As a rule, corresponding studies have only had one measurement in which the ethnic and linguistic divisions were combined.[14] Moreover, it sometimes happens that religious gaps too are included under the heading 'Ethnic fragment-ation'.[15] In that way, one loses potentially interesting information on whether cleavages of different kinds vary with respect to the political consequences.

The information on which we draw pertains to how the population is divided (in percentages for different groups) in the said respects. On this basis we have in each case calculated a fragmentation index according to the formula suggested by Douglas Rae and Michael Taylor. This measurement gives the probability for the affiliation to different groups of two individual citizens selected at random.[16]

Not unexpectedly, distinct differences appear between various areas on the world map. Africa, south of the Sahara, exhibits by far the highest fragmentation in all respects. On the other hand, we find the lowest figures in North Africa and the Middle East; thus in these countries the population is in general relatively homogenous.[17] Against this background it is interesting to observe that these two geographic areas display the same average level of democracy (2.6). As deviations from the expected pattern of linkages I can also, as isolated examples, mention the large country India and the small country Belize, both of which are deeply divided, particularly in ethnic and linguistic respects, but at the same time exhibit high values for democracy.[18]

The statistical relationships for the three measurements of frag-mentation are reported in Table 20. We find the strongest link with

Table 20. *Fragmentation and level of democracy. Simple regression.*

	Standardized regression coefficient	Explained variance (percentage)	
Ethnic fragmentation	−0.15	2.2	(N:127)
Linguistic fragmentation	−0.22[*]	4.9	(N:132)
Religious fragmentation	−0.14	2.1	(N:132)
Average fragmentation	−0.23[**]	5.4	(N:127)

[*] significance at the 0.05 level
[**] significance at the 0.01 level

democracy – in the expected negative direction – in linguistic fragmentation. Nevertheless, even in this case the level of association (as the explained variance in particular shows) is fairly low.[19]

In the debate on the political impact of inhomogeneity in the population, it has often been asserted that the reciprocal *relationship between* different cleavages must be taken into account. The situation is adjudged the most serious when different dividing lines, e.g., ethnic and religious, coincide and reinforce each other. If, on the contrary, they cross-cut – so that individuals with different ethnic identities speak the same language or profess the same religion – the group loyalties are instead modulated with the effect that the tensions are subdued.[20] Unfortunately, it is not possible with the aggregate data at our disposal to test this thesis at all rigorously. What we have information on is the size of the different segments of the population (in percentage of the total). On the other hand, we do not know how the cleavages which can be registered thereby relate to each other, that is, how the division in one respect, e.g., linguistic, coincides with or diverges from the grouping in another, e.g., the religious. In order to acquire knowledge of this we would need data at the individual level.

Notwithstanding, it seems reasonable to assume that in those cases where there is strong fragmentation in all the respects which we discuss, greater tensions are created in the society (irrespective of the reciprocal 'angles' of the cleavages) than in those where the division in one (or two) spheres is substantially less than elsewhere. A simple measure of this consists in the calculation of the average degree of fragmentation for each country. We can see the impact of this measurement in the previous table. The connection here is stronger than for any of the separate fragmentation variables, but it is hardly a question of a major difference.[21]

Now, the fact is that states which are more ethnically and linguistically fragmented in general are characterized by a lower degree of economic and social development.[22] The relationship between democracy and linguistic fragmentation therefore declines once literacy is controlled – as does the link concerning average fragmentation – to a distinctly lower, insignificant level. When the economic system and trade variables are also taken into account this effect is strengthened still further.[23]

According to one line of thought which has been articulated in the debate, the problem consists not primarily in the degree of homogeneity in the population but in the balance in size between different segments. I am referring to the ideas of Arent Lijphart. His research has been greatly concerned with the problems of democracy in divided societies. The solution consists, in his view, in the invention of political methods of bridging the existing cleavages. This is in turn easier to achieve if the different groups are more or less equally matched in the population. Above all, it should not be the case that one fraction totally predominates and is hence in a position to oppress the rest. Ideally, there should be parity in the mobilization strength of the different groups which, furthermore, should not be too numerous; in Lijphart's view three to four equally large segments give the best basis for reconciliation and co-operation.[24]

It should be noted that the mutual balance between the groups is not captured by the fragmentation measurement reported above. By that, we cannot distinguish one case where the population is divided into two equally large fractions and another where one segment incorporates two-thirds while the remainder is separated into two groups. Indeed, in both cases the probability is equally great that two individuals chosen at random will belong to different segments (the value of the fragmentation index becomes 0.5).[25] Nevertheless, these two divisions yield obviously different implications in the perspective postulated by Lijphart.

Thus, in order to test the hypothesis we need other measurements. Therefore, we adopted the following approach. We started by eliminating the cases where the largest fraction was so predominant that the minority can hardly constitute a major problem. Accordingly, those countries where one group constitutes more than 90 per cent of the population were excluded. With the remaining countries we calculated, for one measurement, the standard deviation in size for the three largest segments and, for another, we distinguished the cases where the largest segment represents more than 50 per cent of the population (consequently we here obtain a dichotomous variable). It should be added that our calculations are based throughout on the linguistic division.

When tested against level of democracy these measurements do not produce any strong results; the connections are moderate and insignificant. Nevertheless, it is interesting to observe that a segmental imbalance – the fact that one group is far larger than the others – has a positive impact on the level of democracy, which obviously contradicts the assumptions made by Lijphart.[26]

The division of the population and the political 'tribalism' which this is adjudged to engender has sometimes been presented as one of the most awkward problems in the Third World. In response to such a pessimistic view Arent Lijphart expressed a different opinion. A main theme of his writings has been to seek to demonstrate the possibility of bridging different cleavages with suitable political measures. For this reason, he maintains, it is advantageous if the segments are of about the same size. This latter link in his argumentation was tested here – and not confirmed. But neither did we find support for the conventional idea. The negative relationship between fragmentation and democracy was reduced to an insignificant level once the socio-economic variables were controlled. Notwithstanding, as will later be evident, this is not a final result. Therefore, we shall return to this question.

RELIGION

In an often quoted article from 1984 entitled 'Will More States Be Democratic?', Samuel Huntington discusses (among other themes) the influence of religion. In his opinion there is a striking association between Protestantism and democracy: 'In the contemporary world, virtually all countries with a European population and a protestant majority (except East Germany) have democratic government'. The Roman Catholic Church and its doctrine, on the other hand, has an ambivalent attitude to democracy. Historically, says Huntington, it has often sought to counteract popular influence. Consequently, democracy is less prevalent in Roman Catholic countries and, when it does exist, has generally been introduced later than in predominantely Protestant states. The difference vis-à-vis Islam appears even more clearly in this respect; in the countries where this religion predominated in the early 1980s, the vast majority were more or less authoritarian.[27]

Huntington explains this by saying that religions differ with regard to the goals they pursue: 'cultures that are consummatory in character – that is, where intermediate and ultimate ends are closely connected – seem to be less favourable to democracy'. He also points to the fact that there is no distinction in Islam between religion and politics: the doctrines of the faith must also permeate the secular life.[28] This can be supplemented by arguments put forward by other authors (following Weber). Protestantism is said to foster individual responsibility and is – *inter alia* thereby – also more sceptical and less fundamentalist in character. Furthermore, it has since the Reformation promoted a tradition of rebellion against established authorities. In contrast, the Roman Catholic Church has been considered to be more intolerant and dogmatic; as representative of the true faith it has a stronger tendency to control the lives of its members.[29]

As regards Islam, it is often alleged that this religion has always been more explicitly political than Christianity: 'The community founded by Muhammed in Medina in the seventh century exemplified all the principles of citizenship and democracy ... For while in Christianity religion is separated from the state, in Islam the state is one with the *umma*, the community of believers: religion, state and people form one body. In the Medinian community the state was but the plurality of its citizens unified by faith and obedience to the commands of God.'[30] Through its universal claims, the religious law also applies to civil life. In consequence, no secular constitutional tradition has evolved in the Muslim world, nor the kind of representative system to which the Church in the West for its part contributed.[31] Nevertheless, there are now, it has been remarked, several competing ideological currents in Islam. Side by side with a traditional, absolutist attitude – whereby the idea of popular government, 'a man-made law' stands in sharp contrast to the basic principles of doctrine – there are also modernistic trends. In these latter parties we find a more open, flexible attitude to the religious ordinances. The ideal society, they maintain, is not laid down (at least not in all its details), which implies that there is also considerable scope for the individual's free political judgements.[32]

It would seem obvious from the logical viewpoint that religious and other 'fundamentalism'[33] is difficult to reconcile with democracy. The tolerance and respect for the opinions of others required by democracy can hardly be created in the culture where 'ultimate ends do ... color every concrete act'.[34] According to the principles of popular government, the distinguishing feature of 'the good society' is basically a matter of opinion (whereby the majority's view must prevail). No absolute 'right and true' in politics is recognized here. Trends which claim to present such a thing naturally have difficulty in submitting to the democratic mode of decision-making.

Is there then, in practice, any difference between the countries with regard to democracy which can be attributed to the religion professed by the population? From a scrutinizing of the map we find that many countries in the Arab world, where Islam predominates, have very low values for democracy. But we see exceptions too. In The Gambia and Senegal, for instance, both of which display high values for democracy, the majority of the populations are Muslims. And we can also find countries with low achievement in the Christian world at the time we study – we may mention Chile and Paraguay and a good many states in Africa, both Roman Catholic and Protestant.

In a statistical study, Kenneth Bollen could demonstrate a significant connection between the level of democracy and the percentage of Protestant citizens in different countries. This link was fairly weak, however; other included variables, e.g., degree of economic development, gave much stronger readings.[35] Yet, no similar study has been made of whether Christianity (as a whole) differs from the other major world religion, Islam.

Our investigation of the subject is based on information about the number of followers of different faiths expressed as a percentage of the total population. The states could be further classified with respect to the main religion. Application of the latter measurement reveals a distinct difference between the countries. In the category where Christianity predominates, the degree of democracy clearly exceeds the average for the Third World as a whole, while the Muslim countries fall far short of this level.[36] This pattern is confirmed in Table 21, which illustrates the outcome in simple regression with regard to the percentage of the population which profess the respective religion. Here we can also perceive a difference between Protestantism and Roman Catholicism which obviously favours the former.[37] The assertions of Huntington, and others too,

Table 21. *Religion and level of democracy. Simple regression.*

	Standardized regression coefficient	Explained variance (percentage)	
Percentage of Christians	0.46[**]	21.5	(N:124)
Percentage of Muslims	−0.29[**]	15.1	(N:132)
Percentage of Protestants	0.44[**]	19.4	(N:123)
Percentage of Catholics	0.32[**]	10.0	(N:125)

[**] significance at the 0.05 level
[**] significance at the 0.01 level

on the varying compatibility of the religions with democracy thus seems to be verified. The question is whether these results will hold fast when other attributes too are included. For, as we well know, it is not only on the issue of the population's religious affiliation that the states differ.

Muslim countries have in general a lower degree of economic and social development than do Christian; this is not least true of the population's literacy. Regarding trade relations, it may be mentioned that Muslim-dominated states are characterized by a far lower commercial exchange with the USA, and also a lower percentage of direct investments, together with a somewhat higher concentration of goods in their exports. Is there also a difference in economic system which can be related to the spread of the religions? As is well known, Max Weber has maintained that, historically speaking, capitalism was bred in the Protestant culture. Under the current circumstances, certain signs of such a connection emerge: there is a stronger positive association with Protestantism than with Roman Catholicism. Nevertheless, the difference is by far the greatest between countries dominated by Christianity (as a whole) and Muslim countries.[38]

Table 22 presents the outcome of three multiple regressions where the percentages of Muslims, Christians and Protestants are tested separately together with the socio-economic attributes which previously displayed stronger linkages with level of democracy. As can be seen, the negative connection for Islam is then reduced to a low, insignificant level. On the other hand, the positive links for Christianity and – even more clearly – Protestantism persist in considerable measure. In other words, there is in these latter cases reason to assert that the religious affiliation of the population impinges on the level of democracy independent of the countries' characteristics in socio-economic respects.

Thus, the answer to the question 'does religion matter?' is in the affirmative. The results show that Christianity – and Protestantism in particular – has a positive effect on the level of democracy in the countries studied. In this respect there is a difference *vis-à-vis* Islam. At the same time, it should be remarked that for its part, the latter religion has not exhibited the distinctly negative effect which has sometimes been claimed. The fact that Muslim countries usually have low democratic achievement seems chiefly due to the coincidental socio-economic circumstances.

Table 22. *Religion and level of democracy. Three multiple regressions.*

	Standardized regression coefficients	Explained variance (percentage)
(A)		
Percentage of Muslims	-0.10	
Literacy	0.21^{**}	
Trade USA, imp.	0.28^{**}	
Commodity concentration	-0.23^{**}	
Direct investments	0.15^{*}	
Capitalism	0.25^{**}	
		54.2
(B)		
Percentage of Christians	0.16^{*}	
Literacy	0.21^{**}	
Trade USA, imp.	0.24^{**}	
Commodity concentration	-0.25^{**}	
Direct investments	0.14^{*}	
Capitalism	0.22^{**}	
		55.2
(C)		
Percentage of Protestants	0.23^{**}	
Literacy	0.18^{*}	
Trade USA, imp.	0.30^{**}	
Commodity concentration	-0.26^{**}	
Direct investments	0.13^{*}	
Capitalism	0.18^{*}	
		57.7

**significance at the 0.05 level
*significance at the 0.01 level

SIZE

If it is natural property of small states to be governed as republics, of middling ones to be governed by monarchs, and of large empires to be ruled by despots, it follows that in order to preserve the principles of any established government, it is necessary to maintain the existing size of the state; and that the nature *(l'esprit)* of the state will change to the extent that the state constricts or extends its limits. (Montesquieu)

From Antiquity onwards it has been long held among political philosophers that a democracy, or a republic, must be small in terms of both territory and population. This seemed self-evident. The Greek city-states, ruled by their citizens, had been very small units.

It was also striking that almost all the autonomous cities which came into existence in Europe in the Middle Ages, and survived until Napoleon's times, were republics which, at least in the early stages, were characterized by extensive popular participation in government (although eventually the trend was in many cases toward an oligarchy or an aristocracy).[39] On this point – concerning the natural link between the size of the state and the mode of its government – we therefore find agreement among such otherwise different thinkers as Plato, Aristotle, Montesquieu and Rousseau.[40] Along with the factual evidence offered by history there were also logical reasons for this standpoint. As long as democracy (until the aftermath of the American Revolution) was equated with direct popular government, arguments pertinent to the technicalities of assembly could be adduced: in order to meet in one place and be able to listen to the speaker, the audience – and thereby the population – must be small. At the same time, other effects favourable to democracy ensued from this fact. Humans in small groups feel a closer affinity to each other – such a natural fellowship was in Rousseau's view a well-nigh essential condition for a genuine popular government. Moreover, a limited circle in general involves greater possibility for each to attain a responsible position (in many city states, offices were distributed by lot), which creates a deeper sense of participation and accountability among the citizens[41] – here we obviously find 'the origin' of the dynamic education theory which has so highly characterized the argumentation of the participatory democrats of later times.[42]

Notwithstanding, the connection need not apply only on the said condition, namely direct government by the people. Even in its representative form – which we discuss – it may very well be that the size of the state is relevant. Among the modern researchers into democracy, Arent Lijphart in particular has articulated such a view. His argument is that small states offer better requisites for the creation of the 'spirit of co-operativeness and accommodation' which, he thinks, is crucial for the maintenance of democracy. In such states it is probable that the political leaders will be more united through personal acquaintance and interaction (it should be noted that the behaviour of the elite is the centre of interest in Lijphart's analysis). Furthermore, with a limited number of actors – to use an expression from game theory – the shadow of the future is more perceptible, which is thought to promote co-operation.[43] When the actors realize that the interaction will soon be repeated, they refrain from riding roughshod over their rivals, because of the risk of repayment in like coin: 'For the winners in such a game would forfeit to the losers goodwill, and this would entail high costs relative to the rewards to be gained.' Moreover, another factor enters the picture. Small states are usually more vulnerable to external threats (from larger states), which provides an incentive for increased unity. As Lijphart points out, it is striking that a culture of democratic co-operation was often founded upon international crises, and at times when the countries' existence was at stake.[44]

Island states are of special interest in this regard. They are usually small, in many cases extremely small, in area and population. Through isolation and clearly defined frontiers, it has been maintained, they can achieve a stronger spirit of solidarity of the kinds described above.[45]

Nevertheless, the idea of a fortunate bond between smallness and democracy is not unchallenged. On the contrary, in James Madison's view, it was an advantage if the state was large. For the social and political pluralism could thereby increase so that the tyranny of the majority which he feared would be less likely to ensue:

The smaller the society, the fewer probably will be the distinct parties and interests composing it; the fewer the distinct parties and interests, the more frequently will a majority be found of the same party; and the smaller the number of individuals composing a majority, and the smaller the compass within which they are placed, the more easily will they concert and execute their plans of oppression. Extend the sphere and you take in a greater variety of parties and interests; you make it less probable that a majority of the whole will have a common motive to invade the rights of other citizens; or if such a common motive exists, it will be more difficult for all who feel it to discover their own strength and act in unison with each other.[46]

The ideas on the subject which have evolved in recent times in connection with the theses of the dependency school should also be mentioned. A small state is naturally more likely to become dependent on outside powers. Therefore, it has been alleged, smallness almost inevitably involves a position as a peripheral subordinate in the international economic system – with the political effects which this, according to the expected pattern, brings about. Thus, Robert Ebel has offered the following prediction:

other things being equal, the size of a country will have a direct bearing upon the kind of power structures that will develop there. To be more

Table 23. *Size and level of democracy. Simple regression.*

	Standardized regression coefficient	Explained variance (percentage)	
Population (Log)	−0.28**	7.7	(N:132)
Area (Log)	−0.34**	11.3	(N:132)
Island	0.43**	18.2	(N:132)

**significance at the 0.01 level

specific, the smaller the country, the more concentrated (viz. undemocratic) its power structure is likely to be.[47]

What, then, has the empirical research into the subject demonstrated? Not much, actually. The only scholars to seek zealously to illustrate the facts in this field are Robert Dahl and Edward Tufte. In their book (of highly suitable format) *Size and Democracy* in 1973, these authors report on several differences in political respects between small and large states. Thus, it emerges that large states – as Madison thought – incorporate a more extensive network of political organizations and interest groups. At the same time, the small states offer a closer proximity – and more reciprocal communication – between the citizens and their political leaders.[48] Anyhow, neither these authors, nor any others (as far as I know) have subjected the question of primary interest to us, the relationship between size and level of democracy, to systematic study. In other words, we seem to be the first in the field with empirical inquiry.

Then what do the results indicate? Does the size make any difference, and if so, how? Table 23 presents three simple regressions where the size of the population, the area, and whether or not the state is an island, are matched against the level of democracy. We may thereby conclude that these attributes demonstrate a connection in accord with the thoughts which Lijphart, among others, has expressed. Thus, large states are less democratic.[49] Notwithstanding, this calls for an immediate reservation. The association is only strong at a very low level of size; in other words, the connection has a 'roof'. Thus it appears, if we consider the size of the population, that the real micro-states, with a population of less than 100,000, have surprisingly high values for democracy; the average is 8.9. For states with a larger population, up to one million, this figure is, however, no higher than 5.5 and the tendency is uneven at the subsequent size intervals. We find a similar pattern with regard to area – naturally, these two variables are strongly correlated.[50]

If we consider whether or not the state is an island, the outcome is more distinct. For such states the average level of democracy is 7.1, while for others it is 3.6. As the table shows, this attribute exhibits a clearly stronger connection than the size of the population and area. An internal control reveals that the coefficient for the two latter variables falls steeply (that for size of population to a wholly unessential level), while the relationship for island states by and large persists.[51] Thus, the latter attribute appears decisive. However, this may ensue from the different classifications applied. In the one case, for island states, we have a dichotomy, while in the other, for the population and the area, we are dealing with continuous variables. We also know that regarding the latter, the association with democracy declines over a certain level. Since island states are usually small, it is perhaps a reflection of this 'roof effect'.[52] In that case, the important point is not that certain states are islands (with the isolation, etc. which this involves), but that they are often very small in area and population.[53]

In order to test this we have reclassified the variables concerning the size of the population and the area in order to distinguish (dichotomously) between small and large states.[54] But this makes no difference: the association with democracy remains essentially the same as before, and in this form too the effect of the size variables is drastically curtailed when an island state (or not) is simultaneously included in the regression.[55] Thus, the fact remains – it is the island states that are special.

What does this depend on? Perhaps the connection is in the main spurious to such an extent that it reflects the effect of other attributes essential in the context? It may be mentioned that island states are little different from others as regards degree of economic development. On the other hand, popular education in general is better. The belief that island states are more commercially dependent proves only partly valid, namely in the form of a higher level regarding partner concentration and direct investments (which attributes, however, as we saw, have no connection with democracy in the degree or the direction postulated by the dependency theory). It is more interesting to observe that island states are far more Protestant dominated than others.[56] This may be the explanation.

Table 24. *Island state (or not) and level of democracy. Two multiple regressions.*

	Standardized regression coefficients	Explained variance (percentage)
(A)		
Island	0.22**	
Literacy	0.18*	
Trade USA, imp.	0.30**	
Commodity concentration	−0.24**	
Direct investments	0.11	
Capitalism	0.23**	
		57.1
(B)		
Island	0.14	
Literacy	0.15*	
Trade USA, imp.	0.30**	
Commodity concentration	−0.25**	
Direct investments	0.10	
Capitalism	0.19**	
Percentage of Protestants	0.17*	
		58.8

* significance at the 0.05 level
**significance at the 0.01 level

To a considerable extent, this seems to be the case. The relationship is illustrated in Table 24. In the first regression, our relevant variable is tested together with a number of socio-economic attributes. Here, a markedly positive relationship between island states and level of democracy remains. When Protestantism too is included, the picture changes. The connection now becomes much weaker and no longer significant.

The idea that popular government flourishes best in small states is, as we saw, of long standing. Tested on the conditions of today, and with regard to democracy in the representative form, the idea at first seemed to be confirmed – and particularly concerning island states. Nevertheless, to a substantial extent the connection proved to be spurious. It may be concluded that the often very small island states are not, as such, as special as they appear to be on simple inspection of the political geography.

CHAPTER 7

Institutional conditions

Virtually all the countries of the Third World were once colonies and thereby subject to a foreign power,[1] usually European. This led to the creation of political and administrative structures which the new states took over in one way or another after the advent of independence. Side by side with the different institutional legacies handed down by the imperial nations, it has been alleged, their political conduct, not least during the actual decolonization process, left its mark (through the force of example) in the countries concerned.

Before examining the arguments which are wont to be adduced concerning the significance of the colonial background, I should begin by acknowledging a limitation regarding the empirical study which follows. As is well known, the colonial period did not run parallel in different parts of the world. In Latin America it began in the sixteenth century and was concluded in the late 1800s. Consequently, it came to an end before the great expansion in Africa and also in large parts of the Middle East, Asia and Oceania, which occurred in the second half of the nineteenth century. The decolonization of the countries in the latter areas (and also in the Caribbean) did not take place until after the Second World War, particularly in the late 1950s and early 1960s. If the colonial link is to be adjudged relevant to the conditions of today, it really should not be too far back in time. For this reason – and thereby also to achieve comparability – we include only those countries which have been under colonial rule in the twentieth century. Accordingly, states which have been independent throughout the present century are classified as not colonized.[2]

It is generally believed among those who have discussed the

subject that a British colonial background was on many counts an advantage for democracy. The second great colonial power in the twentieth century, France, is frequently mentioned in comparison, and to great extent in contrast. Notwithstanding that both these once-great European powers for their part have a long tradition of popular rule – which in a more developed form has actually been in force longer in France than in Great Britain – they behaved rather differently as colonial rulers. The British soon endeavoured to counter discontent in the subject countries primarily with reforms. Wise from their failure in North America in the late eighteenth century, they had already begun a gradual decolonization by the middle of the nineteenth century, with the result that countries such as Canada and Australia were assigned the status of so-called Dominions which later, after the First World War, were *de facto* liberated. Immediately thereafter, in the mid-1930s, India's future right to independence was also recognized in reality. This was an act of great symbolical and practical significance – India was indeed 'the crowning jewel' of the Empire. The country became independent in 1947, the transition being in the main peaceful and institutionalized. The same could be said of well-nigh all the British colonies, many of which were set free in the following decades.[3]

In line with their reformist strategy, the British fairly soon set up organs for native representation in the government of many of the colonies. These organs had limited competence and, in many cases (particularly at first), were rather corporative in their composition. Nevertheless, it has been maintained, they made the local elite familiar with parliamentary and pluralistic forms of government.[4]

The French, too, eventually introduced different forms of representation for the native population, but these organs on the whole had a far weaker position. Moreover, in several cases an obvious manipulation of the electoral process occurred. The French long offered overt resistance to the idea of independence for the colonies. In order to withstand such claims, very extensive repression was exercised in several places after the Second World War. As a result of this rigid attitude, France was drawn into prolonged wars in North Africa and Indochina; thus independence here was achieved by far from peaceful means.[5]

Furthermore, it has been alleged that the British built up a fairly well-functioning administrative system – and, in particular, a judiciary – in the colonies. At the same time, a kind of 'indirect rule' was imposed, which involved links with old, local modes of organization. The native population was thus incorporated to a significant extent in the administrative apparatus and thereby imprinted by the rational, legalistic traditions which in England and elsewhere had constituted a counterbalance to the arbitrary use of power. France, in contrast, applied a markedly centralized administrative system, which in addition was sustained in all essentials by officials from the home country. Consequently, the population of the French colonies became less involved in the exercise of authority. Thus, there was a pronounced lack of administrative and political 'human capital' in these countries when independence came.[6]

Such are the arguments. The states which the British left behind them would for these reasons be better equipped for democratic government than those which had belonged to France (and this difference was adjudged still greater with respect to former Portuguese and Belgian colonies). But what support is there for this, as it is called, conventional wisdom? The question was previously raised in an investigation by Kenneth Bollen and Robert Jackman. Controlling for several other attributes, a British colonial background proved to have a significant positive connection with democracy.[7]

Let us now see what information our data can provide. A comparison of the means as regards level of democracy for former British and French colonies respectively reveals a distinct difference. For the British, the level is above the average for all countries studied, but for the French it is markedly lower.[8] A simple regression – see Table 25 – shows a similar tendency: a British background has a positive association with democracy and a French a negative. At the same time the fact that states have not been colonies during this century has a much weaker impact.

As is well known, Great Britain was a sea power. Her navy

Table 25. *Colonial background and level of democracy. Simple regression.*

	Standardized regression coefficient	Explained variance (percentage)	
British colony	0.29[**]	8.4	(N:132)
French colony	−0.30[**]	9.0	(N:132)
Non colony	0.11	1.2	(N:132)

Note: [**] significance at the 0.01 level

dominated the oceans. In consequence, the Union Flag, the symbol of Britain, flew in many of the small countries which are surrounded by water.

Moreover, we know that island states are in large measure Protestant. Here we can undoubtedly assume a historical connection![9] At the same time, we can by means of other available information establish that former British colonies are ahead of their French counterparts when it comes to economic and social development, e.g., literacy. There is also a noteworthy difference concerning economic systems: the former countries bear a stronger imprint of capitalism than those which were under French rule.[10]

Controlling for the attributes now at issue, the significant connections for colonial background, be it British or French, vanish. Accordingly, the difference with respect to degree of democracy which we just mentioned seems to be mainly a consequence of the effect of other variables – the religious factor in particular plays a major role here.[11]

However, the point with which we have so far been concerned – British contra French colonial background – is perhaps not the most interesting one, but rather the length of the colonial period. This idea was put forward by Huntington. After considering the fact that, after all, the majority of the former British possessions at the start of the 1980s exhibited relatively low democratic attainment, he suggests as a possible explanation that the period under British rule makes the difference. It is, he maintains, a striking fact that countries such as India and Sri Lanka, like many of the states in the West Indies, where the presence of the British had begun as early as the eighteenth century, are substantially more democratic than the nations in Africa which were colonized far later. On the whole, says Huntington, the latter differ little regarding democracy from other states on that continent.

In order to test this idea, we have compiled information on the length of the colonial period in the countries concerned. However, this issue is somewhat complicated to settle. It is not difficult to obtain information on when the period ends. The problem is to decide when it starts. For colonization was in many cases gradual, and occasionally interrupted by long intervals. Moreover, it often happened that the first landing, so to speak, was made by more or less independent trading companies, whose position on the spot was only given official sanction later on. For this reason we have used two measurements. The one pertains to the time when the colonial power first gained an official[12] (and lasting) foothold in the country. The second instead derives from the time when the greater part of the country was colonized. Naturally, in some cases the period is identical with both these criteria, but it is usually shorter with the latter.

It now proves that independent of which measurement we use, the outcome is by and large the same (I shall therefore confine myself in what follows to the first measurement). What do the results say? If, as Huntington did, we concentrate on the former British possessions, his hypothesis is confirmed beyond doubt; the longer they were colonized the higher, and distinctly so, the level of democracy. Interestingly enough, however, the same holds true for the former French territories; here too a long colonial period seems beneficial from a democratic point of view.[13]

Since we thus obtain the same outcome regarding the time factor for these states, it may well be that another dividing line between the former colonial powers is crucial, namely whether they for their part applied the principles of democracy (i.e., in the home country). In that case we should reach the same result if we were to add to the former British and French colonies (sample 1) the Belgian, Dutch and American (sample 2). On the other hand, the time factor should yield a weaker result if we also included Italian, Portuguese and Spanish colonies (sample 3) and, as a further expansion, the countries which during the twentieth century belonged to the Japanese or the Ottoman Empire (sample 4).

Such proves to be the case. The relationship between the colonial period and the level of democracy – see Table 26 – is indeed somewhat stronger in sample 1 than in sample 2, but there is no major difference. Much greater is the change on inclusion of the countries whose former masters were themselves under authoritarian rule for well-nigh the entire colonial period (samples 3 and 4). When these too are taken into account, the association finally becomes virtually insignificant, particularly in terms of explained variance.

Thus far, then, we can establish that the crux seems to be how long the countries were colonized by states which themselves had a democratic bent; within this circle, on the other hand, it makes little difference who was in control. It remains to be seen, however, to what extent his result holds good when other attributes are considered too.

Table 26. *Duration of the colonial period and level of democracy. Different samples. Simple regression*

	Standardized regression coefficient	Explained variance (percentage)	
British colonies	0.49**	24.2	(N:58)
French colonies	0.64**	40.8	(N:22)
Sample 1	0.56**	30.9	(N:80)
Sample 2	0.51**	25.6	(N:88)
Sample 3	0.18	3.3	(N:97)
Sample 4	0.14	1.9	(N:102)

Note: ** significance at the 0.01 level

If we confine ourselves to the 88 countries contained in sample 2, we find that the time factor still has a manifest, statistically significant effect when we also include in the regression the socio-economic variables which previously set the tone, together with Protestantism. Nevertheless, the picture changes when all 132 states, including those which have not been colonies in the twentieth century, provide the basis for the analysis: the impact of the time factor then declines to a low, insignificant, level.[14] The results are presented in Table 27.

We have thus obtained a somewhat mixed outcome. The issue with which the debate has primarily been concerned, the difference between former British and French territories, essentially lost its importance when the other variables mentioned here were considered simultaneously. In a way, the duration of the colonial period was of greater interest. A study of only those countries which were subject to democratic states in Europe and North America showed that the time factor had a considerable positive impact also when other differences between them were controlled. But in a global perspective, that is, when we examine the variation regarding the level of democracy in all 132 countries, this factor does not have the same weight; then the differences in socio-economic respects and concerning religion appear to be far more decisive.

THE PUBLIC SECTOR

Political democracy *sensu stricto* signifies that the people should control the activities of the state authorities. This requires that the

Table 27. *Duration of the colonial period and level of democracy. Different samples. Multiple regression.*

	Standardized regression coefficients	Explained variance (percentage)
Sample 2:		
Colonial period	0.21[*]	
Literacy	0.21[*]	
Commodity concentration	−0.24[**]	
Trade, USA, imp.	0.17	
Capitalism	0.20[*]	
Percentage of protestants	0.20[*]	
		58.6
All 132 states:		
Colonial period	0.08	
Literacy	0.18[*]	
Commodity concentration	−0.23[**]	
Trade, USA, imp.	0.30[**]	
Capitalism	0.21[**]	
Percentage of protestants	0.22[**]	
		56.6

citizens are able, in various respects, to function as free and equal rulers. The majority of the empirical theories pertinent to the prerequisites of democracy which have been reviewed so far deal mainly with this aspect of the problem. But the possibility of control can naturally also depend on the nature of the object of influence. In simple terms, governments may differ in the extent to which they are amenable to democratic control.

In this case, too, there is reason to begin with a reference to Huntington. In an article which strongly emphasizes institutional conditions, he comments on the need for balance between the input and output sides of the political system – the one relating to the resources for popular influence, and the other to the executive arm, i.e., the central bureaucracy *sensu lato*. In states where the bureaucracy occupies a strong, independent position, says Huntington, it is very difficult for popular influence to hold its own. The point at issue is a distorted structural distribution of power – not primarily between different groups in civil society, but between the state and its officials on the one hand and the great majority of the citizens on the other.[15]

Legacies from the past can promote such a development. Thus, Barrington Moore asserts that the survival of a preindustrial bureaucracy into modern times has created conditions which disfavour democracy. In his view, the history of Germany, Russia and China offers clear evidence of this.[16] Yet, the bureaucratic system, which the colonial powers left behind them in many countries of the Third World was fairly modest. As a rule, the colonial administrations were indeed sparsely populated; in many cases the governor of the respective country only had several hundred officials at his disposal. The whole of French Africa, with a native population of 18 million, was ruled in the 1930s (at the height of the Empire) by 4,500 colonial officials, and in Nigeria, with 20 million inhabitants, the corresponding figure was 1,400.[17] After independence, however, a steep rise usually occurred in the public bureaucracy. There were several reasons for this growth. At first, independence involved decentralization and thereby an increase in the administrative tasks; certain functions which were formerly filled centrally, in London or in Paris, etc. were now transferred to the field, so to speak. But first and foremost, the objectives set by the new states were far more extensive. Changes on a broad front – in the economy, the infrastructure, the health service, education, etc. – would now ensue. Grandiose development plans under public control – often in cooperation with international aid agencies – were the order of the day. In some cases, this approach was chosen for explicit, ideological reasons, in others more out of necessity. The alternative, in the form of a developed civil organizational structure, was often conspicuous by its absence. The means of realizing this policy was a strongly growing public sector. In Africa in particular, so vigorous an expansion of the corps of civil servants occurred in the 1960s and 1970s that even Professor Parkinson must have been amazed.[18]

There was yet another driving force behind this development. As numerous observers have remarked, the political life in many countries of Asia, Africa and Latin America is characterized by patterns of client/patron relationships.[19] Irrespective of ideological banners and other marks of distinction, the political work is heavily concentrated on the offer of patronage, that is, benefits addressed exclusively to the groups where leaders have their political footing. It may be a matter of creating job opportunities or giving grants for the building of roads, schools, hospitals, etc. in certain places and – not least – the ability to confer positions in the government establishment which are not only often well paid but, moreover, provide possibilities of further distribution for both the individual concerned (personally) and the group to which he belongs. Thus, the public sector is used as a means to satisfy diverse particularistic interests and therefore becomes a source for building popular support for the factions which compete for power. Naturally, this is promoted by a public sector in expansion: there is then a larger cake to share.

In consequence, the state in the administrative sense is strikingly 'soft' in many developing countries;[20] it frequently functions as an antithesis to the rational rule-governed type of bureaucracy which Weber advocated. Extensive corruption, nepotism, and a general mismanagement of public funds constitute a common pattern. There are countless reports thereof.[21] Despite the state bureaucracy's often impressive extent, it normally has at the same time a surprisingly weak steerage capacity – this phenomenon was called by one scholar 'the swollen state' (one which is simultaneously both large and impotent),[22] and by another 'a state that is suspended in mid-air above the society' (by reason of a general civic withdrawal from the control of public agencies).[23]

There is another problem, too. The establishment of a large state in an economically weakly developed society makes it particularly difficult, it has been alleged, to apply the democratic form of division of power. Since public positions in these societies represent well-nigh the only way to social and economic improvement, the control of government becomes crucial. When so much is at stake in political life, there is no scope for the tolerance and peaceful competition which democracy requires – for the difference of result between gain and loss is too great. Politics instead assumes the nature of a relentless zero-sum game.[24]

For these reasons, a large public sector can be thought to present an obstacle to democratic development in the countries which we study. In order to test this hypothesis we used the following data: (1) the ratio of the size of public expenditure to GNP; (2) public consumption (which is a subset of the former); and (3) as an indicator of the administrative undertakings: the percentage of publicly owned hospitals.[25]

A study executed by Kenneth Bollen yielded results which support the above assumption; the size of public expenditure shows a significant negative relationship with the degree of democracy.[26] However, this result is not confirmed in the test we performed. As

Table 28. *Different measurements of the size of the public sector and level of democracy. Simple regression.*

	Standardized regression coefficient	Explained variance (percentage)	
Public expenditure	0.19	3.6	(N:85)
Public consumption	−0.15	2.2	(N:115)
Public hospitals	−0.20*	3.9	(N:112)

Note: * = Significance at the 0.05 level

Table 28 shows, in simple regression the level of public expenditure has a positive association with democracy. As regards the other two measurements, which illustrate more limited aspects of the size of the public sector, we find, in contrast, an (expected) negative link. The explained variance is, however, remarkably low throughout. This gives reason to assume that the relationships are sensitive to control for other attributes, which also turns out to be the case. When the variables which previously proved to be strong are included in the regression, the connection for publicly owned hospitals is wholly eliminated[27] and the result is the same for the other two indicators of the size of the public sector which are used here.

'Statism' in the form of a rapidly growing public sector has featured increasingly as a problem in the debate concerning the countries of the Third World. This development is considered to promote clientelism and corruption and, among other things, thereby contribute to a markedly weak administrative capacity. The state authorities in these countries are frequently described as severely wasteful and, foremost, a burden on society. We have not seen fit *per se* to scrutinize these accounts of the situation; they served only as background descriptions for the thesis that 'statism' has a negative effect on the form of government in the respect in focus here. As is evident, however, this thesis has not been confirmed. Side by side with the other attributes differentiating the countries which were presented previously, the size of the public sector, according to the measurements which we applied, has practically no impact on the level of democracy in the Third World.

THE MILITARY

The situation is particularly distressing from the viewpoint of democracy when the military arm of the state, the armed forces, is politically dominant. The military has a special position with regard to political power resources: 'The nature of the political tactics employed by the military reflects their organizational coherence and the fact that while other social forces can pressure the government, the military can replace the government.'[28] Together with the fact that the most effective means of coercion – weapons and trained soldiers – are at the military's disposal, it also occupies a strong position in purely organizational terms. Characterized by centralization, hierarchy and discipline, it possesses an administrative capacity which has few counterparts in the rest of social and political life – especially in the developing countries where this capacity is often in very short supply. Moreover, socialization into a military *esprit de corps* creates an identity and an internal solidarity which, in turn, alienate the armed forces from the rest of society. When such a tradition has been built up over a long period, the military can become a closed segment, a 'state' within the state; and, furthermore, with reference to its claims, superior to the state.[29]

Latin America has a long history of innumerable military interventions in politics. As a recent measure of the activity in question, it may be mentioned that between 1960 and 1979 coups were executed, with subsequent military government, in 13 of the 17 states; in some cases (as in Argentina) this happened several times during the period. The four exceptions were Colombia, Venezuela, Costa Rica and Mexico. Africa south of the Sahara has also experienced many coups d'état since independence; in a study comprising 45 states, there were successful interventions in 25 countries (the total number of such coups was 52) during the period 1960–82; when unsuccessful attempts are also included[30] the number of states affected was 38 (that is, 84 per cent). A strong military dominance in political life is also to be found in a good many states in the Arab world and the Mediterranean area, particularly Libya, Egypt, Iraq, Syria and Turkey. And there are several similar examples in the Far East and Oceania: Pakistan, Bangladesh, Burma, Thailand, Indonesia, South Korea and Fiji.[31]

There has been much controversy concerning the causes of military coups d'état and military regimes. Some explanations pertain directly to the theories of the requisites for democracy which were discussed above, e.g., the modernization and dependency school, and alternative theses related to these have also been presented. Thus, Edward Muller formulated a kind of dependency theory which in contrast to the current one (which deals with purely economic conditions) directs attention to aid relationships, particularly those having military elements. Through this type of dependency, the great powers can steer the political development in the recipient countries to their interests of military and security policy. In Muller's opinion, the relations between the Latin American countries and the USA should be seen in this light. In conformation, he demonstrates an (however moderate) connection between aid of the said nature and the tendency to coups in the countries concerned.[32] Other explanations relate rather to the conditions within the actual armed forces, e.g., their social recruitment basis, internal solidarity and political 'ethos' (Morris Janowitz), or the emergence of a more technocratic, commercial and professional military culture which in its turn – this is yet another aspect – provides the basis for fairly wide coalitions outside its own ranks; with the native business world and also with parts of the working class; this is called 'the new corporatism' (Alfred Stepan). There is another 'school' too (Aristide Zolberg, Samuel Decalo), which primarily emphasizes situation-specific conditions; discontent with subsidies or benefits within the armed forces, burgeoning conflicts (of a personal or ideological nature) between political and military leaders etc.; the point according to this approach is that there are no universal explanations of military interventions in politics.[33]

However, irrespective of the reason, we can state that the military has in many countries become a permanent power factor in politics, directly by its own rule, or indirectly, as a supervisor of the civilian government, 'entitled' to intervene when the situation so demands. The motives which are normally adduced are to protect 'the nation', the community and the state from political anarchy and degeneration: violence and lawlessness, serious conflicts between different political groupings, corruption and mismanagement of public funds, general economic crisis, etc. It is often alleged that the military must intervene to restore the country to such order that it can return, at least eventually, to a civilian and democratic government. As several observers of the subject have remarked, there is nevertheless much evidence that the conditions in these respects may rather deteriorate in the event of a military take-over of power. Above all, they are wont to emphasize the tendency to a dissolution of the institutional rule system that the interventions involve. To begin with, a military coup d'état is normally a violation of the current constitution. By this, 'a moral barrier' breaks down which may be difficult to repair. Once the first step has been taken intervention may easily become a habit.[34]

The consequences of the military's role as political guardian, says Huntington, are in practice a very unclear division of power and responsibility which, in contradiction to their explicit purpose, contribute to an erosion of political order:

While guardianship has the loftiest justifications and rationales, it also has the most debilitating and corrupting effect on the political system. Responsibility and power are divorced. Civilian leaders may have responsibility, but they know they do not have power and are not allowed to create power because their actions are subject to military veto. The military juntas may exercise power, but they know that they will not have to be responsible for the consequences of their action, for they can always turn authority back to the civilians when the problems of governance become too much for them.[35]

As implied by the quotation, the alleged reasons for intervention (law and order, etc.) are rarely reflected in the conduct of military regimes. There is abundant evidence here (as for civilian governments) of corruption and other kinds of misrule. General (and, for many years, also President) Mobuto of Zaire represents a regime which at present, despite serious competition, would seem to be internationally unparalleled with regard to embezzlement of public funds; the estimated sums are well-nigh inconceivable.[36] Extensive political violence and a rule of sheer terror has in many cases ensued from the armed forces' take-over of the national government; the events in Indonesia, Argentina, Chile and Uruguay in the 1960s and 1970s are the most blatant examples in recent times. Thus, it is not merely by their 'entry' that military regimes contribute to the dissolution of the legal rules of political life; the government which follows is rarely a paragon of virtue either.

This in turn creates a severe transitional problem when civilian, democratically elected politicians are to assume power once more. The question of punishment – with reference to the sometimes very serious crimes which have been committed – then becomes extremely sensitive. In view of the military's latent power resources,

Table 29. *Military expenditure and level of democracy. Simple regression.*

	Standardized regression coefficient	Explained variance (percentage)	
Military expenditure	-0.43^{**}	18.2	(N:128)

Note: ** significant at the 0.01 level

there is reason to apply a strategy of reconciliation, i.e., not to make an issue of what has happened. Nevertheless, this means *de facto* acceptance of manifest breaches of the law which (again) undermines the rule system. Furthermore, the politicians risk losing their popular legitimacy by doing nothing. This political dilemma hardly constitutes a favourable beginning for a democratic government.[37]

Against this background, there is undoubtedly reason to assume that large armed forces – with the potential for intervention this confers – have an adverse effect on democracy.[38] As the basis for tests of the situation in this respect, we used data on the size of military expenditure – to be precise, their percentage of the total public expenditures – in the countries under study. As we can see in Table 29, this indicator has a clear negative connection with the level of democracy, which consequently – so far – confirms our assumption.[39]

As often happens, the explanatory factor which is the object of scrutiny is, in its turn, related to other attributes which have proved to be of importance for democracy. There is, in particular, a linkage here with the religious affiliation of the population: in countries where Protestantism, (and indeed Christianity in general) is widespread, the military are assigned fewer resources. Furthermore, it is worth mentioning that the size of the military expenditure is negatively correlated (albeit at a lower level) with capitalism, trade with the USA, and the degree of socio-economic development.[40] Do these underlying relationships perhaps explain the outcome just recorded? Not wholly. When the other attributes, by categories, are controlled, a negative, significant association persists between the size of military expenditure and the level of democracy: and the same applies if the whole list of variables, which previously proved to have a considerable impact, is taken into account; the result is illustrated in Table 30.

Table 30. *Military expenditure and level of democracy. Multiple regression.*

	Standardized regression coefficients	Explained variance (percentage)
Military expenditure	-0.15^{*}	
Literacy	0.17^{*}	
Commodity concentration	-0.23^{**}	
Trade, USA, imp.	0.29^{**}	
Capitalism	0.20^{**}	
Percentage of Protestants	0.20^{**}	
		57.7

Note: * significance at the 0.5 level
** significance at the 0.01 level

Thus we have found that the size of the armed forces (measured in economic terms) has a statistically confirmed, independent impact on democracy, and this in an expected, negative, direction. At the same time we can say that this factor has a comparatively modest position in the competition. Other variables seem to have a greater effect on the varying levels of democracy in the countries of the Third World.

CHAPTER 8

General picture and problems of causality

Several ideas pertinent to the requisites of democracy have been reviewed and subjected to empirical testing in the preceding pages. The chaff has thereby been separated from the wheat. The method of this division took the form of a stepwise regression. The possible explanatory factors which already at the first scrutiny could not display significant association – or which lost this quality in later stages – were then disregarded. However, a problem is inherent in this approach. The risk is that those which fall short of the limit would have done better if they had been included at a later stage of the analysis. Indeed, it usually happens that on controlling for more variables, associations either persist (by and large) throughout or decline to an ever-marked extent. This circumstance motivated the layout chosen here. But there are, of course, exceptions; those which appear 'dead' can 'revive' when further attributes are included in the regression.

Moreover, it is not self-evident to demand the significance level – at least 0.05 on double-sided (two-tailed) testing – which is here applied. In some similar studies a lower limit was used (e.g., in the form of only a one-sided test at the said level). Thus, it would be worth trying to find out whether the final result is essentially changed if a lower standard of significance is used.

For this reason, we have performed a series of regressions, where from the start all the attributes of any interest were included. Variables such as the percentage employed in service, trade with the EC, fragmentation, island states, colonial background, etc. thereby gained a new chance. The layout was such that step by step we removed the weakest variable,[1] in order for those which finally remained to fulfil the requirement of double-sided significance at the 0.10 level. We see the result in Table 31, where for clarity's sake the T-values are also reported.

Table 31. *Variables which after gradual sorting display significant associations with level of democracy on at least the 0.10 level.*

	Standardized regression coefficients	T-values	Explained variance (percentage)
Literacy	0.13(*)	−1.806	
Commodity concentration	−0.24**	−3.759	
Trade, USA, imp.	0.29**	4.196	
Capitalism	0.18*	2.574	
Percentage of Protestants	0.20**	2.754	
Military expenditure	0.17*	−2.415	
Average fragmentation	−0.13*	−2.023	
			59.2

Note: (*) significance at the 0.10 level
 * significance at the 0.05 level
 ** significance at the 0.01 level

The most prominent difference *vis-à-vis* the outcome which was reported just before (in Table 30) is that average fragmentation now appears among the more important variables. Accordingly, the usual idea that cleavages in the population constitute a complicating circumstance for democracy is finally confirmed. It is also notable that literacy now falls short of the significance level (0.05) which was previously used as a criterion.[2] Otherwise the picture is more or less the same.

Thus, we have now seen the general, global pattern. But there are, of course, regional deviations.[3] The negative connection between commodity concentration and democracy is particularly marked in North Africa and the Middle East;[4] many of the states here concentrate their exports almost exclusively to oil products at the same time as they often have remarkably low values for democracy. Moreover, trade with the USA plays a minor role in Sub-Saharan Africa while it is of importance in other parts of the world. The so-called Black Africa also stands out in that the religious factor generally has a weaker impact. The reason would seem to be that the major religions have here penetrated only to a minor extent; on the whole, their advent was comparatively recent and considerable sections of the population in many of the countries still hold traditional, native beliefs. On the other hand, this factor is so much more influential in Asia and Oceania, and even in North Africa and the Middle East. In these areas, fragmentation too gives a clearly stronger result than in Latin America, the Caribbean and (which may seem more surprising) in Sub-Saharan Africa. The tendency as regards military expenditure is fairly even over the continents. Much the same can be said of the connection between the economic system (capitalism) and democracy, although the link is somewhat stronger in Asia and Oceania than elsewhere. Finally, it may be mentioned that Latin America and the Caribbean diverge somewhat concerning the importance of literacy; the relationship is here slightly weaker than in other areas.

It is thus possible to observe certain geographical differences with respect to the strength of the connections. But their significance should not be exaggerated. Analysis of the interaction between regions and the said variables yield consistently weak results – in no case do we find any significant outcomes even at the 0.10 level.[5] This indicates that the relationships are primarily global and therefore not regionally concentrated.

A common feature of the theories and explicit hypotheses discussed here is that they relate to different structural conditions in the states in question. The main idea of the explanatory approach they represent is that political life is affected by its environment; government by the people or not (in simple terms) is assumed to be a consequence of the economic and social circumstances in society, the cultural and demographic characteristics of the population, etc. According to this logic, states which share such attributes should on the whole exhibit similar democratic performances.[6]

In contrast – I would point out – there is another line of research, whereby it does not suffice to seek explanations in the external constraints of politics. Considerable importance must also be attached to the conduct of the actors involved. Such an 'antideterministic' view has been vigorously maintained by Arend Lijphart, who for his part emphasizes the significance of political leadership: democracy can evolve and be lasting – even under disadvantageous external conditions – if the political elite strives to co-operate to this end. Apart from a necessary commitment to the task (of constantly setting the value of democracy high on the agenda), skilful engineering is also required; that is, according to Lijphart, the ability to find suitable political forms which can contribute to compromise and reconciliation between opposing groups.[7]

In general terms, this approach links up with the thesis of the role of the individual actors – the personalities – in history. The crux is not the external circumstances, but rather who holds the helm of the state. Consequently, in this perspective it makes a great difference whether the political leadership is executed by men like Jawharalal Nehru, David Ben-Gurion and Léopold Senghor or by such as Kwame Nkruma, Luis Somoza and Ferdinand Marcos.

To this controversial question – whether it depends chiefly on the politicians themselves or on the circumstances under which they work – we cannot here offer a distinct answer. For the investigation which was executed has been wholly addressed to the testing of hypotheses which pertain to the one perspective. What we can show is how far this approach seems to reach, that is, how much it explains and – within this scope – what explanatory factors emerge as more important than others.

What, then, can we say about the requisites of democracy in the part of the world which was examined? It is clear that no single explanatory factor strikes like an iron fist through the material. On the contrary, several attributes of different kinds stand out as important. With the variables which have finally crystallized, we can explain some 60 per cent of the variation concerning the level of democracy. We can but speculate on what other factors we have thereby left 'unrevealed'. It may be such as pertains in one way or another to the type of explanations which were discussed, but which for lack of ingenuity or for the absence of necessary data we could not include in our investigation. It may also be a matter of specific circumstances which prevail in the individual countries e.g. such as relates to political leadership. All we can say is that other things too probably have an impact on democracy, and that these factors could be of either a structural or an actor-oriented nature. On the other hand, it is worth accentuating the fact that a complete fit between explanans and explanandum (that is, 100 per cent explained variance) is far from attainable in the kind of broad-based causal study that we have undertaken. Relatively speaking, the accumulated explanatory level we have achieved must be seen as satisfactory.

In consequence of the tests which were carried out, we can start by recording a number of negative findings. Several possible explanations were not confirmed through empirical confrontation. These include those which relate to the size of the public sector. As regards the colonial background, the difference between a previous French or British affiliation did not prove to have the significance for democracy which was formerly assumed. On the other hand, the duration of the colonial period has a positive effect among the countries which for their part have been democratic for much of the twentieth century. Nevertheless, these circumstances do not have the same relative importance when our entire sample of countries constitutes the basis of the analysis. The size factor – and, in particular, island states contra others – seemed in simple tests of connections to have a favourable effect on the level of democracy. But this, we later found, was primarily a consequence of the impact of other variables. The ideas which gained no support at our scrutiny also include the theory concerning the significance of the distribution of income and wealth. Neither independently, nor on consideration of other kinds of attribute which could be adjudged important in the context, did any such association with level of democracy emerge.

Among the chiefly positive results, the indications of what is thought in the modernization school to be the explanatory link – economic and social development – those in particular which pertain to popular education, proved to be of importance. Here, the literacy rate in the population appears as the most decisive. When we gradually included more and more variables of other kinds in the analysis, however, this attribute successively declined. In the end, the said measurement of modernization is the explanatory factor which has the poorest position. I would emphasize this as a first striking observation: when, as here, we consider only the countries of the Third World and, moreover, include far more potential explanatory factors than has previously been the case,[8] a manifestly weaker connection emerges between modernization and democracy than has been reported in earlier studies. The conclusion is that differences in terms of socio-economic development in this part of the world are, although not inconsiderable, far from crucial for democracy.

In order to test the theses of the dependency school, several measurements of the countries' commercial relationships were used. In this case, several important associations with democracy appeared, even after internal control, which nevertheless rarely followed the direction predicated by the dependency school. Yet, in the course of the study, the list of variables which pertain to trade gradually thinned out. Thus, trade with the EC and the Soviet bloc respectively, and eventually also direct investments, retreated to the wings, while trade with the USA and commodity concentration in exports remained 'on stage'. As we saw, these are the attributes which give the strongest outcomes in the final regression. This appears as the second striking result of our investigation: for countries in the Third World the trade relations evidently play a major role for the mode of government.

The way in which the life of production is organized – in capitalistic contra socialistic forms – has been considered by many to be an important requisite for democracy. But, despite the lively discussion on this topic, the question has not previously been the object of any proper empirical test.[9] Our study has shown that a relationship of the expected nature does exist and we could even establish that capitalism in particular is associated with the existence of political freedoms.

Among cultural and demographic conditions, fragmentation of the population proved to give fairly moderate connections with democracy which, moreover, were further reduced once socio-economic attributes were controlled. But, in this case, the result changed when we later also included other kinds of variables. At a *per se* weak level, the average fragmentation finally joins – and, as expected, with a negative signature – the most important explanatory variables. This is an outcome which closely accords with the observations of earlier researchers. The same can be said of the religious factor, namely the percentage of Protestants, which for its part shows a positive relationship with democracy. Indeed, this holds true – but somewhat less strongly – for Christianity in general. In other words, a common view concerning the impact of religion on the mode of government is confirmed thus far. On the other hand, we do not find support for what is usually the antithesis of the religious thesis, namely that the Islamic faith has in like measure the reverse effect on democracy. The negative connection which first appeared proved to depend chiefly on other traits in the states where Islam predominates.

Finally, we come to the military factor. This is yet another problem about which much has been said but where systematic empirical studies with reference to democracy are lacking. Our investigation demonstrates that countries where a high proportion of the resources are assigned to the armed forces tend to have a low degree of democracy. This association stands fast even when other important variables are taken into account.

This is, in short, the picture which emerges through the statistical techniques and borderline criteria which have been used here. What it represents is a number of documented connections between the said factors and the level of democracy. The question is how these links should be understood. In the previous pages, I have on this point simplified the issue for myself (and the reader); the relationships have been interpreted throughout in line with the assumptions in the explanatory theories, namely that democracy is the dependent factor – the one which is influenced by others. But this is by no means self-evident. As Dankwart Rustow rightly has pointed out in his criticism of the conclusions based on statistical connections which Lipset presented, we do not know *a priori* what causes what:

correlation evidently is not the same as causation – it provides at best a clue to some sort of causal connection without indicating its direction.[10]

Consequently, before we can make any more definite assertions, we must submit reasons which imply that the connections follow a certain line, i.e., that democracy is indeed an effect of the variables X, Y and Z, and not the reverse. In some cases it seems fairly obvious how the situation should be read. Cleavages in the population and religious affiliation cannot be adjudged to be a consequence of the actual mode of government. Here it is a matter of circumstances which as a rule have prevailed for a long period, and which can be influenced by political means only to a minor extent – and then in the very long term. Thus – given the associations which have been observed – we need not doubt the fragmentation and Protestantism impact on democracy.

The situation concerning some other factors is less certain. In the case of literacy, a reverse causality could well be postulated; namely that states which have adopted democracy invest more than others in popular education. A similar situation may prevail with respect to the size of the military; it may be the case that authoritarian regimes (since they need it the most) strengthen the armed forces, while states which have become democratic disarm. As regards trade with the USA, too, this may be a consequence (and not a cause) of democratization. As is well known, the USA follows a trade policy where countries are ranked with reference *inter alia* to political and human rights.

Thus, the question is whether changes over time with respect to literacy, military expenditure and trade can depend on the mode of government. In order to examine this issue to some extent, we compiled data on these factors at the start of the 1970s for some 30 countries. These were later compared with similar data from the late 1980s. It should be mentioned that in the sample of countries, about one half could be classified as chiefly democratic for the greater part of the intervening period, while the others do not meet this criterion (they are henceforth called democratic and non-democratic respectively).[11]

Concerning the percentage of literates in the population, we find that the level increases overall during the period. Nevertheless, in the cases where the change was greatest, we see no connection to the mode of government – progress seems to be as favourable in non-democratic as in democratic states.[12] The tendency for military expenditures is more divided, but this usually increases during the period. Nor do we here see any linkage of the kind which we seek; military expansion is just as common in both kinds of state, and the same is true in the cases where a reduction occurred.[13] As a rule, trade with the USA diminishes over time for the countries included in the sample. Among the states where this tendency is particularly prominent, the percentage of democracies is, in relative terms, as high as that of non-democracies.[14] In other words, no association can be documented. Thus, the result is that neither for literacy, nor military expenditure, nor trade with the USA, can we find any signs of a reversed causality.

In the case of commodity concentration in exports, the direction of the link should not prove to be a problem; the idea that these conditions depend to any essential extent on the mode of government seems far-fetched. Hence, we can assume that the 'causal arrow' flies in the expected direction. However, there is another problem. What does the relationship actually illustrate? According to the interpretation by the dependency school, the explanation is that the countries whose exports are heavily concentrated in one item are particularly vulnerable in the world of international trade. Thus, outside powers can bring to bear pressure which has an adverse effect on democracy. This need not be the case, however. Instead of placing the causal source externally, such a unilaterality in production could very well be thought to exert effects of primarily an internal nature. Countries whose exports are heavily dependent on a certain kind of product – maybe oil, cocoa, copper, etc. – naturally have a low degree of diversification in their economies.

This may contribute to a limited social pluralism, and could even be expected to impede the growth of active popular organizations. It is worth emphasizing that commodity concentration has been used in certain studies as a measurement of the degree of social and economic development[15] With reference to our own data, this does not seem unreasonable. Commodity concentration indeed does not display any striking connection with the variables in the said field, but the correlations are in some cases higher here than with the other measurements of dependency which were used.[16] I leave open the question of which interpretation is the more reasonable. My point is merely to emphasize that it is not evident that the explanation of the negative link which we observed is the one submitted by the dependency school.

If we return to the question of the direction of the linkages, the assumption concerning the role of the economic system is, as I see it, the most doubtful. As is well known, the usual idea is that economic freedom engenders political liberties, and thereby also democratic conditions. In our study, a strong association undoubtedly emerged between political freedoms and capitalism. But this is not to say what causes what. In the recent upheavals in Eastern Europe we have rather seen a development where first a political change occurs in democracy's favour and then, as a consequence, an orientation towards capitalist forms of production. It is also worth recalling that all the states in our study which apply a distinctly socialist economic system have markedly low values for democracy, while the connections are otherwise more mixed. The safest link is perhaps simply that a maintenance of far-reaching socialist forms of production (involving an extensive planned economy and widespread restrictions of the right of ownership) requires an authoritarian political system. In all probability, no democratic state could enforce the strict regulations which this state of affairs prescribes. In a democracy, a government which adopted such measures would presumably be dismissed. From this viewpoint it seems natural that socialist states which become democratic step away from the old production system. This – reversed logic – does not, of course, cover the whole spectrum of connections between the designs of the economic and political systems. It explains the parallelism to be found at the two ends of the scales; between a purely socialistic economy and a distinctly authoritarian government.

As is clear, we may draw fairly accurate conclusions regarding the direction of the relationship when it comes to fragmentation, religion and commodity concentration. Nevertheless, as far as the last-mentioned variable is concerned, it is not thereby clear what actually constitutes the explanation. In the cases of literacy, the size of the military and trade with the USA, our examination revealed nothing to prove the existence of a reversed causality. Concerning the association between the economic system and democracy, there is, however, reason to believe that the link to a certain extent diverges from the pattern which has usually been assumed to prevail.

Having thus scrutinized the nature of the observed statistical associations, what conclusions in a wider context can be drawn from our study? Here it is natural to pay attention in particular to the variable 'trade with USA' that gave the strongest outcome and which also points to something really new in relation to earlier inquiries of this kind. In the case of this connection, the general implication can hardly be questioned. In all probability, it is a matter of an external effect to the extent that these trade relationships are combined with influence on the mode of government. This, in turn, indicates that the US administration is using trade as a policy instrument in its interaction with the states of the Third World.

This factor – the occurrence of a linkage between international relations and domestic political structures – has lately been emphasized especially by Laurence Whitehead.[17] With empirical reference to the political changes (up and down with respect to democracy), which have taken place in Latin America and Southern Europe, this author gives account of a number of methods which could be applied in order to stimulate (or prevent) political transformation in the target countries. Beside military inducements, covert activities and aid engagements, trade relationships made conditional stand out as an important instrument for external political influence.[18]

Whitehead demonstrates that the US representatives have over the post-war period (and also at earlier times), in many instances expressed a firm commitment with the promotion of democracy overseas. In practice, however, these objectives have often been overshadowed by the security interests which the USA as the leading power in the Western sphere has seen as its main responsibility. Anti-communism (in a wide sense) and reliability as alliance partners became during the Cold War the guiding principles of

Washington's relationship with the countries in Latin America (and elsewhere). In consequence, the US did in many cases co-operate with (and sometimes even take part in the establishment of) outright undemocratic regimes.[19]

However, in pace with the growing *détente* between the two international blocs, there has been a change in the US foreign-policy priorities. Since the mid-1970s (starting with President Carter), Washington has put greater emphasis on the 'moral' aspects of international relations, that is, to stand up for democracy and human rights, both within and outside the US sphere of influence. Notwithstanding that these proclamations have been somewhat selectively and contingently applied, the US authorities have lately exerted a considerable international pressure in support of democratization.[20]

The question is, then, what real effect these measures might have. On a general plane, Whitehead expresses a fairly modest view. In peacetime (when it is not a matter of military intervention as in Japan, Germany and Grenada) 'it is the process internal to each country that is most important in determining the success of democratic transitions; external support is of secondary importance'.[21] However, in his analysis of some concrete cases, he makes an interpretation which would give foundation for a different conclusion. This refers to the states where the restoration of democracy in Latin America started in the late 1970s and the early 1980s (the Dominican Republic, Ecuador and Peru), in which the USA was evidently involved, albeit more or less openly. This occurred, Whitehead remarks, in countries where the internal circumstances – with regard to socioeconomic structures and political traditions – hardly suggested that the process of transformation would be initiated there.[22]

Moving ahead to the late 1980s when our inquiry was conducted, and where the accumulated impact of Washington's new foreign-policy attitude concerning democracy could reasonably be more accurately examined, we have found that the US by means of its trade relationships has exerted an important influence on political institutions overseas. This also supports the view that international pressure – even in peacetime – can strongly affect the political process in individual countries.

In the perspective of such a linkage, the other major explanatory variable that is also related to trade – i.e., commodity concentration in exports, which exhibited a negative connection with democracy – might be given another (in fact a third) interpretation. According to the dependency school, commodity concentration should be seen as a weakness on the part of the states at issue, with the effect that they are more susceptible to external economic and political pressure. But perhaps it is the other way around. As may be recalled, the connection was particularly marked in the Arab states; that is, in the region which accounts for the lion's share of the world's oil production. In my understanding, there is reason to assume that this position, involving control over a commodity of vital economic importance, makes these states more resistant to international imposition, including pressure with respect to domestic political structures.[23] If so, this would presumably also hold true for major exporters of other raw materials of great industrial significance, for instance, certain essential materials (as in the case of South Africa and Zaire).[24] In other words, countries whose export is heavily concentrated on a specific item may thus be more capable of maintaining national independence and thereby be able more strongly to safeguard the preservation of authoritarian modes of government.

Having focused on the international aspects, which in this study have come out as particularly interesting, we should not, of course, disregard the fact that other attributes of a primarily internal nature also have proved to be of significance (and, accordingly, from the point of view of promoting popular rule from outside, could be seen as constraints of a more or less affectable kind). As has been evident, democracy is more likely to flourish in countries dominated by Christianity – and, in particular, by Protestantism – and where the population is relatively homogeneous and well-educated. The establishment of this mode of government is further facilitated in the case of a tiny military apparatus and if (with some reservation for the logic of causality) economic life is organized mainly in accordance with private ownership and market principles. Beside these findings we should not, I would like to point out, neglect the number of negative outcomes, which in view of the scholarly discourse upon the requisites of democracy could as well provide some enlightenment.

Finally some methodological reflections with reference to future research into this area. We have now carried out an empirical study in form of statistical analyses of (so far as was possible) systematically compiled mass data. The study comprises a large number of countries about which we gathered an abundance of information which could be of interest. The advantages of this approach are that we gain a wide overview, generalizability, and a high degree of certainty in the conclusions; if, from an interestingly formulated theory, and reasonable operationalizations thereof, we can demonstrate manifest connections – or if such are conspicuous by their absence – this result cannot be dismissed.

But the quantitative method has, of course, its limitations.[25] First and foremost I would here emphasize the rigidity of the research design inherent in this approach. In order to achieve the wide overview required, each stage must be carefully planned. We must have decided in advance which theories are to be discussed, how these are to be operationalized, and what type of data we thus shall seek to compile. At the subsequent analysis of the data a good many new ideas can certainly be given free rein. Variables may be reclassified and combined and we may test clusters of relationships which were not envisaged originally. But, notwithstanding, for practical reasons the frame of the study is to a great extent set by the perspective which we applied from the outset. What is more, far from always ideal circumstances prevail at the operationalizational stage. On the whole, the more countries, and the more attributes, are included, the greater the problems in finding comparable valid data.[26] At the same time, the reports become inevitably sweeping; what is presented, we may say, is a bird's-eye view of the empirical landscape.

The methodical alternative, the qualitative analysis of a few cases, naturally has the advantage that it is here possible to give a far more penetrating and variegated picture of the situation under study. It is thus feasible to follow in detail the processes which contribute to (or prevent) change in the respects of interest. Furthermore, such studies normally need not be as firmly structured beforehand as those quantitatively oriented. Through this more flexible approach the researcher is in a better position to find new trails and clues along the way. The scope for 'discoveries' is therefore greater. The major disadvantage is, of course, the limitation of the empirical focus. Case studies tend to assume an ideographical stamp insofar as the explanations made pertain exclusively to the country or countries which are examined (which may *per se* be defensible: the purpose is perhaps merely to elicit the circumstances in certain cases, not to contribute to a more comprehensive debate). But even when the case studies have an explicitly generalistic ambition the said problem persists. With a few observations it is not possible – with any high degree of certainty – to verify connections of a general nature, and even less to control for spuriosity (i.e., underlying patterns of relationship). This requires the application of some kind of quantitative method.

It should, however, be clear from the above that the two research trends can at best complement each other. Statistical analysis of mass data has its strength when it comes to testing of theories and hypotheses which are well formulated in advance. Usually, then, results emerge which in their turn generate new issues, some of which can be advantageously addressed via the freer, more intensive form of case study. It may be a matter of illuminating the deeper significance of certain general connections which have appeared, or of making new 'discoveries' which may provide a basis for alternative theories or lead to the reformulation of old ones. These contributions can in their turn serve as starting-points for future studies based on mass data.

In the light of the results which emerged in this investigation, as I see it, three questions in particular merit a more penetrating study through selection of suitable, illustrative cases. The first relates to the problem of how the negative relationship between democracy and commodity concentration should really be understood. We have asked ourselves whether the impact is primarily of an internal or an external nature and, in the latter case, does export concentration involve a weak and dependent international position, or does it, as I would assume, entail external strength and greater international autonomy? Moreover, I would point to the US trade relationship, which as I have tried to elucidate, could be seen as a means of outside political pressure. The question is how this is materialized in different ways – for example, how it is accomplished in co-operation with local actors;[27] to what extent it is a part of a wider 'cluster of interference' which includes also security policy, military assistance and civilian aid and, in addition, whether the actions taken by US authorities even may affect the way multilateral organs (e.g., the World Bank) take their stand in individual cases. Furthermore, I would again emphasize the association between democracy and capitalism where I maintain that there is reason to assert that the causality – given the usual theoretical conception – may to a certain extent be the reverse. Here a detailed study of a number of countries which represent different combinations regarding political and economic change could be expected to contribute to increased insight into how these things are related.

Concerning further quantitative studies of the subject, I believe the strength of the analysis could be improved primarily by means of a longitudinal approach, i.e., on the basis of data from several points of time. We would then obtain a more direct measurement of the phenomenon to which many empirical theories of democracy pertain, namely patterns of political change. With access to such so-called time-series data for both explanatory factors and that to be explained it would also be possible, with greater certainty than here, to answer questions which relate to the direction of causality.

In other words, much work remains to be done. Through formulation and testing of new ideas, and by application of, and interaction between, different methodical approaches, our insight into the requisites of democracy may in the long term be enhanced. It is my hope that the results presented here will serve to contribute to such a cumulative process of increased knowledge.

Appendix A

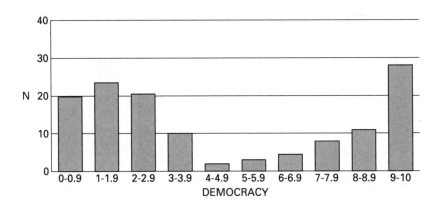

1. Our Index: Third World Countries 1988.

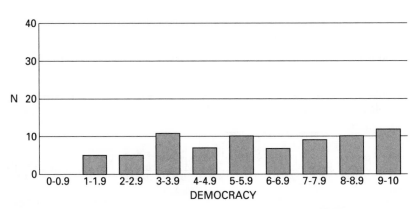

2. Bollen 1980: Third World Countries 1960. The values for different countries have been transformed to an index from 0 to 10.

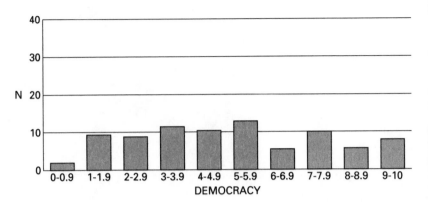

3. Bollen 1980: Third World Countries 1965. The values for different countries have been transformed to an index from 0 to 10.

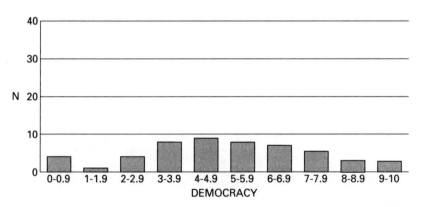

4. Coulter 1975: Third World Countries 1946–65. The values for different countries have been transformed to an index from 0 to 10.

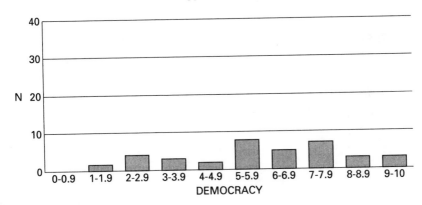

5. Jackman 1974: Third World Countries 1960. The values for different countries have been transformed to an index from 0 to 10.

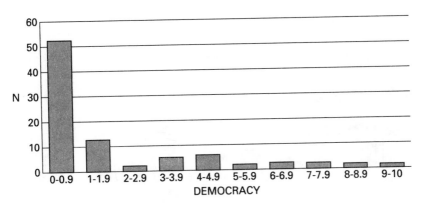

6. Vanhanen 1984: Third World Countries 1960–69. The values for different countries have been transformed to an index from 0 to 10.

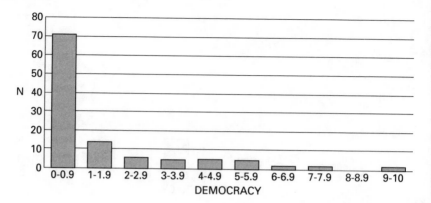

7.　Vanhanen 1989: Third World Countries 1980–85. The values for different
countries have been transformed to an index from 0 to 10.

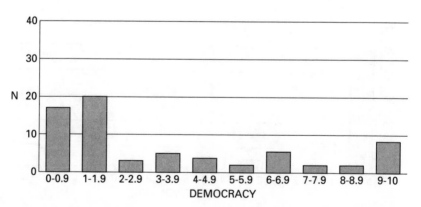

8.　Arat 1985: Third World Countries 1965. The values for different countries
have been transformed to an index from 0 to 10.

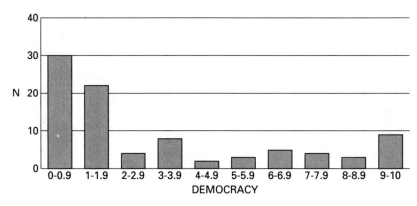

9. Arat 1985: Third World Countries 1977. The values for different countries have been transformed to an index from 0 to 10.

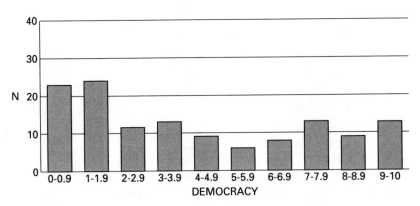

10. Gastil 1989: Third World Countries 1988. The values for different countries have been transformed to an index from 0 to 10.

Appendix B

EXPLANATORY VARIABLES: SOURCES

Socio-economic conditions

The GNP per capita

Sources: *Britannica – Book of the Year 1989*. Encyclopedia Britannica Ltd, Chicago. 1989.

World Development Report 1989, The World Bank. Oxford University Press, Oxford. 1989.

Annual Report 1988. The World Bank, Washington D.C. 1988.

UNCTAD Handbook of International Trade and Development Statistics 1988. UN, New York. 1989.

The Europe World Yearbook 1988. Europa Publications, London. 1988.

Länder i Fickformat. Utrikespolitiska institutet, Stockholm. Various years.

The Britannica – Book of the Year 1989 was used by preference if no later information was available in the other sources.

The GNP per capita Average Growth in 1970–80 and 1980–86

Sources: *Britannica – Book of the Year 1989*.

Industrial Production in Per Cent of the GNP.

Sources: *Britannica – Book of the Year 1989*.

UNCTAD Handbook of International Trade and Development Statistics 1988.

World Development Report 1989.

Länder i Fickformat.

The Britannica – Book of the Year 1989 was primarily used unless later information was to be found in the other sources.

Mining, manufacturing, construction and public utilities were included under industry.

The Labour Force: Percentage Employed in Agriculture, Industry and Service.
Sources: *The Europa World Yearbook 1989.*
        FAO Yearbook of Production 1988. Rome, 1989.
        Britannica – Book of the Year 1989.
        Länder i Fickformat.
The Europa World Yearbook was the principal source. If the information was lacking or out of date the other sources were used.

Energy Consumption per capita.
Sources: *The UNCTAD Handbook of International Trade and Development 1988* was used in the main. Data for certain countries were derived from the *World Development Report 1989* and *UN – 1986 Energy Statistics Yearbook.* New York, 1988.

Urbanization in Per Cent of the Population.
Sources: Most of the information was taken from the *World Development Report 1989.* When data were lacking the *Britannica – Book of the Year 1989* was used.

Literacy in Per Cent of the Population.
Source: *Britannica – Book of the Year 1989.*

Percentage in Education in the Population; Primary, Secondary, Higher.
Source: *Britannica – Book of the Year 1989.*

Calorie Consumption per capita.
Sources: *World Development Report 1989.*
        Britannica – Book of the Year 1989.
        UN Statistical Yearbook for Latin America and the Caribbean 1988. (1989)
        World Statistics in Brief. UN Statistical Pocketbook. New York, 1987.
        The Least Developed Countries 1987. UNCTAD, New York, 1988.
        World Development Report 1986.
Data were taken for 1965 and as late as possible in the 1980s.

Infant Mortality.
Sources: *UN Demographic Yearbook 1986.* New York, 1988.
        UNICEF, The State of the World's Children 1988. Oxford University Press, Oxford. 1988.
        UN Statistical Yearbook for Asia and the Pacific 1988.
        UN Statistical Yearbook for Latin America and the Caribbean 1988.

Britannica – Book of the Year 1989.
Data for 1960 were taken from UNICEF, *The State of the World's Children* and as late as possible in the 1980s.

Telephones, Radio and TV. Number of individuals per set.
Source: *Britannica – Book of the Year 1989.*

Daily Newspapers per Thousand Inhabitants.
Source: *Britannica – Book of the Year 1989.*
Data which were not calculated on the total number of daily newspapers have been excluded.

The Total Trade in Relation to the GNP.
Sources: The main source is *Britannica – Book of the Year 1985–9.* Certain data were supplemented with *Europa Publications 1988–9: Africa South of the Sahara* (1989), *The Far East and Australasia* (1989), *The Middle East and North Africa* (1989), *South America and the Caribbean* (1988).

Trade with Blocs. EC, USA, USSR and others. Imports and Exports in Per Cent.
Source: *Britannica – Book of the Year 1989.*

Trading Partners: The Two Largest Export and Import Countries Respectively in Per Cent.
Sources: The main source is *Britannica – Book of the Year 1989* with some supplementary data from Europa Publications 1988–9.

Commodity Concentration: The Two Largest Export Items in Percentage of the Total Exports.
Source: *Britannica – Book of the Year 1989.*

Direct Investments in Relation to the GNP.
Sources: The main source is the *UN Handbook of International Trade and Development Statistics 1988. The Transnational Corporations in World Development – Trends and Prospects 1988* (United Nations Centre on Transnational Corporations, New York, 1988). *The World Development Report 1989* and *OECD's Geographical Distribution of Financial Flows to Developing Countries 1984/87.* (Paris, 1989) were also used. Data on the GNP are taken from *Britannica – Book of the Year* 1984, 1987, 1988 and 1989.

Aid: Total ODA in Relation to the GNP.
Sources: The main source is the *World Development Report 1989.*

OECD's Geographical Distribution of Financial Flows to Developing Countries 1984/87 was also used.

Aid: Grants. Partner Concentration; The Two Largest DAC Countries, Percentage.
Source: *Geographical Distribution of Financial Flows to Developing Countries 1984/7.*

Income Distribution. The Highest 10 per cent and the Lowest 20 per cent Respectively.
Source: *Britannica – Book of the Year 1989.*
Countries with data only from urban or from rural areas were included if such was the area where most of the inhabitants live. When information was only available on income after tax this was omitted.

Family Farms.
Source: Vanhanen, Tatu. 'The Level of Democratization Related to Socioeconomic Variables in 147 states in 1980–85'. *Scandinavian Political Studies* 12:95–127. 1989.

Economic System.
Source: Gastil, Raymond D. *Freedom in the World. Political Rights & Civil Liberties 1988–1989.* Freedom House. 1989

Demographic and cultural conditions

The Ethnic Composition of the Population
Source: *Britannica – Book of the Year 1989.*

The Linguistic Composition of the Population.
Source: *Britannica – Book of the Year 1989.*

The Religious Affiliations of the Population.
Source: Most of the data were taken from *Britannica – Book of the Year 1989. The World Christian Encyclopedia*, ed. David B. Barrett. Oxford University Press, Oxford. 1982, was used as a supplementary source.
Anglicans and 'marginal Protestants' were counted as Protestants. Native Christian churches and so-called 'crypto-Christian' are included among the total of Christians. Jews are also included among the Christians.

Area.
Source: *Britannica – Book of the Year 1989.*

Size of the Population.
Source: *Britannica – Book of the Year 1989.*

Density of the Population.
Source: *Britannica – Book of the Year 1989.*

Institutional conditions

Colonial background.
Sources: *International Historical Statistics*; Africa and Asia. Mitchell, MacMillan. 1982.
International Historical Statistics; The Americas and Australasia. Mitchell, MacMillan. 1983.
Länder i Fickformat.
Country Reports on Human Rights Practices for 1988. US Department of State, Washington D.C. 1989.
Encyclopedia Britannica.
Atlas Zur Weltgeschichte. Braunschweig Westeruns. 1963.

Public Expenditure in Per Cent of the GNP
Sources: *World Development Report 1989.*
UN Statistical Yearbook 1985/6. New York. 1988.

Military Expenditure in Per Cent of the GNP and of Public Expenditure Respectively.
Sources: *SIPRI Yearbook 1989.* Oxford University Press, Oxford. 1989.
World Military and Social Expenditures 1987–88. R. Leger Sivard. World Priorities, Washington D.C. 1987.
The Military Balance 1988–89. The International Institute for Strategic Studies (IISS). London. 1988.
The Military Balance 1989–90. The International Institute for Strategic Studies (IISS). London. 1989.
Britannica – Book of the Year 1989.
The source with the most recent data was used.

Notes

INTRODUCTION

1 As an example of troublesome, crude classifications, I may mention the division with regard to 'Electoral irregularity' which is to be found in a data base published by Taylor and Hudson. Here a three-grade scale combines issues pertinent to ballot-rigging, prohibition of parties from running, boycott of parties, racial discrimination in the franchise, agreements on a joint list between parties, and whether candidates in a one-party election are to be nominated centrally or via local initiative (Taylor & Hudson 1972, Table 2.9). In all fairness, these different aspects of the holding of elections should be kept separate. Furthermore, it is not self-evident that all the issues mentioned are equally troublesome from a democratic viewpoint (no arguments whatever are advanced on this matter). A scale produced by Banks may illustrate the second problem: a ranking of countries in relation to the 'effectiveness of the legislature' uses a division into four classes (effective, largely effective, etc.) with no definition whatsoever of what this involves (Banks 1971, Segment 10, field L).

2 This signifies that at the time of the investigation, the state was recognized by a large number of other nations and, moreover, was not *de facto* occupied. For these reasons Western Sahara, Namibia, the Turkish sector of Cyprus, Cambodia and – after some hesitation – also Mongolia (I adjudged it to be in reality an integral part of the Soviet Union) are excluded. It should also be emphasized that only the conditions which prevail in the state's own territory are taken into account; areas which the state occupies and where the situation may be essentially different are not included: this limitation concerns, for example, countries such as Morocco, Israel and Vietnam.

3 On this point see Bollen 1980, p. 375.

4 As an example of such a study see Muller 1988, pp. 54f.

1 POINTS OF DEPARTURE

1 See Chapter 2.

2 Two exceptions should be mentioned here: Robert Dahl and Kenneth

Bollen. In his book *Polyarchy* the former executes a detailed analysis of the concept of democracy, and in an Appendix presents a number of empirical measurements of democracy (which were devised with the help of two colleagues). The problem is that these indicators are only weakly connected with explications of the concept of democracy previously given in the book. They are rather taken from the data catalogue (Banks and Textor 1963) whence the information came. Thus the operationalizations seem to be inferred from 'the material' rather than from his own theory. A similar objection can also be addressed to Bollen, who nevertheless uses several sources of catalogue type. Dahl 1971, Appendix A, Bollen 1980, pp. 371ff.

3 Dahl 1970, p. 95.

4 Graham 1986.

5 I omit such very general requirements as pertain to clarity and consistency (etc.) of the definitions. See on this point Vedung 1982, Chapts. 4–6. Moreover I am content to accept the method of construction of definitions – starting from a core formula – which was suggested by Felix Oppenheim. For a review of the arguments for this approach see Carlsnaes 1986, pp. 130ff.

6 Sartori 1987, pp. 21f.

7 To seek support, as is sometimes done, in statements in an encyclopedia (e.g., the *Encyclopedia Britannica*) is no solution in this case. One work in the West can, of course, be outweighed by another – with different statements – in the East. Cf. May 1978, pp. 6f. and (for criticism thereof) Anckar 1984, pp. 19ff.

8 Dahl 1970, p. 78. See also Dahl 1956, Chapt. 3.

9 Plamenatz 1973, p. 152, Sartori 1987, p. 7.

10 Sartori 1987, pp. 7f. and 48ff.

11 In other words the realism which here is recommended is equivalent to the requirement (*sensu stricto*) for a scientific procedure.

12 Cf. Holden 1974, pp. 4 and 183ff.

13 Cf. Vedung 1982, pp. 89.

2 POLITICAL DEMOCRACY

1 Needless to say, it makes no difference if each has 1 or 10 votes, provided the number is the same (thus the slogan 'one person – one vote' is somewhat simplified).

2 The extreme opposite of the rule – which is just as partial – is what Douglas Rae called 'the rate of individual initiative', which means that 'a policy is imposed when any single participant approves of it'. Rae 1969, p. 40. See also Lively 1975, pp. 17f.

3 Bryce 1921: I, p. 26, Dahl 1956, pp. 64f., Bobbio 1987, p. 63, Elster 1988, p. 1.

4 With this method there is no absolute quantitative 'threshold' for

decisions; all that is required is a relative majority. See on this point
Hermansson 1988, pp. 168f.

5 Sartori 1987, pp. 138f. and 220ff.

6 Rae 1969, Taylor 1969.

7 Lively 1975, p. 25, Pennock 1979, p. 8, Holden 1974, p. 106, Graham
1986, p. 29. See also Sartori 1987, pp. 138f.

8 Rae 1969, pp. 52f.

9 Another argument worth mentioning was submitted by Barry Holden.
The starting point is, despite disagreement and votes, how it is possible to
say that a decision was reached by all. The answer is that the majority's
preference should prevail rather than the minority's since 'the majority is
nearer to being all'. The margin at close votes may, of course, be minute
but there is nevertheless a difference, says Holden. This is essentially true.
However, according to this mode of reasoning, the majority rule is far
from ideal. Holden 1974, pp. 99ff and 118. For a review of other (nowadays less interesting) arguments in favour of the majority rule see Mayo
1960, Chapt. 11, Holden 1974, pp. 100f. and Berg 1965.

10 We ignore equal votes (50–50), where lots are sometimes drawn or the
chairman gives a casting vote.

11 The issue can be illustrated as follows:

	A Votes required for approval	B Votes required for rejection	Difference A–B, %
Simple majority	51	51	
Value of each vote*	0.0196	0.0196	–
2/3 majority	67	34	
Value of each vote	0.0149	0.0294	197
3/4 majority	75	25	
Value of each vote	0.0133	0.0385	289
Unanimity (veto)	100	1	
Value of each vote	0.0100	1	10 000

* Value of each vote 1/A and 1/B respectively.

12 As is clear, the reasoning is based on the condition that consent and
rejection respectively signify a decision to the same extent (and a stance
vis-à-vis the trend of public policy). With strange arguments Sartori
(1987, p. 222) seeks to sustain another position, i.e., that rejection,
when a proposal is prevented from passing, would be a non-decision; a
kind of passive measure which does not mean that control is exerted
over public policy. So would, for instance, a rejection of a proposal to
reduce taxes not be a decision? Of course it would: it is a decision to
retain the tax level. To choose the *status quo* is not a 'non-decision', nor
need it involve passivity on the part of the state.

13 Furthermore it fulfils the requirement of anonymity (whereby the identity of the voter makes no difference) and responsivity (that changed preferences yield a result in the 'right' direction). See K. May 1982, pp. 300f., and Hermansson 1988, pp. 165 and 168.

14 Hamilton, Madison and Jay 1961, particularly no. 51. See also Dahl 1956, Chapt. 1.

15 See May 1978, p. 5, Burnheim 1985, p. 111, and the arguments of similar content which are summarized in Dahl 1970, pp. 64ff.

16 Dahl 1970, pp. 66f., Anckar 1984, p. 19.

17 For an attempt (albeit ultimately fruitless) to declare the geographical demarcation from democratic principles see Whelan 1983, pp. 13ff.

18 A review of the arguments in the Swedish debate (immigrants who have not become citizens may here vote at the municipal but not the national level) is given in Nord 1987.

19 Lively 1975, p. 10.

20 Schumpeter 1947, pp. 284f.

21 Ibid., pp. 269f.

22 Ibid. pp. 242f.

23 Boström 1988, pp. 79f.

24 This is the point on which Schumpeter has his grave doubt.

25 What Schumpeter has in mind when he comments on the significance of democracy is the popular government which is applied in North America and Western Europe, particularly his new homeland, the USA. When we now scrutinize his theses it is therefore natural to consider the research pursued concerning rationality and representation in these parts of the world.

26 For a review see Lewin 1970, Chapts. 1–2, Holden 1974, pp. 140ff. and Graham 1986, p. 130f.

27 Key 1966, p. VII.

28 Holden 1974, pp. 169ff., Pennock 1979, pp. 287ff., Holmberg and Gilljam 1987, pp. 61f. and 300 ff. See also Holmberg 1981, pp. 288ff. and 381ff.

29 Pennock 1979, p. 293.

30 Pateman 1970, pp. 42f. See also Barber 1984, p. 152: 'Community grows out of participation and at the same time makes participation possible; civic activity educates individuals how to think publicly as citizens even as citizenship informs civic activity with the required sense of publicness and justice. Politics becomes its own university, citizenship of its own training ground, and participation of its own tutor.'

31 It is typical that Keith Graham, a fervent advocate of the participationist ideals, exhorts those who share his views to submit arguments which make it likely that the desired popular commitment can really be achieved. Graham 1986, p. 167.

32 Holmberg and Gilljam 1987, p. 62.

33 A thorough examination of these problems is presented in Riker 1982,

Chapts, 4–8. See also Hermansson 1990, pp. 229ff. and Graham 1986, pp. 54f.

34 Riker 1982, pp. 238f.

35 On this point see Sartori 1987, p. 152.

36 Riker, 1982, pp. 243f.

37 As regards this rule of argumentation see Vedung 1982, pp. 105f.

38 The question whether we then – once the two models have been assigned a reasonable formulation at the outset – can find any differences in general which will react on the capacity to reflect preferences, will be dwelt upon below, pp. 24f.

39 This measurement can vary from 0 (total correspondence) to 100 (total divergence).

40 We here present the comparison of the representation studies in France, the USA and Sweden which are reported in Holmberg 1989, pp. 14ff. As regards Sweden see also Holmberg and Esaiasson 1988, Chapt. 4. For other reviews of the research in the field which yield a similar picture at a general level see Pennock 1979, pp. 289f. and Holden 1974, pp. 170ff. It should be remarked that Holmberg for his part makes a point of the fact that a random selection of 349 individuals – corresponding to the seats in Sweden's *Riksdag* – would give a lower difference of opinion (in relation to the rest of the population) than the 15 percent which his representation study showed. The reference point which is then fixed has, however, nothing to do with elections or other active participation in the political decision-making process. It is a matter of drawing a sample from the population and it is hardly surprising that it is highly representative of this population in terms of opinions (so long as the sample is large enough); this is the requisite in the plethora of opinion polls which are constantly presented. In other words the contrast which Holmberg offers is a kind of 'Gallup democracy', which is something far less complicated than, and different in content from, the process of political democracy. Cf. below p. 175, n. 80.

41 Graham 1986, p. 128.

42 Dahl 1970, pp. 86ff., Plamenatz 1973, pp. 44f., Bobbio 1987, p. 53 and Sartori 1987, pp. 25f. and 111.

43 Lijphart 1984, pp. 197ff.

44 In purely technical terms it is conceivable that all the citizens were linked in a gigantic computer net and daily made decisions (by pressing 'the button') in all kinds of issue – so-called computerocracy. If, furthermore, it was mandatory to comprehend information and debate, people would have to devote most of their time to making the system work. For various views of this speculative form of democracy see Lewin 1970, pp. 238f., Graham 1986, pp. 137f., and Bobbio 1987, p. 31.

45 Sartori 1987, pp. 111f.

46 Bobbio 1987, pp. 52f. The delegate system corresponds to Position E in the figure.

47 This complement corresponds to Position B in the figure.

48 This assumption derives from the (assuredly not particularly timely) comparative studies of political behaviour which are presented in Almond and Coleman 1960 and Almond and Verba 1963.

49 See, e.g., Pateman 1970, Chapt. 2, Barber 1984, pp. 145f. and 150ff., and Graham 1986, p. 64.

50 Dahl 1970, p. 78 and 1971, p. 2.

51 Pateman 1970, pp. 35ff., Macpherson 1977, Chapt. 5, Graham 1986, Chapt. 8 and 240ff., and Mansbridge 1980, pp. 23ff. See also Lewin 1970, pp. 228ff.

52 Boström 1988, pp. 30ff. and 256.

53 Nor indeed does political democracy stipulate how large its 'sphere' in the society is to be (i.e., how large the democratically governed public sector should be). Nor does it say whether other organizations, companies and denominations should be democratically constructed. Naturally it is feasible to assert (as Dahl does) that a society as a whole is more democratic if many of its associations bear the imprint of democracy. But that is a matter of the design of the society concerning which we citizens may have many and varied desires. As phenomena, the democracy of the state and that of the society should be differentiated. The fact that they may be conceived as connected (so that the one promotes the other) is a separate issue; this should be open for testing.

54 Macpherson 1977, pp. 108ff. Regarding Cole's model of guild socialism see Pateman 1970, pp. 36ff. Somewhat surprisingly the otherwise very reflective Keith Graham considers that these pyramidal models would greatly increase the citizens' political influence as compared with the conventional election system. Graham 1986, p. 157.

55 Holden 1974, p. 29, Bobbio 1987, p. 53 and Sartori 1987, p. 26.

56 Bobbio 1987, p. 31. Cf. Sartori 1987, Chapt. 4 (particularly 4.5).

57 Sartori 1987, p. 118, Holmberg and Gilljam 1987, p. 54. See also Verba, Nie and Kim 1978, Chapt. 4.

58 Sartori 1987, pp. 117ff.

59 Riker 1982, p. 251, Sartori 1987, pp. 115ff., Dahl 1970, p. 72, and Barber 1984, p. 154.

60 It must be remarked that the uncertainty may vary with respect to which order of voting is applied. The so-called approval voting is the most robust as regards manipulation of the agenda, which is the problem just mentioned here. See Hermansson 1990, Chapt. 7.

61 Dahl 1970, p. 75, Sartori 1987, p. 115. See also Burnheim 1985, pp. 91f.

62 Cf., Sartori 1987, pp. 41ff.

63 Lewin 1977, pp. 51ff.

64 Holmes 1988, pp. 232ff., Holden 1974, pp. 34ff and 166, Sartori 1987, pp. 86ff., and Mayo 1960, Chapt. 7.

65 For a more detailed survey of these arguments see Holden 1974, pp. 37ff.

66 Sejersted 1988, p. 145, Holden 1974, pp. 51f., and Sartori 1987, pp. 22ff. and 133.

67 Sejersted 1988, pp. 135f. and 148f., and Sartori 1987, p. 192. See also Hermansson 1986.

68 In the literature on constitutionalism authors sometimes shift from one of these two meanings to the other (see, e.g., Holmes 1988). Naturally this is unfortunate: the latter meaning is indeed far stronger and thereby linked with other problems than the former. For a clear acceptance of the first definition see Sartori 1962 and Sejersted 1988. Elster 1988 tends to accept the second definition.

69 Elster 1988, pp. 2f., and Riker 1982, p. 250.

70 Hamilton, Madison and Jay 1961, No. 49. See also Holmes 1988, pp. 215ff.

71 For a review see Holmes 1988, pp. 199ff. See also Riker 1982, pp. 247ff.

72 Hamilton, Madison and Jay 1961, Nos. 49 and 51. See also Barber 1984, p. 160.

73 Cf. Holden 1974, pp. 189f. It may be remarked that the Athenian democracy survived for several centuries without any constitutional restrictions (Sartori 1987, p. 192). Roughly the same system, in legal terms, prevails in Great Britain today; there are indeed here several constitutional rules – albeit not in a collected, written form – which are scrupulously obeyed (Sartori 1962, pp. 853ff.), but the Parliament could change these at any time (with a simple majority).

74 I have disregarded such far-fetched alternative solutions as replacement of elections by lotteries. For a book of such suggestions which in its oddity is highly readable I would mention Burnheim 1985.

75 Sartori 1987, p. 30.

76 For a recent explication of this approach, see Chirkin 1986.

77 We find extensive argumentation along this line in Macpherson 1966. See also Pennock 1979, pp. 12f.

78 For a more detailed argument, with which I agree, see Holden 1974, pp. 41ff. and 230ff. Sartori 1987, pp. 10, 23f. and 470ff. (Chapt. 15:4–15:6) and Graham 1986, Chapt. 10.

79 Lively 1975, p. 34, Sartori 1987, p. 35, and Dahl 1989, Chapts. 4 and 5.

80 In contrast to individual opinion polls this involves a total sample of the population. The issue consists of a broad assessment of various matters of political fact and allows wide scope for information and debate. Cf. Sartori 1987, pp. 88f.

81 Lenin 1970, pp. 60ff.

82 Graham 1986, pp. 21f and Holden 1974, pp. 212f.

83 Bobbio 1987, p. 59.

84 Holden 1974, p. 231.

85 Thus it is not feasible to have, like Lipset (1959) one criterion for states

in Europe and North America and another, less rigid, for Latin America. Moreover it is essential to hold throughout to a definite form of democracy and not, as happens in Sklar's (1983) review of democracy in Africa, for example, oscillate between political, economic and social democracy. What Sklar calls social democracy obviously presupposes a mode of government which diverges considerably from political democracy. Such may not be concealed by sweeping, vague definitions of concepts.

86 Cf. Bobbio 1987, p. 24, and Mayo 1960, p. 61.

87 We could envisage criteria such as participation in elections, openness in the nomination process or the scope and institutional strength of the formation of opinions. Depending on which of these (or other) criteria we choose, we could reach fairly different results concerning the degree of 'optimal democracy' in countries such as Australia, Norway and USA.

88 This rule affects *inter alia* the kind of reform proposal which Macpherson puts forward. Cf. above p. 25.

3 AN INDEX OF DEMOCRACY

1 Plamenatz 1973, Chapt. 7, and Ross 1963, pp. 82ff.

2 As Sartori has put it: 'we are going too far in the direction of overstatement when we assert that democracy postulates conflict'. Sartori 1976, p. 15.

3 Bobbio 1987, p. 62, and Ross 1963, pp. 207ff.

4 From this viewpoint it must be deemed unsatisfactory, as in several studies, to distinguish those cases where (only) extremist parties are forbidden – see e.g., Dahl 1971, Appendix A, Jackman 1973, p. 37, and Arat 1985, p. 50. For it is not hereby stated whether the parties' political bent or their practices are at issue. Several Communist, religious and regional parties (and also others) may seem, partly by reason of the observer's premises, extreme with regard to their programme. Nevertheless, at the same time they may well appear to be wholly democratic.

5 It is important from the methodic viewpoint to maintain this distinction. Otherwise there is a risk, as seems to have occurred in several earlier studies (see, e.g., Arat 1985, pp. 49f., and Dahl 1971, Appendix A), of allowing the relative distribution of points to result from the number of criteria and the degree of refinement of the scale, which in turn may heavily depend on a varied quality of the data. Thus the available empirical material will come to dictate the relative significance of the various democratic components.

6 For example I may mention Pakistan, Chile and Haiti, where the conditions have improved towards the end of the year, and Burma and Kenya, where the situation has instead deteriorated.

7 With reference to eventual shifts between different years (and as

remarked also within one and the same year) the lack of a clear uniform point of temporal objective is a problem in earlier studies. Dahl's study (Appendix A) gives the occasion as '*circa* 1969'. Bollen's study (1980, p. 376) concerns the years 1960 and 1965. Nevertheless, as regards the majority of variables, the conditions during several years (1959–61 and 1964–66 respectively) are described, in the form of an average for these years. The disadvantage with this procedure (see also Vanhanen 1984) is that the values produced may be wholly artificial. Countries where the degree of democracy has oscillated between high and low will be assigned to the middle of the scale, which, however, is a level which has never existed. (Strangely enough Bollen himself, p. 375, offers an analogous objection to the measurement of long periods which was made by Cutright 1963.) With reference to the temporal aspect the studies by Smith (1969, pp. 102f.) and Coulter (1975, pp. 1f.) are far more doubtful, to say the least. They present a mixture of data in the form of collective measurements for the period 1946–65 (taken from Cutright) together with divergent information from individual years in the 1960s.

8 The material for Latin America, the Caribbean, the Middle East and North Africa (some 55 states) was chiefly collected by Annika Molin, while Per Nordlund and Kristina Karlsson were responsible for the countries in Asia (some 20 states). I myself compiled the information on Africa south of the Sahara and Oceania (about 55 states).

9 We consistently draw on the latest issues, 1987–89. In certain areas, however, we have used several issues. In Keesing's, data are derived from the entire decade of the 1980s and in *The Chronicle of Parliamentary Elections* from 1984 (Vols. XVIII-XXII). Furthermore, where applicable, we used the studies of countries reported in *Political Parties of the Third World* (ed. Vickey Randell, 1988) and *Marxist Regimes Series* (ed. Bogdan Szajkowsky). The *Political Handbook of the World* (published by Arthur Banks, recent issues) was also used to some extent.

10 On occasions we also used *Internationella Studier, The Times, The Economist, The New York Times, The Guardian, The International Herald Tribune, Tempus,* and *Kommentar*. All the information was published in 1988 except as regards *Electoral Studies* where we went back to 1984 (and forward to 1989) and *Internationella Studier*, where the 1987 and 1988 issues were used.

11 We here refer to the issues of 1987, 1988 and 1989 and as regards *Area Handbook* also 1986. Furthermore the following publications were used, *inter alia* as background material: *Democracy in Latin America and the Caribbean* (US State Department, Special Report 158, 1987), *Comparing New Democracies* (ed. Enrique Boloyra, 1987), *Elections and Democratization in Latin America* (eds. Paul Drake and Eduardo Silva, 1986), *Latin American Political Movements* (ed. Ciaran O'Maolain, 1985), *Afro-Marxist Regimes* (eds. Edmond J. Keller and Donald Rothchild, 1987), *Democracy and Pluralism in Africa* (ed. Dov Ronen, 1986), *Elections in Independent*

Africa (ed. Fred Hayward, 1986), *The Arab Gulf States: Steps Toward Political Participation* (published by John E. Peterson, 1988), *The Government and Politics of the Middle East and North Africa* (eds. David D. Long and Bernard Reich, 1986) and *Government and Politics in South Asia* (eds. Craig Baxter, Yogenda K. Malik, Charles H. Kennedy and Robert Oberst, 1987).

12 It should be remarked that this criterion is conspicuous by its absence in the majority of earlier studies. The exceptions are Neubauer 1967 (p. 105) and Dahl 1971 (Appendix A). When this factor is disregarded, countries such as South Africa and occasionally Zimbabwe (Rhodesia before 1979) obtain an unreasonably high grade. Arat's study (1985, Table A 2) may here be mentioned as a striking example: on a scale from 0 to about 19.5 (where the latter marks the highest level of democracy), the two countries receive values of over 16 for the years 1967–77! Concerning South Africa see also the grading in Bollen 1980, Appendix 2, Perry 1980, pp. 166 and 388, and Coulter 1975, p. 5.

13 On the other hand it is generally accepted that children and certain mentally defective individuals may not vote; they do not fulfil, it may be said, the requirement of rationality and the personal independence which full political participation postulates. Mayo 1960, Chapt. 6. As regards the voting age the countries apply somewhat different rules (it ranges between 15 and 21 years). Nevertheless the difference is disregarded here. Nor shall we take account of the variation that occurs with respect to the franchise for individuals with a criminal record.

14 Of South Africa's approximately 18 million Blacks barely half are domiciled in the homelands. There are 10 homelands at present, 4 of which have been declared independent. They are, however, only recognized by South Africa.

15 A franchise is awarded to the head of each so-called *matai* – a kind of extended family which *inter alia* collectively owns all land. There are at present nearly 20,000 *matai* communities. With a population of about 165,000 the percentage of adult citizens entitled to vote may be estimated as 20.

16 In Thailand there is a literacy requirement for franchise but, as far as we have found, this is not applied in practice. In the latest election in Kuwait (1985), however, a strict requirement of literacy was enforced. Moreover, women were excluded from the franchise. The Parliament was, however, dissolved by the Emir in 1986. In Brazil the Indian population has long been incapacitated; yet it represents less than 1 per cent of the total population. By reason of the minor extent of the restriction I also disregard the ban on voting which Indonesia has imposed on those who were members of the Communist party in 1965. These are today probably less than 1 per cent of the adult citizens. For the same reason we may disregard the requirement of literacy which applies to men in Tonga, since 99 per cent are literate.

17 This happened in Sri Lanka, for example, in 1982 when the Parliament which was elected in 1977 had its mandate prolonged until 1989 via a plebiscite.

18 As an illustrative example I may mention Sudan, where 28 of 260 seats in the last election were set aside for 'graduate constituencies' (professional and academic groups which stood in the forefront when the previous military regime was overthrown). There is also a minus for Sudan inasmuch as 41 of the parliamentary seats could not be filled by reason of the civil war in the south of the country.

19 The openness and correctness of the elections (see below pp. 44ff. and 47ff.) must be taken into account here. If the organ which appoints certain Members of Parliament is classified one category lower in these respects, these seats are assessed at half their value; if it is classified two categories lower, then they are discounted.

20 Lerner 1958, p. 57, Neubauer 1967, p. 105, Needler 1968, p. 893, Winham 1970, p. 814, Coulter 1975, p. 1, Vanhanen 1984, p. 31.

21 For example I may mention the 1988 election in Paraguay. The Government here declared a 90 per cent turnout. A study which was made by the independent Catholic University, on the other hand, says that about 40 per cent took part in the election.

22 According to Ivor Crewe, who investigated the matter, it may be assumed that the incidence of compulsory voting will increase the turnout by at least 10 per cent. This judgement is confirmed by *inter alia* the fact that participation in the post-war period in 28 states studied was 17 per cent higher on average in the category in which voting was compulsory. Crewe 1981, p. 240. See also Blais and Carty 1990, p. 176.

23 Lewin 1970, Chapts. 2 and 4, and Bollen 1980, pp. 373f. For a recent empirical study of the impact of nonvoting see Bennett and Resnick 1990, pp. 776ff.

24 Thus it is a manifest source of error to give without further ado non-party states a low grade. See Cutright 1963, p. 256, Smith 1969, p. 103, Hannan and Carroll 1981, pp. 21f., and Arat 1985, p. 51.

25 However, the winds of change have risen in recent years, although they are still moderate. In 5 of the 11 states in the area, there was no party organization in the last election (the Marshall Islands, Federated States of Micronesia, Nauru, Tonga and Tuvalu). Notwithstanding, an opposition block was recently formed in the parliament in some cases.

26 Linz 1975, p. 184.

27 Cutright 1963, p. 256, Vanhanen 1984, p. 32, and Arat 1985, p. 50. In Dahl 1971, Appendix A, the corresponding limit is 85 per cent.

28 A pertinent source of error which is not considered with this criterion (see, e.g., Vanhanen 1984) is the incidence of pure vassal parties which are permitted to run in certain countries and awarded votes and parliamentary seats. This has been the case for many years in, for example, Indonesia, Syria, Iraq and (in Somoza's time) in Nicaragua.

29 Among other examples of a 'distorted' outcome despite open and largely fair elections I may mention The Gambia (for a long time), and the last elections in Antigua and Barbuda, Barbados, Dominica, Grenada, Jamaica and Trinidad and Tobago. The said criterion is particularly misleading when (as in Cutright 1963 and Dahl 1971) we consider the distribution of mandates in the parliament, which is greatly influenced by the electoral system which is applied. With majority elections there is often a strong overrepresentation in the number of seats for the winning party.

30 This objection may be addressed in particular to Cutright and Vanhanen. The latter indeed works (together with the demarcation criterion) with a scale whereby the states are awarded points according to how high a percentage of votes went to the party or parties which did not win. Naturally, this measurement favours countries with proportional representation. On the other hand all one-party states receive o value or just above. Since Vanhanen's Index of Democracy is constructed so that the said value is multiplied by the degree of electoral participation (only these two attributes are considered), the result is that for the period 1970–79, 40 of the 129 states studied receive the value o (on a scale up to about 40), and another 20 or so a value less than 1. Almost half of the cases are thereby distributed indiscriminately at the bottom of the scale which – apart from the objections in other respects which may be voiced – must create problems in the application of the statistical technique (regression) which the author uses in the explanatory analysis. Vanhanen 1984, pp. 108f. See also Vanhanen 1989, Appendix.

31 Of the 132 countries investigated 36 can be classified as one-party states. In 15 of these, elections are held according to the one-list model while in 17 (direct) elections with rival candidates are arranged – yet, in all cases, only to the Parliament.

32 Another simple 'rule of thumb' which is used concerns how often the Government changes (see e.g. Gastil 1989, pp. 13f.). The idea is that a long period in office indicates that the elections were not open (or otherwise fair). Thus countries such as Botswana, The Gambia and Bahamas appear suspect, since there has been no change of the party in office since Independence. Nevertheless, this criterion can be very misleading. Here, too, we must see what form the elections actually took in the individual cases.

33 According to British tradition, the Government itself can decide the date of the election within a given period.

34 Thus we cannot, like Vanhanen (1984, p. 29), simply assume that boycott of the elections is invariably due to the government forbidding opposition groups to compete.

35 Cutright 1963, p. 256, Needler 1968, p. 891, Dahl 1971, Appendix A, Jackman 1974, p. 37, and Arat 1985, pp. 49f. See also Hannan and Carroll 1981, p. 21.

36 It could perhaps be maintained that among states which apply the one-list model there may be a difference as regards a varying degree of co-operation 'from below' in the drafting of the list. A country such as Cape Verde would then be considered as less closed and hierarchical than, for example, Somalia. Yet, it is invariably very difficult to obtain reasonable insight into whether consultations, which do occur in some cases (or at least are alleged to do so), perform any significant function for the rank and file of the population.

37 Placement in this category requires that there be two or more intermediate stages in the electoral process, and that in the first stage there be competition for the majority of the seats to be filled by election.

38 See the previous chapter, p. 25.

39 As should be obvious, the majority of these measures presuppose control of the government.

40 More on this point below, pp. 135f.

41 Cf. Rouquie 1978, pp. 18ff.

42 See above, p. 24.

43 For an interesting discussion of this subject see Okun 1975, p. 9.

44 Mackenzie 1958, Chapt. 11.

45 As examples of the reverse I may mention Egypt, where the Supreme Court (which is the decisive authority) decided that a number of seats which had been awarded to the party in office should be given to the opposition. This transfer has not occurred, however.

46 It has happened that the victorious Colorado Party in certain constituencies received far more votes than there were registered voters – a result which the President publicly defended by maintaining that the opposition had obtained a correspondingly generous count in other areas. Indeed, irrespective of the outcome of the election, the opposition parties were awarded a quota of the seats in the National Assembly.

47 Among other things, the opposition's principal channel for formation of opinion, the newspaper *La Presna* was closed during the election campaign.

48 Weiner 1987, pp. 5 and 8.

49 Such a consideration may concern how democracy is best preserved with constitutional arrangements – but then the question does not pertain to democracy *per se*, but to its constitutional requisites. Cf. the comments on Madison above, pp. 31f.

50 In contrast I may mention Zambia. Here too the regime has in recent years sought to change the electoral regulations. The aim was (as in Kenya) to strengthen the party's control over the procedure. The proposal was, however, rejected by the Zambian Parliament. Thus, in this case placement is in a higher category, III.

51 He died in 1989.

52 Thus, those countries where the military's position has become vaguer over time, such as Argentina and Uruguay, are assigned to this category.

53 If the Executive is appointed by the Parliament the former is throughout awarded the same value as the elections to the latter.

54 The most exaggerated example here is Fitzgibbon's democratic measurements from 1945 onward where *inter alia* educational level, living standard and social legislation were taken into account. See, e.g., Fitzgibbon and Johnsson 1961, p. 516.

55 See Gastil 1988, pp. 22f., Perry 1980, p. 165, and Anderson 1987, pp. 66f.

56 Above p. 7.

57 Dahl 1971, p. 73, Mayo 1960, pp. 147ff.

58 Gastil 1988, pp. 17f. See also Ross 1963, pp. 78f.

59 See above p. 56.

60 Thus a state where the freedom of opinion corresponds to Category II according to the above is placed in IIb if there is a minor degree of surveillance.

61 Bollen 1980, p. 375, and Arat 1985, pp. 52f. See also Arat 1988, p. 25.

62 We find a measurement which is remarkable in this respect in Arat (1985, pp. 52f., 1988, p. 25). The author grades the number of 'government sanctions' in relation to the degree of 'social unrest' (political murders, guerrilla actions, riots, anti-government demonstrations, etc.) which occurs annually in each country. Thus an abundance of oppression on the part of the state may be outweighed by a high level of civic political violence. A country where open war is waged between the regime and sections of the society may thus achieve a fairly favourable result since the one is balanced by the other. This is strange. With reference to the political freedoms, it seems instead reasonable to see oppression by the state and political violence by civic groups as aggravating negative attributes. Much violence on both sides makes the situation worse, not better.

63 In India the incidence of political violence is concentrated chiefly in the Punjab.

64 Thus two journalists who had written articles (on the RENATO guerrillas, active in Mozambique) of which the Government disapproved were detained in 1988. They were released after 60 days. Further cases of imprisonment (by agency of the police and by authority of a special law) occurred later in the year, albeit in another context.

We have already said in general how the intermediary positions are used. It may be added as an illustration that in Category IVb (the second highest) there may not be any political prisoners or government interference (or other iregularities) in the judiciary. The reason for placement here is in most cases that the police authority (at least parts of it) are known for brutality in their activities. Moreover a country may be assigned to this category because the law allows persons who disturb the public order (or the like) to be imprisoned, although this right is never invoked. Senegal is an example thereof.

65 The value which emerged for each state at the first calculation was therefore multiplied by the factor 0.2083333.

66 Furthermore, we have not taken into account the decision rules applied in the parliament, namely whether any other than the majority formula is followed in ordinary policy questions. Exceptions to this rule, however, would seem to be rare. Yet it may be mentioned as an example that the National Assembly in Nepal requires a 60 per cent approval for a positive decision.

67 Here and henceforth correlations pertain to Pearson coefficients which may range from 0 (no connection) to $+/-$ 1 (total connection).

68 For example the distribution for correct elections was lowered in a calculation to 2 points (against 4 for open elections); at the same time the collective value for political freedoms was reduced so as to reach parity. The correlation with our Index of Democracy then became 0.9997. In another case we confined ourselves to assessing elections only in terms of franchise and openness (taking account, as before, of the 0 value for correctness and effectiveness but with no additional points for these attributes) and only of freedom of opinion among the political freedoms. The correlation with our index became 0.9854.

69 The Head of State (Dr Banda) was then appointed 'life president'.

4 INTRODUCTION

1 Thus, I endeavour to give what Evert Vedung has called a 'systematic interpretation'. Vedung 1982, pp. 103 ff.

2 Throughout, I am presenting the standardized regression coefficients.

5 SOCIO-ECONOMIC CONDITIONS

1 Deutsch 1961, p. 474. See also Randall and Teobald 1985, p. 18.

2 Lipset 1960, p. 56. See also Lerner 1958, p. 45, Pennock 1979, p. 243, Powell 1982, p. 37, and Apter 1987, p. 25.

3 Lipset 1959, p. 84, Kornhausser 1959, p. 131 and de Schweinitz 1964, pp. 234ff. See also Powell 1982, pp. 35f., Huntington 1984, p. 199 and Alford & Friedland 1985, pp. 61ff.

4 Lerner 1958, pp. 60ff.

5 Lipset 1959, p. 75 and Cutright 1963, pp. 253ff.

6 Coleman 1960, pp. 541ff.

7 Russet 1965, p. 140.

8 Smith 1985, pp. 537f. and Randall and Teobald 1985, p. 21. See also Valenzuela and Valenzuela 1974, pp. 538f.

9 Smith 1985, pp. 533ff.

10 Ibid. p. 537. Hydén 1983, pp. 9f.

11 Smith 1985, pp. 538ff. and Randall and Teobald 1985, p. 33.

12 Huntington 1968, pp. 37f. See also Nordlinger 1972, p. 112, Pennock 1979, pp. 251f. and Horowitz 1985, p. 179.
13 Muller 1985, p. 446 and Pennock 1979, p. 232.
14 Dahl 1971, p. 70.
15 Bollen 1979, p. 584 and Bollen and Jackman 1985, p. 450.
16 Jackman 1975, pp. 70f., Coulter 1975, p. 23, Arat 1988, pp. 26f. and Vanhanen 1989, p. 118.
17 Deutsch 1961, p. 495. A similar hypothesis has been submitted by Huntington (1984, p. 201). The idea is that once the socio-economic development reaches a certain level, it enforces a change in the mode of government. States thereby find themselves in 'a zone of transition or choice', where, however, a development towards democracy is only one of the options; it may also incline towards a more rigid authoritarian government. Consequently, in contrast to Deutsch, Huntington does not envisage a convergent development above 'the threshold'. See also Dahl 1971, p. 67.
18 Neubauer 1967, p. 1007.
19 Jackman 1975, pp. 70ff. and Arat 1988, pp. 26f.
20 Lerner 1958, p. 88. See also Deutsch 1961, p. 495, and Coulter 1975, p. 11.
21 Huntington 1968, pp. 47f. See also Coulter 1975, p. 20, Pennock 1979, p. 208 and Apter 1987, p. 17.
22 Appendix B contains an account of how these data were compiled.
23 Vanhanen's studies also include the Eastern bloc (the Second World).
24 The correlations are on the 0.45 to 0.60 level.
25 As a rule the correlations here too are in the interval 0.45 to 0.60. The education variables are excepted; the proportion at the primary stage is weakly correlated with education at the secondary and higher levels.
26 The following factor solution may be reported as an example:

	Factor 1	Factor 2
GNP-level	0.94	−0.27
Employed in agriculture	−0.72	−0.32
Employed in service	0.64	0.36
Industrial production	0.67	−0.04
Urbanization	0.78	0.09
Calorie consumption	0.69	0.16
Education, Higher	0.39	0.33
Education, Secondary	0.32	0.51
Education, Primary	−0.37	0.97
Literacy	0.13	0.82
Radio sets	−0.12	−0.56
Telephones	−0.10	−0.68
Infant mortality	−0.34	−0.67
Eigenvalues	2.89	2.61

The number of factors is here, as henceforth, determined according to

Kaiser's criterion (Eigenvalue > 1). The table presents standardized regression coefficients in oblique rotation (Promax). The correlation between the factors is 0.46.

As is clear the proportion of highly educated individuals diverges from the other variables. It does not load particularly strongly on either of the factors. Thus it may be concluded that Factor 2 pertains first and foremost to popular education at a rather elementary, general level. Moreover, it is, in parenthesis, interesting to note that the level of infant mortality relates more to the latter than to the economic conditions.

27 Cf. Lipset 1959, p. 80.
28 The correlation coefficients are in the interval 0.45–0.60 in the former cases and around 0.30 in the latter. Concerning the correlation between the dimensions (the factors in the analysis) see note 26.
29 The selection consists of 16 countries in Western Europe and North America, three OECD countries in Asia and Oceania together with Chile, Venezuela, Mexico, Israel and India – thus 23 states in all, five of which (those named) are included in our sample. Neubauer 1967, p. 1007.
30 Variables which display curvilinear connections with democracy are duly expressed in logarithms. Cf. Jackman 1975, p. 73 and Bollen 1979, p. 578.
31 This applies when both variables are expressed as logarithms. In its original form the correlation is 0.78.
32 The selection was executed so that in the results which are presented I could include the variable which proved to be the strongest together with the others. It should be borne in mind that with respect to GNP-level and energy consumption it makes no difference which variable is chosen.
33 See, e.g., Pennock 1979, p. 243 and Deutsch 1961, p. 495.
34 The outcome is as follows:

	Standardized regression coefficients	Explained variance (percentage)
Literacy	0.46[**]	
Radio	0.08	
TV	0.14	
		23.7

[**]significance at the 0.01 level

35 See, in particular, Coulter 1975, pp. 11f. and 26f., but also Deutsch 1961, pp. 494f. and Pennock 1979, p. 233.
36 The correlations are on the 0.05–0.25 level and highest for changes in infant mortality which is most strongly associated with literacy ($r = 0.66$).

37 We obtain the following regression results:

	Standardized regression coefficients	Explained variance (percentage)
Literacy	0.53[**]	
GNP growth 1970–85	0.14	
Reduction of infant mortality 1960–87	0.09	
Calorie growth 1965–87	−0.18	
		25.4

[**]significance at the 0.01 level

38 These measurements are constructed so that we compare the percentual deviation, positive or negative, from the average value for each variable considered as follows:

$$\frac{Indiv.value\ V_1 - Mean\ V_1 \times 100}{Mean\ V_1} \qquad \frac{Indiv.value\ V_2 - Mean\ V_2 \times 100}{Mean\ V_2}$$

As controls we have instead used variations in range of the respective variables. These measurements yield essentially the same result.

39 This applies in particular to the relation between the levels of consumption and of literacy. The correlation with the level of democracy is here 0.46. Furthermore this measurement is very strongly correlated with literacy *per se* ($r = 0.90$); the higher this is the greater, almost perfectly linear, becomes the imbalance in favour of literacy. The connection with democracy therefore again seems to be largely a reflection of the influence of literacy. It may be added that the balance measurements' correlations with democracy are otherwise modest: they lie at best between 0.15 and 0.25.

40 The regression appears as follows:

	Standardized regression coefficients	Explained variance (percentage)
Low percentage employed in service high degree of urbanization	0.18[*]	
Literacy	0.43[**]	
		24.6

[*] = significance at the 0.05 level
[**] = significance at the 0.01 level

It should be remarked that the connection for the measurement of imbalance declines (and loses its significance) when more attributes pertinent to popular education and mass communications are included.

41 Lerner 1958, p. 46.

42 See Jackman 1975, Bollen 1979 and Arat 1988.

43 Kaufman, Geller and Chernotsky 1975, p. 304, and Randall and Teobald 1985, pp. 99ff.

44 The general theory is outlined in Frank 1969 and Wallerstein 1974. See

also Valenzuela and Valenzuela 1974, pp. 543ff., Smith 1985, pp. 544ff., and Randall and Teobald 1985, pp. 103ff.

45 Evans 1979, pp. 47ff., Kaufman, Geller and Chernotsky 1975, pp. 308f., Cardoso and Faletto 1979, pp. 166ff., Chirot 1977, pp. 8of., Thomas 1984, pp. 82ff., and Amin 1987, pp. 1of.

46 Frank 1969, pp. 21 and 317f., Thomas 1984, pp. 50ff., and Randall and Teobald 1985, p. 103.

47 Smith 1985, pp. 556ff., and Hydén 1983, pp. 266f. and 273f.

48 Jackson and Rosberg 1985, pp. 302ff, Fatton 1987, pp. 22f. and Goulbourne 1987, pp. 30ff.

49 Smith 1985, pp. 557f., Vanhanen 1987, pp. 3of. and Sklar 1979, pp. 5, 551.

50 Timberlake and Williams 1984, p. 141.

51 Almond 1989, p. 237 and Snyder and Kick 1979, p. 1097.

52 Kaufman, Geller and Chernotsky 1975, pp. 316ff.

53 Bollen 1983, p. 477. See also Timberlake and Williams 1984, pp. 144f.

54 Gasiorowski 1988, pp. 493f. and 501f.

55 Bollen and Jackman 1985, pp. 448f. See also Hannan and Carroll 1981, p. 31.

56 The common measurement here is the percentage for which the largest trading partner, or the two largest, is responsible – sometimes a joint measurement is used for partner concentration in imports and exports.

57 Gasiorowski 1985, pp. 332f., Gasiorowski 1988, pp. 499f. and Kaufman, Geller and Chernotsky 1975, pp. 31of. See also Bornshier, Chase-Dunn and Rubinson 1978, pp. 656f. and 66of.

58 Snyder and Kick 1979, pp. 1104ff. It should be mentioned that this is the measurement used in Bollen's study.

59 Nemeth and Smith 1985, pp. 534f. Another, more specific interpretation of the contexts was proposed by Guillermo O'Donnell (1973). He focuses chiefly on how different stages in a country's industrial development impinge on the internal political life as well as on the external economic and political relations. On the whole this theory has little attachment to the central premises of the dependency school. Cf. Gasiorowski 1988, pp. 502ff.

60 For a far more complicated variant see Nemeth and Smith 1985, pp. 525ff.

61 Thomas 1984, pp. 5of., Gasiorowski 1985, p. 337.

62 The link between total trade and direct investments is the highest ($r = 0.29$) of the traditional dependence variables. On the other hand, these attributes have no connection with commodity concentration ($r = 0.04$ and 0.03 respectively), which in turn only partly relates to the partner concentration in imports and exports ($r = 0.02$ and 0.19 respectively). The correlations between the latter variables and the total trade and direct investments respectively range between -0.08 and 0.19. The link between the just-mentioned variables and trade with

blocs varies in both level and direction. For direct investments the notations are negligible, for total trade they range between 0.29 and −0.23 (trade with other countries and the Soviet bloc respectively) and for commodity concentration between 0.29 (imports from EC) and −0.22 (imports from USA). The connections with partner concentration are in general stronger; they vary between −0.32 (import/import EC) and 0.32 (export/export USA). Finally as regards the internal connections between different measurements of trade with blocs the notations here too tend to be low or moderate (at corresponding levels). The exception is trade with other countries which with respect to both imports and exports is connected at the 0.65 level with trade with EC.

63 The following outcome illustrates the matter:

	Factor 1	Factor 2	Factor 3	Factor 4
Partner concentration, imp.	0.75	0.05	0.04	−0.10
Partner concentration, exp.	0.77	0.07	−0.07	0.32
Commodity concentration	0.09	−0.21	0.04	0.82
Direct investments	0.20	−0.20	0.70	−0.01
Total trade	0.04	0.31	0.72	0.17
Trade, EC, imp.	−0.43	−0.79	0.04	0.29
Trade, USA, imp.	0.61	−0.15	0.23	−0.59
Trade, Soviet bloc, imp.	0.27	−0.09	−0.60	0.29
Trade, others, imp.	−0.13	0.95	0.12	−0.03
Eigenvalues	1.85	1.75	1.45	1.32

The correlation between the factors is very low (below 0.15 throughout). Thus the figures presented are the result of orthogonal rotation (varimax). It should be mentioned that the outcome is essentially similar if, for partner and commodity concentration, we take the second largest partner or item respectively or, for trade with blocs, instead consider the export side.

64 The result does not change if we instead consider the two largest trading partners' shares of imports and exports respectively.

65 Throughout, what is reported is the largest export item. If in this case we also include the second largest item the connection is somewhat lower (−0.37[**]).

66 The starting point was to include the variables which exhibited significant connections at simple regression. As regards trade with blocs, however, only imports, which yield the strongest connections, have been included in each case. Moreover imports from other countries must be omitted since this attribute is too strongly correlated with the remainder.

67 When considered separately, the included variables for relations to blocs give an explained variance of 38.6 per cent, while each of the other three, traditional indicators of dependence, yield one of 26.0 per cent.

68 Bornshier, Chase-Dunn and Rubinson 1978, pp. 654 and 661f., and Gasiorowski 1985, p. 334.

69 r = 0.17
70 The correlation between total aid and the traditional measurement of dependence lies at best on the 0.10 level, and with trade with blocs the highest notation is −0.26 (USA, imports). The pattern and the level are about the same for aid concentration. Yet a connection of 0.26 with partner concentration (exp.) and of 0.32 with trade with USA (imp.) should be emphasized. As illustration it may be mentioned that the correlations with different modernization variables, such as GNP, degree of urbanization and percentage employed in agriculture are consistently higher; in both cases they lie on the 0.30 to 0.45 level – highest with GNP (Log). In other words, to regard the percentage of total aid and concentration on the donor side as dependence variables appears empirically doubtful.
71 r = 0.03.
72 Beta = 0.23*.
73 A particularly powerful reducing effect ensues from trade with the USA, the dependence variable which has the strongest connection with aid concentration.
74 Aristotle 1946, p. 173, Tocqueville 1969, Vol. Two, Part III.
75 Dahl 1971, p. 55.
76 Ibid. p. 54.
77 Pennock 1979, pp. 232f. We find a similar argumentation in Lenski 1966, pp. 308ff. and Lipset and Rokkan 1967, pp. 44f.
78 Mann 1986, pp. 40ff. and Vanhanen 1984, pp. 21f.
79 Mann 1986, pp. 44ff. Usher 1981, p. 35, Hall 1985, pp. 27ff and Jones 1981, pp. 11ff. See also Eisenstadt and Ronninger 1984, pp. 244ff.
80 Wittfogel 1957. It should be pointed out that Wittfogel's thesis – both its description and explanation (that despotism is a consequence of the major irrigation systems) – has been vigorously questioned (Mann 1986, pp. 93ff. and Hall 1985, p. 36). Moreover, all agrarian societies are far from similar. Depending on several circumstances where the type of production orientation is a factor, they can display wide variations in terms of social and political hierarchy. This has been emphasized by Barrington Moore 1967, pp. 419f. See also Goodell 1980, pp. 287ff.
81 Dahl 1971, pp. 88f.
82 Russet 1964, p. 453.
83 Vanhanen 1984, p. 126.
84 Vanhanen 1987, p. 28.
85 A summary of earlier studies is given in Bollen and Jackman 1985, pp. 443 and 450ff. See also Powell 1982, pp. 47ff.
86 For the second group, the 10 per cent who earn most, we only have data from 49 countries.
87 If we instead take the share of the 10 per cent with the highest income, the coefficient becomes 0.00. An alternative measure is to use the ratio

between the two groups, i.e., the share of the highest income group divided by the share of the lowest. This gives an 0.06 connection with level of democracy. It may be added that the connection between the two original measurements (the share of the lowest 20 per cent and the highest 10 per cent respectively) is −0.63. These are in their turn moderately correlated with the share of family farms: r = 0.19 and −0.13 respectively (in the aforesaid order).

88 *Income share of* Employed in Employed in Employed Industrial GNP
   lowest group agriculture industry in sevice production (Log.)
   (20 per cent):

	Employed in agriculture	Employed in industry	Employed in sevice	Industrial production	GNP (Log.)
Correlation with this variable	0.10	−0.01	−0.14	−0.02	−0.13
Standardized regression coefficient on control for this variable	−0.14	−0.17	−0.12	−0.18	−0.15
Family farms:					
Correlation with this variable	0.47	−0.44	−0.43	−0.22	−0.33
Standardized regression coefficient on control for this variable	0.07	−0.04	0.08	−0.09	−0.01

89 It may be added that neither does the outcome change on control for other attributes (e.g., literacy and different measures of dependency).

90 Lindblom 1977, pp. 161f. See also Berger 1987, p. 73.

91 The argument is summarized in Tingsten 1965, pp. 147f. and Ross 1963, pp. 74ff. See also Bowles and Gintis 1986, Chapt. 2.

92 Usher 1981, pp. 78 and 96.

93 Schumpeter 1947, p. 297. See also Berger 1987, pp. 79f.

94 Hayek 1944, pp. 71ff. and Chapt. 5.

95 Tingsten 1965, pp. 161ff. See also Schumpeter 1947, p. 302 and Berger 1987, pp. 81f.

96 Lindblom 1977, pp. 162f. and 165.

97 Moore 1967, pp. 491ff. See also Lipset and Rokkan 1967, pp. 44f.

98 Moore 1967, p. 418. This Marxist analysis seems irreconcilable with the tenets of the dependency school. This difference was also emphasized by one of the dependence theoreticians: 'in the context of dependent development, the association of bourgeois democracy and capitalist accumulation no longer holds' (Evans 1979, p. 47. See also Amin 1987, pp. 10f.). Nevertheless, this could be seen primarily as a difference of object; the idea is that the conditions in the Third World are wholly

different from those in the First (to which Moore and Therborn primarily refer).

99 Therborn 1977, pp. 44f. For a similar analysis prompted by Marx's study of Louis Bonaparte, see Poulantzas 1979, p. 321.

100 Therborn 1977, pp. 43, 96. See also Marshall 1977, p. 105. Therborn 1977, p. 41, Huntington 1984, pp. 204f. and Berger 1987, Chapt. 2.

101 Usher 1981 p. 96. See also Marshall 1977, p. 105, Therborn 1977, p. 41.

102 See, e.g., Usher 1981.

103 Bollen 1979, and Brunk, Caldeira and Lewis-Beck 1987.

104 Berger 1987, pp. 18f.

105 Berger 1987, p. 76.

106 Gastil 1989, pp. 68ff.

107 The difference between the two former categories pertain to the magnitude of the occurrent exceptions in the form of private ownership.

108 $r = 0.09$

109 For GNP (Log.), calorie consumption and GNP growth the correlation is on the $0.15 - 0.20$ level.

110 The same can be said of the opposite view held by Laski, Cole and others. Capitalism undoubtedly contributes to greater inequality in society: with the income share which accrues to the lowest group (20 per cent) the correlation is -0.24. Nevertheless, as we saw, the latter attribute has no connection with democracy in the postulated direction.

111 With variables such as infant mortality, literacy and percentage employed in service r is on the $0.15 - 0.20$ level. See also above, p. 108 and note 108.

112 The correlations are as follows:

	Trade Soviet block imports	Trade USA, imports	Direct investments	Commodity concentration
Capitalism	-0.50	0.31	0.26	-0.30

6 DEMOGRAPHIC AND CULTURAL CONDITIONS

1 Diamond, Lipset and Linz 1986, pp. 15f.

2 Pennock (1979, p. 241) expresses the issue as follows: 'Democracy needs citizens who respect the law and resist its abuse, whoever's rights are being abused'.

3 Tingsten 1965, p. 113.

4 Cf. Madison: 'A zeal for different positions concerning religion, concerning government, and many other points, as well of speculation as of practice; an attachment to different leaders ambitiously contending for pre-eminence and power; or to persons of other descriptions whose fortunes have been interesting to the human passions, have in turn

divided mankind into parties, inflamed them with mutual animosity, and rendered them much more disposed to vex and oppress each other than to co-operate for their common good' (Hamilton, Madison and Jay 1961, Nr. 10, p. 79).

5 Rustow 1970, pp. 352f. See also Emerson 1971, p. 247 and Pennock 1979, p. 246.

6 Rae and Taylor (1970, p. 1) give the following definition: 'Cleavages are the criteria which divide the members of a community or subcommunity, and the relevant cleavages are those which divide members into groups with important political differences at specific times and places'.

7 Powell 1982, p. 43, Lipset and Rokkan 1967, p. 6, Horowitz 1985, pp. 223f. and Jackson and Rosberg 1984, pp. 177f.

8 Rabushka and Shepsle 1972, pp. 208ff. and 217. See also Kuper 1969, p. 14 and Horowitz 1985, pp. 291ff. Cf. J. S. Mill: 'Free institutions are next to impossible in a country made up of different nationalities. Among a people without fellow-feeling, especially if they read and speak different languages, the united public opinion necessary to the working of representative government, cannot exist' (Mill 1958, p. 230).

9 Horowitz 1985.

10 Jackson and Rosberg 1984, pp. 179f.

11 Hannan and Carroll 1981, pp. 179f.

12 Vanhanen 1987, p. 29. See also Dahl 1971, pp. 110f.

13 Powell 1982, pp. 51 and 154ff. See also Coulter 1975, pp. 103ff.

14 These date are taken from *World Handbook of Political and Social Indicators* (different editions, the latest being 1983, published by Charles Lewis Taylor and David A. Jodice).

15 Thus Donald Horowitz defines 'ethnicity' as an identity based on 'color, appearance, language, religion, some other indicator of common origin, or some combination thereof'. Horowitz 1985, pp. 17f. See also Powell 1982, pp. 43f.

16 The value may vary from 0 (total homogeneity in the population) to 1 (total fragmentation).

17 The averages are as follows:

	Ethnic	Linguistic	Religious
All 132 states	44.1	38.9	31.4
Latin America/Caribbean	40.6	21.3	25.9
Africa south of Sahara	57.7	57.6	37.5
North Africa/Middle East	27.0	24.0	22.2
Asia/Oceania	39.5	39.8	34.3

18 The fragmentation measurements (ethnic, linguistic and religious) are in India 0.88, 0.89 and 0.30 and in Belize 0.72, 0.64 and 0.54. As comparison I may mention Nigeria (0.85, 0.85, 0.55), Uganda (0.86,

0.92, 0.37), Ethiopia (0.72, 0.70, 0.61) and – as examples of low marks –
Somalia (0.03, 0.03, 0.00) and South Yemen (0.10, 0.08, 0.01).

19 The correlations between the three measurements are as follows:

	Linguistic	Religious
Ethnic	0.70	0.19
Linguistic		0.29

20 Lipset 1960, p. 74, Rae and Taylor 1970, pp. 12ff., Goodin 1975,
pp. 516ff. See also Lijphart 1977, pp. 75f.

21 In view of the many known examples of open conflicts in divided states
we would expect high fragmentation in particular to have a negative
effect on political violence and oppression, and to have a stronger such
influence on political freedoms than concerning elections (see Powell
1982, pp. 154ff.). Such is not the case, however. Insofar as a tendency
can be observed, fragmentation in fact has a stronger negative effect as
regards elections. Yet, it is most important to mention that it is invariably a matter of moderate differences between the various components
of democracy.

22 For example, the following correlations may be presented:

	GNP (Log)	Employed in agriculture	Literacy	Percentage educated, primary
Fragmentation				
Linguistic	−0.29	0.40	−0.39	−0.26
Average	−0.26	0.29	−0.34	−0.27

It should be remarked that religious fragmentation hardly has any
connection with the degree of socio-economic development.

23 This result may be reported as an illustration:

	Standardized regression coefficients	Explained variance (percentage)
Average fragmentation	−0.07	
Literacy	0.23[**]	
Trade USA, Imp.	0.29[**]	
Commodity concentration	−0.25[**]	
Direct investments	0.16[*]	
Capitalism	0.23[**]	
		53.8

[*] significance at the 0.05 level
[**] significance at the 0.01 level

The result remains essentially the same if we instead include linguistic
fragmentation.

24 Lijphart 1977, p. 57. See also Hannan and Carroll 1981, p. 31. Cf.
Chirot 1985, p. 188.

25 Hannan and Carroll 1981, p. 31.
26 It may be mentioned that for the balance measurement which is based on the standard deviation beta = 0.16 (2.6%).
27 Huntington, 1984, pp. 207f. *Re* the role of the Roman Catholic Church, see also Lipset 1959, p. 88 and Shefter 1977, pp. 441ff.
28 Huntington 1984, p. 208.
29 Lipset 1959, pp. 85 and 92f., and Lenski and Lenski 1974, p. 349. See also Schumpeter 1947, pp. 265f.
30 Zubaida 1987, p. 31.
31 Badie 1986, p. 251 and Eisenstad 1986, pp. 28f.
32 Ahmed 1985, pp. 209f. and 215. See also Mozaffari 1987, Chapt. 4.
33 As I see it, doctrinaire Marxist-Leninism and certain strong nationalistic currents may also be included here.
34 Apter 1965, p. 85.
35 Bollen 1979, p. 582 and Bollen and Jackman 1985, pp. 444 and 450.
36 The averages are as follows:

| Christian countries | 5.5 |
| Muslim countries | 2.6 |

37 For other religions reported separately the result is as follows (with the explained variance in parentheses): Hinduism 0.01 (0.1); Buddhism −0.05 (0.0); Greek Orthodox 0.06 (0.0). It should be remarked that in the majority of countries these religions are represented extremely weakly or not at all. No fixed conclusions should therefore be drawn from the figures presented.
38 The following correlations are worth presenting:

	Christians	Protestants	R. Catholics	Muslims
Literary	0.38	0.33	0.28	−0.43
Trade USA, imp.	0.46	0.16	0.47	−0.33
Direct Inv.	0.24	0.23	0.13	−0.16
Commodity concentration	−0.07	−0.06	−0.03	0.22
Capitalism	0.27	0.31	0.14	−0.12

39 Palmer 1959, Chapt. 2. See also Burke 1986, p. 140ff, and Jones 1981, p. 109.
40 Dahl and Tufte 1973, pp. 4ff.
41 Ibid., pp. 5f. See also Dahl 1970, pp. 69f and Elster 1988, pp. 9ff.
42 See above p. 18.
43 Axelrod 1984. See also Axelrod and Keohane 1985, pp. 232f. and Lewin 1988, pp. 133ff.
44 Lijphart 1977, pp. 65f. See also Weiner 1987, p. 29.
45 Ostheimer 1975, pp. 17f. See also Weiner 1987, pp. 29f.
46 Hamilton, Madison and Jay 1961, No. 10, p. 83.
47 Ebel 1972, p. 328. See also Seligson 1987, pp. 149f. and Ostheimer 1975, p. 22.

48 Dahl and Tufte 1973, pp. 39f. and 86f. See also Ostheimer 1975, pp. 14f. and Powell 1982, Chapt. 3.
49 As we see, the undichotomised variables are expressed in logarithms which indicate a curvilinear connection.
50 For Population (Log.) and Area (Log.) r = 0.83.
51 The outcome is as follows:

		Standardized regression coefficients	Explained variance (percentage)
a.	Population (Log.)	−0.01	
	Island	0.39**	
			18.4
b.	Area (Log.)	−0.12	
	Island	0.35**	
			19.1

** significance at the 0.01 level

52 The correlations are:

	Population (Log.)	Area (Log.)
Island	−0.55	−0.66

53 It is worth noting that all microstates (with a population < 100,000) are islands.
54 The limits are one million for population and 1,000 km² for area.
55 The result is as follows:

		Standardized regression coefficients	Explained variance (percentage)
a.	Small population	−0.01	
	Island	0.39**	
			18.5
b.	Small area	−0.14	
	Island	0.34**	
			19.4

** significance at the 0.01 level

56 The following correlations are worth reporting:

	Literacy	Partner concentration	Direct investments	Protestantism	Average fragmentation
Island	−0.36	0.23	0.32	0.56	−0.31

7 INSTITUTIONAL CONDITIONS

1 The exceptions are Liberia, Turkey, Afghanistan and Thailand.
2 If the colonial connection is to be adjudged to have had any impact a time limit must also be imposed: the colonial supremacy must have

endured for at least 10 years (this excludes Ethiopia which was briefly occupied by Italy). Given this time limit, if changes occurred then the last colonial power is counted throughout. When amalgamations took place after the liberation, the state is referred to the colonial power which had the largest share of the territory (thus Somalia, for example, which consists of a former Italian and a British part, is classified as a former Italian colony).

3 The exception was Southern Rhodesia, where the white minority unilaterally declared its independence in 1965.

4 Smith 1978, pp. 71f., Weiner 1987, pp. 19f., Emerson 1960, pp. 230f., Diamond, Lipset and Linz 1986, p. 49 and Bollen and Jackman 1985, p. 445.

5 Smith 1978, pp. 84 and 87, Emerson 1960, pp. 232f. and Zolberg 1966, pp. 40, 79 and 107. See also Collier 1982, Chapt. 4.

6 Emerson 1960, pp. 235f., Zolberg 1966, pp. 107f. and 120, Killingray 1986, pp. 416ff, Weiner 1987, p. 19 and Young 1988, pp. 35 and 42f. See also Dahl 1971, pp. 170f.

7 Bollen and Jackman 1985, pp. 447 and 450. The GNP level, dependency (according to Snyder and Kick 1979) and the percentage of Protestants are included as other variables in the regression. In one case the distribution of income is considered as well.

8 The value for former British colonies is 5.7 and for former French possessions 2.2. The average for all countries is 4.6.

9 Cf. Weiner 1987, p. 30.

10 The following correlations may be mentioned:

	Employed in service	Infant mortality	Literacy	Prot- estantism	Island state
British colony	0.25	−0.23	0.24	0.49	0.31
French colony	−0.28	0.26	−0.31	−0.30	−0.30

11 This is clearest as regards the percentage of protestants. When this is included in the regression as the only other variable, the significant connection with British colonial background disappears. At the same time, I would mention that a theory submitted by Myron Weiner (1987, p. 30) is not confirmed by our study. Weiner maintains that the higher level of democracy in island states derives from the fact that the majority of these were under British rule. An internal control of these two attributes gives the following result:

	Standardized regression coefficients	Explained variance (percentage)
British colony	0.21[*]	
Island	0.37[**]	
		22.1

[*] significance at the 0.05 level
[**] significance at the 0.01 level

12 Naturally, this criterion is not crystal clear. As a practical indicator we have in doubtful cases used the date when an official, a governor or the like, took up residence in the country.

13 It is worth observing that the colonial period is longer on average in the British case.

14 We then adopted the following approach. The states which were not colonized during the twentieth century, and those which were added in samples 3 and 4 (former Portuguese and Japanese colonies etc.), are assigned the value 0. For the remainder, the states in sample 2, we applied two alternatives. In the one we used the original value as regards the duration of the colonial period; in the other we executed a categorization (1–5) at 50-year intervals. These two measurements, however, yield a very similar result. That reported is the outcome on application of the latter, categorized, variant.

15 Huntington 1965, pp. 410f. See also Riggs 1963, p. 120.

16 Moore 1967, p. 346.

17 Jackson and Rosberg 1986, pp. 6f. See also Killingray 1986, p. 436, Young 1988, p. 38.

18 Migdal 1988, pp. 11ff., Hydén 1983, pp. 76ff. and 93ff., Lofchie 1970, p. 280, Ayoande 1988, pp. 107f., Tangri 1985, p. 118, and Diamond 1988, p. 22.

19 For general surveys of this subject see Eisenstadt and Ronninger 1984, Schmidt, Scott, Landé and Guasti 1977, and Blomkvist 1988.

20 The designation 'the soft state' was coined by Gunnar Myrdal (1968, pp. 225f.). For a discussion of the concept and illustrations of the subject see Blomkvist 1988, pp. 285ff. and Hydén 1983, pp. 89ff.

21 The following may be mentioned as examples from different continents: Frankel 1969, pp. 459 and 465, Eisenstadt and Ronninger 1984, pp. 106 and 128, Jackson and Rosberg 1985, p. 301, and Hydén 1983, pp. 61 and 91. For a general analysis see Clapham 1985, pp. 45ff.

22 Diamond 1988, p. 20.

23 Hydén 1983, p. 36.

24 Diamond, Lipset and Linz 1986, p. 73, Ingham 1990, pp. 5f., Chazan 1988, p. 120, and Zolberg 1966, pp. 92 and 142. See also Pennock 1979, p. 220, and Usher 1981, pp. 12ff. and 42ff.

25 The correlation between these measurements is as follows:

	Public hospitals	Public consumption
Public expenditure	0.04	0.62
Public consumption	0.04	

26 Bollen 1979, p. 582. It should be remarked that his sample also comprises the states of Western Europe and North America. See also Brunk, Caldeira and Lewis-Beck 1987.

27 The outcome is as follows:

	Standardized regression coefficients	Explained variance (percentage)
Public hospitals	0.02	
Literacy	0.18[*]	
Commodity concentration	−0.24[**]	
Trade, USA, imp.	0.31[**]	
Capitalism	0.22[**]	
Percentage Protestants	0.25[**]	
		56.1

[*] significance at the 0.05 level
[**] significance at the 0.01 level

As background it may be mentioned that the percentage of publicly owned hospitals is connected positively with the commodity concentration ($r = 21$) and negatively with capitalism and trade with the USA ($r = -0.27$ and -0.23 respectively).

28 Huntington 1968, p. 217.

29 Lissak 1976, pp. 29f., Welch 1970, p. 170. See also Rustow 1967, pp. 170ff.

30 A total of 158 unsuccessful coups and military conspiracies are reported for the period in question.

31 Boström 1987, pp. 7ff., Johnson, Slater and McGowan 1984, p. 622, Perlmutter 1980, pp. 96ff., and Welch 1970, p. 157. For a summary analysis of the military establishment's sometimes very important position in Communist states see Albright, 1980, pp. 557ff.

32 In addition, according to Muller, ideological factors play a role too. Thus, it is possible to see a distinct difference in the USA's conduct under, on the one hand, Presidents Kennedy and Carter who attached importance to democracy and human rights and, on the other, Johnson and Nixon who followed a narrower line of security policy and were thereby more inclined to support coups for reasons of *realpolitik*. Muller 1985, p. 467.

33 For a survey of the subject see Norlinger 1977, pp. 85ff., Perlmutter 1980, pp. 98ff. and Philip 1984, pp. 2ff.

34 Welsch 1971, p. 229, Diamond, Lipset and Linz 1986, p. 46, and Jackson and Rosberg 1982, pp. 64f.

35 Huntington 1968, p. 228.

36 Jackson and Rosberg 1982, p. 23 and 1982b, p. 10.

37 Diamond, Lipset and Linz 1986, p. 52.

38 We find some support for this assumption in a study of military coups d'état executed by Johnson, Slater and McGowan. Cf. Dahl 1971, pp. 49f. As far as I know, however, no investigation with respect to the level of democracy, corresponding to that presented here, has been made.

39 It may be mentioned that the result is very similar if we instead examine the size of military expenditure in relation to the GNP.

40 The correlations are as follows:

	Protestants	Capitalism	Trade USA, imp.	Literacy
Military expenditure	−0.44	−0.30	−0.22	−0.22

8 GENERAL PICTURE AND PROBLEMS OF CAUSALITY

1 We here used the T-value as a criterion.

2 Controls by means of stepwise regressions reveal that the crucial item in this context is military expenditure. When this variable is included in the regression, literacy drops and fragmentation rises. The background is that military is associated with literacy, which in turn is connected with fragmentation. On the other hand, there is almost no correlation between fragmentation and military expenditure.

3 Cf. Coulter 1975, pp. 45ff.

4 Here and henceforth it is the differences emerging from the comparison of the correlations between the said attributes and level of democracy in every geographical area which are reported.

5 In this analysis we subjected the entire sample to multiple regressions with three variables included: Type (1) Latin America/The Caribbean (as a dichotomy: 1-0), (2) Trade with the USA, and (3) Latin America/The Caribbean * Trade with the USA.

6 It is worth mentioning that these structural conditions could be either of an objective nature or man-made (even politically made). The point is that they, at a given point in time, work as constraints on the political process. Carlsnaes 1986, pp. 107ff.

7 Lijphart 1977, pp. 2ff and 165. See also Linz 1978, pp. 4ff and Diamond 1989.

8 In addition, of course, the criteria which are involved in the establishment of our dependent variable (the index of democracy) are somewhat different.

9 See above p. 106.

10 Rustow 1970, p. 342.

11 Concerning the mode of government, the period at issue is 1970–85 (i.e., 16 years). The following states are included in the group of those who are democratic in the main: Colombia, Venezuela, Costa Rica, Barbados, The Dominican Republic, Jamaica, Trinidad and Tobago, Botswana, The Gambia, Mauritius, Cyprus, Israel, India, Sri Lanka, Fiji and Nauru. The second group comprises Argentina, Bolivia, Brazil, Chile, Ecuador, Peru, Uruguay, Guatemala, Honduras, Guiana, Burkina Faso, Ghana, Nigeria, Senegal, Lebanon, Turkey, Malaysia and the Philippines. With regard to the criteria and the material used

in the classification, I must refer to a forthcoming study of the duration of democracy, the purpose for which these data were compiled.

12 If we have as a criterion a rise of over 10 per cent and discount the countries where the level in 1970 was so high that no improvement could be made, we find such an increase in 11 of 15 non-democracies (73 per cent) and seven of 12 democracies (58 per cent).

13 If, as a limit we have an increase or a decrease respectively of at least 25 per cent – and one position in between – we find as a result that an increase occurs in 56 per cent of the non-democratic states, and in 50 per cent of the democracies. In the event of a decrease, the corresponding figure are 22 per cent and 25 per cent.

14 With regard to a decrease of at least 20 per cent we find that 61 per cent of the non-democracies and 65 per cent of the democracies fall into this category.

15 See, e.g., Powell 1982, pp. 34f.

16 A correlation with the GNP level at 0.30 may be mentioned. Concerning the connection with the dependence variables see p. 187 note 62 above.

17 Whitehead 1986. See also Pridham 1991.

18 Whitehead 1986, p. 25. See also Farer 1989, pp. 117f.

19 Whitehead 1986, pp. 20f and 34 ff. and do. 1989, p. 90. See also Muller, above, p. 198, note 32.

20 Whitehead 1986, p. 40 and do. 1989, pp. 91ff.

21 Whitehead 1986, p. 31.

22 Ibid. pp. 37f.

23 This conclusion is supported by the circumstance that factor analysis reveals a negative association of considerable degree between commodity concentration and trade with USA. See above, page 188, note 63 (factor 4).

24 On Zaire see Ingham 1990, p. 164.

25 For interesting viewpoints on the questions to be discussed here I refer the reader to Dogan and Pelassy 1990, Chapts. 2 and 14, Ragin 1987, Chapts. 1 and 3, and George 1979, pp. 51ff.

26 This is exemplified in our investigation by the limitation to only professional organizations besides parties as indicators of organizational freedoms.

27 On this point see Whitehead, 1986, p. 25.

Bibliography

Ahmed, Ishtiaq. 1985. *The Concept of an Islamic State. An Analysis of the Ideological Controversy in Pakistan*. Department of Political Science, University of Stockholm, Stockholm.

Albright, David E. 1980. 'A Comparative Conceptualization of Civil–Military Relations'. *World Politics* 32:553–76.

Alford, Robert R. and Friedland, Roger. 1985. *Powers of Theory. Capitalism, the State, and Democracy*. Cambridge University Press, Cambridge.

Almond, Gabriel A. 1989. 'Review Article: The International–National Connection'. *British Journal of Political Science* 19:237–59.

Almond, Gabriel A. and Coleman, James S. (eds.) 1960. *The Politics of the Developing Areas*. Princeton University Press, Princeton.

Almond, Gabriel A. and Verba, Sidney. 1963. *The Civic Culture*. Princeton University Press, Princeton.

Amin, Samir. 1987. 'Preface: The State and the Question of Development', in Nyongó, Peter Anyang' (ed.) *Popular Struggles for Democracy in Africa*, pp. 1–13. The United Nations University Zed Books, London.

Anckar, Dag. 1984. 'A Definition of Democracy' in Anckar, Dag and Berndtson, Erkki (eds.), *Essays on Democratic Theory*, pp. 15–33. The Finnish Political Science Association, Jyväskylä.

Anderson, T. 1987. 'Progress in the Democratic Revolution in Latin America: Country Assessments – 1987'. *Journal of Interamerican Studies and World Affairs* 29: 57–71.

Apter, David E. 1965. *The Politics of Modernization*. University of Chicago Press, Chicago.

 1987. *Rethinking Development. Modernization, Dependency, and Postmodern Politics*. Sage Publications, Newbury Park.

Arat, Zehra F. 1985. *The Viability of Political Democracy in Developing Countries*. University Microfilms International, Ann Arbor, MI.

 1988. 'Democracy and Economic Development. Modernization Theory Revisited'. *Comparative Politics* 21:21–36.

Aristotle. 1946. *The Politics of Aristotle*. Clarendon, Oxford.

Axelrod, Robert. 1984. *The Evolution of Cooperation*. Basic Books, New York.

Axelrod, Robert and Keohane, Robert O. 1985. 'Achieving Cooperation under Anarchy: Strategies and Institutions'. *World Politics* 38: 226–54.

Ayoade, John A. A. 1988. 'States Without Citizens: An Emerging African Phenomenon', in Rothchild, Donald and Chazan, Naomi (eds.) *The Precarious Balance. State and Society in Africa.* pp. 100–20. Westview Press, Boulder.

Badie, Bertrand. 1986. 'State, Legitimacy and Protest in Islamic Culture', in Kazancigil, Ali (ed.), *The State in Global Perspective.* pp. 250–65. Gower. Aldershot, Hants.

Banks, Arthur S. 1971. *Cross-Polity Time Series Data.* MIT Press, Cambridge.

Banks, Arthur S. and Textor, R. B. 1963. *A Cross-Polity Survey.* MIT Press, Cambridge.

Barber, Benjamin. 1984. *Strong Democracy: Participatory Politics for a New Age.* University of California Press, Berkeley.

Barber, Cohn and Jeffey, Henry B. (eds.) 1986. *Marxist Regimes.* Pinter, London.

Baxter, Craig, Malik, Yogendra K, Kennedy, Charles H. and Oberst, Robert C. 1987. *Government and Politics in South Asia.* Westview Press, Boulder.

Bennett, Stephen Earl and Resnick, David. 1990. 'The Implications of Nonvoting for Democracy in the United States'. *American Journal of Political Science* 34:771–802.

Berg, Elias. 1965. *Democracy and the Majority Principle.* Scandinavian University Books, Stockholm.

Berger, Peter L. 1987. *The Capitalist Revolution.* Wildwood Press. Aldershot, Hants.

Blais, A. and Carty, R. K. 1990. 'Does Proportional Representation Foster Voter Turnout?' *European Journal of Political Research* 18:167–81.

Blomkvist, Hans. 1988. *The Soft State: Housing Reform and State Capacity in India.* Uppsala University, Department of Government. Uppsala.

Bobbio, Norberto. 1987. *The Future of Democracy.* Polity Press, Oxford.

Bollen, Kenneth A. 1979. 'Political Democracy and Timing of Development'. *American Sociological Review* 44:572–87.

    1980. 'Issues in the Comparative Measurement of Political Democracy'. *American Sociological Review* 45:370–90.

    1983. 'World System Position, Dependency, and Democracy: The Cross-National Evidence'. *American Sociological Review* 48:468–79.

Bollen, Kenneth A. and Jackman, Robert W. 1985. 'Political Democracy and the Size Distribution of Income'. *American Sociological Review* 50:438–57.

Boloyra, Enrique (ed.) 1987. *Comparing New Democracies.* Westview Press, Boulder.

Bornschier, Volker, Chase-Dunn, Christopher and Rubinson, Richard. 1978. 'Cross-national Evidence of the Effects of Foreign Investment and Aid on Economic Growth and Inequality: A Survey of Findings and a Reanalysis'. *American Journal of Sociology* 84:651–83.

Boström, Bengt-Ove. 1988. *Samtal om demokrati.* Bokförlaget Doxa AB, Lund.

Boström, Mikael. 1987. *Demokrati och diktatur i Latinamerika.* Statsvetenskapliga förbundet, Gothenburg.

Bowles, Samuel and Gintis, Herbert. 1986. *Democracy and Capitalism. Property, Community, and the Contradictions of Modern Social Thought.* Routledge & Kegan Paul, London.

Brunk, Gregory G., Caldeira, Gregory A. and Lewis-Beck, Michael S. 1987. 'Capitalism, Socialism, and Democracy: An Empirical Inquiry'. *European Journal of Political Research* 15:459–70.

Bryce, James. 1921. *Modern Democracy. Vol I.* Macmillan, London.

Burke, Peter. 1986. 'City-States', in Hall, John A. (ed.) *States in History.* pp. 137–53. Basil Blackwell, Oxford.

Burnheim, John. 1985. *Is Democracy Possible? The Alternative to Electoral Politics.* University of California Press, Berkeley.

Carlsnaes, Walter. 1986. *Ideology and Foreign Policy. Problems of Comparative Conceptualization.* Basil Blackwell, Oxford.

Cardoso, Fernando H. and Faletto, Enzo. 1979. *Dependency and Development in Latin America.* University of California Press, Berkeley.

Chazan, Naomi. 1988. 'Patterns of State-Society Incorporation and Disengagement in Africa', in Rothchild, Donald and Chazan, Naomi (eds.), *The Precarious Balance. State and Society in Africa.* pp. 121–48. Westview Press, Boulder.

Chirkin, V. E. 1986. 'The Forms of the Socialist State', in Kazancigil, Ali (ed.), *The State in Global Perspective.* pp. 266–75. Gower. Aldershot, Hants.

Chirot, Daniel. 1977. *Social Change in the Twentieth Century.* Harcourt, Brace & Jovanovich, New York.

1985. 'The Rise of the West'. *American Sociological Review* 50:181–95.

Clapham, Christopher. 1985. *Third World Politics. An Introduction.* Croom Helm, London.

Coleman, James S. 1960. 'Conclusion', in Almond, Gabriel A. and Coleman, James S. (eds.) *The Politics of the Developing Areas.* Princeton University Press, Princeton.

Collier, Rut Berins. 1982. *Regimes in Tropical Africa. Changing Forms of Supremacy 1945–1975.* University of California Press, Berkeley.

Coulter, Philip. 1975. *Social Mobilization and Liberal Democracy.* Lexington Books, Lexington.

Crewe, Ivor. 1981. 'Electoral Participation', in Butler, David, Penniman, Howard R. and Ranney, Austin (eds.) *Democracy at the Polls. A Comparative Study of National Elections.* American Enterprise Institute, Washington, D.C.

Cutright, Phillips. 1963. 'National Political Development: Measurement and Analysis'. *American Sociological Review* 28:253–64.

Dahl, Robert A. 1956. *A Preface to Democratic Theory.* University of Chicago Press, Chicago.

1970. *After the Revolution? Authority in a Good Society.* Yale University Press, New Haven and London.

1971. *Polyarchy: Participation and Opposition.* Yale University Press, New Haven and London.

1989. *Democracy and Its Critics.* Yale University Press, New Haven and London.

Dahl, Robert A. and Tufte, Edward R. 1973. *Size and Democracy.* Stanford University Press, Stanford.

Deutsch, Karl W. 1961. 'Social Mobilization and Political Development'. *The American Political Science Review* 55:403–514.

Diamond, Larry. 1988. 'Introduction: Roots of Failure, Seeds of Hope', in Diamond, Larry, Linz, Juan J. and Lipset, Seymore Martin (eds.) *Democracy in Developing Countries. Volume Two. Africa.* pp. 1–32. Lynne Rienner, Boulder.

1989. *Crisis, Choice and Structure: Reconciling Alternative Models for Explaining Democratic Success and Failure in the Third World.* Paper presented to the 1989 Annual Meeting of the American Political Science Association, Atlanta.

Diamond, Larry, Lipset, Seymour M. and Linz, Juan. 1986. *Developing and Sustaining Democratic Government in the Third World.* Paper presented to the 1986 Annual Meeting of the American Political Science Association, Washington, D.C.

Dogan, Mattei and Pelassy, Dominique. 1990. *How to Compare Nations. Strategies in Comparative Politics.* Chatham House Publishers, Inc. Chatham, New Jersey.

Drake, Paul and Silva, Eduardo (eds.) 1986. *Elections and Democratization in Latin America.* Center for Iberian and Latin American Studies, San Diego.

Ebel, Roland H. 1972. 'Governing the City-State: Notes on the Politics of the Small Latin American Countries', *Journal of Inter-American Studies and World Affairs* 14:325–46.

Eisenstadt, S. N. 1986. 'Comparative Analysis of the State in Historical Contexts', in Kazancigil, Ali (ed.) *The State in Global Perspective.* pp. 20–54. Gower. Aldershot, Hants.

Eisenstadt, S. N. and Roninger, L. 1984. *Patrons, Clients and Friends. Interpersonal Relations and the Structure of Trust in Society.* Cambridge University Press, Cambridge.

Elster, Jon. 1988. 'Introduction', in Elster, Jon and Slagstad, Rune (eds.), *Constitutionalism and Democracy.* pp. 1–18. Cambridge University Press, Cambridge.

Emerson, Rupert. 1960. *From Empire to Nation. The Rise to Self-Assertion of Asian and African Peoples.* Harvard University Press, Cambridge, Mass.

1971. 'The Prospects for Democracy in Africa', in Lofchie, Michael F. (ed.), *The State of the Nations. Constraints on Development in Independent Africa.* University of California Press, Berkeley.

Evans, Peter. 1979. *Dependent Development: The Alliance of Multinational State and Local Capital in Brazil.* Princeton University Press, Princeton.

Farer, Tom J. 1989. 'A Multilateral Arrangement to Secure Democracy', in Pastor, Robert A. (ed.), *Democracy in the Americas: Stopping the Pendulum.* Holms and Meir, New York.

Fatton, Robert Jr. 1987. *The Making of a Liberal Democracy. Senegal's Passive Revolution, 1975–1985.* Lynne Rienner Publisher, London.

Fitzgibbon, Russell H. and Johnson, Kenneth F. 1961. 'Measurement of Latin American Political Change'. *The American Political Science Review* 55:515–26.

Frank, Andre Gunder. 1969. *Capitalism and Underdevelopment in Latin America. Historical Studies of Chile and Brazil.* Modern Reader Paperbacks, New York and London.

Frankel, Francine R. 1969. 'Democracy and Political Development: Perspectives from the Indian Experience', *World Politics* 21:448–68.

Gasiorowski, Mark J. 1985. 'The Structure of Third World Economic Interdependence'. *International Organization* 39:321–42.

1988. 'Economic Dependence and Political Democracy. A Cross-National Study'. *Comparative Political Studies* 20:489–515.

Gastil, Raymond D. 1988. *Freedom in the World. Political Rights & Civil Liberties 1987–1988.* Freedom House, New York.

1989. *Freedom in the World. Political Rights & Civil Liberties 1988–1989.* Freedom House, New York.

George, Alexander L. 1979. 'Case Studies and Theory Development: The Method of Structured, Focused Comparison' in Lauren, Paul Gordon (ed.) *Diplomacy: New Approaches in History, Theory and Policy.* The Free Press, New York.

Goodell, Grace. 1980. 'From Status to Contract: the Significance of Agrarian Relations of Production in the West, Japan, and in "Asiatic" Persia'. *European Journal of Sociology* 21:285–325.

Goodin, Robert E. 1975. 'Cross-Cutting Cleavages'. *British Journal of Political Science* 5:516–19.

Goulbourne, Harry. 1987. 'The State, Development and the Need for Participatory Democracy in Africa', in Nyongó, Peter Anyang' (ed.), *Popular Struggles for Democracy in Africa.* pp. 26–47. The United Nations University Zed Books, London.

Graham, Keith. 1986. *The Battle of Democracy: Conflict, Consensus and the Individual.* Wheatsheaf Books, Brighton.

Hall, John A. 1985. *Powers and Liberties. The Causes and Consequences of the Rise of the West.* Basil Blackwell, Oxford.

Hamilton, Alixander, Madison, James and Jay, John. 1961. *The Federalist Papers.* New American Library, New York.

Hannan, Michael T. and Carroll, Glenn R. 1981. 'Dynamics of Formal Political Structure: An Event–History Analysis'. *American Sociological Review* 46:19–35.

Hayek, Friedrich von. 1944. *The Road to Serfdom*. University of Chicago Press, Chicago.

Hayward, Fred M. (ed.) 1987. *Elections in Independent Africa*. Westview, Boulder.

Hermansson, Jörgen. 1986. 'Demokrati i västerländsk mening', *Statsvetenskaplig Tidskrift* 4:253–78.

1990. *Spelteorins nytta*. Almqvist & Wiksell International, Stockholm.

Holden, Barry. 1974. *The Nature of Democracy*. Nelson, London.

Holmberg, Sören. 1981. *Svenska Väljare*. LiberFörlag, Stockholm.

1989. 'Political Representation in Sweden'. *Scandinavian Political Studies* 12:1–36.

Holmberg, Sören and Gilljam, Mikael. 1987. *Väljare och val i Sverige*. Bonniers, Stockholm.

Holmberg, Sören and Esaiasson, Peter. 1988. *De folkvalda. En bok om riksdagsledamöterna och den representativa demokratin i Sverige*. Bonniers, Stockholm.

Holmes, Stephen. 1988. 'Precommitment and the Paradox of Democracy', in Elster, Jon and Slagstad, Rune (eds.) *Constitutionalism and Democracy*. pp. 195–240. Cambridge University Press, Cambridge.

Horowitz, Donald H. 1985. *Ethnic Groups in Conflict*. University of California Press, Berkeley.

Huntington, Samuel P. 1965. 'Political Development and Political Decay', *World Politics* 17:386–430.

1968. *Political Order in Changing Societies*. Yale University Press, New Haven.

1984. 'Will More Countries be Democratic?'. *Political Science Quarterly* 99:193–218.

Hydén, Göran. 1983. *No Shortcuts to Progress*. Heinemann, London.

Ingham, Kenneth. 1990. *Politics in Modern Africa: The Uneven Tribal Dimension*. Routledge, London and New York.

Jackman, Robert W. 1973. 'On the Relation of Economic Development to Democratic Performance'. *American Journal of Political Science* 17:611–21.

1974. 'Political Democracy and Social Equality: A Comparative Analysis'. *American Sociological Review* 39:29–45.

1975. *Politics and Social Equality: A Comparative Analysis*. John Wiley and Sons, New York.

Jackson, Robert H. and Rosberg, Carl G. 1982. *Personal Rule in Black Africa. Prince, Autocrat, Prophet, Tyrant*. University of California Press, Berkeley.

1982b. 'Why Africa's Weak States Persist: The Empirical and the Juridical Statehood', *World Politics* 35:1–24.

1984. 'Popular Legitimacy and African Multi-Ethnic States', *The Journal of Modern African Studies* 22:177–98.

1985. 'Democracy in Tropical Africa: Democracy Versus Autocracy in African Politics'. *Journal of International Affairs* 2:293–305.

1986. 'Sovereignty and Underdevelopment: Juridical Statehood in the African Crises', *Journal of Modern African Studies* 24:1–31.

Johnson, Thomas H., Slater, Robert O. and McGowan, Pat. 1984. 'Explaining African Military Coups d'Etat, 1960–1982'. *The American Political Science Review* 78:622–40.

Jones, Eric L. 1981. *The European Miracle. Environments, Economies, and Geopolitics in the History of Europe and Asia*. Cambridge University Press, Cambridge.

Kaufman, Robert R., Chernotsky, Harry I. and Geller, Daniel S. 1975. 'A Preliminary Test of the Theory of Dependency'. *Comparative Politics* 7:303–30.

Keller, Edmond J. and Rothchild, Donald. (eds.) 1987. *Afro-Marxist Regimes*. Lynne Rienner Publishers, Boulder.

Key, V. O. Jr. 1966. *The Responsible Electorate. Rationality in Presidential Voting 1936–1960*. Harvard University Press, Cambridge, Mass.

Killingray, David. 1986. 'The Maintenance of Law and Order in British Colonial Africa'. *African Affairs. Journal of the Royal African Society* 85: 411–37.

Kornhauser, William. 1959. *The Politics of Mass Society*. Free Press, Glencoe.

Kuper, Leo. 1969. 'Plural Societies: Perspectives and Problems' in Kuper, Leo and Smith M. G. (eds.) *Pluralism in Africa*. University of California Press, Berkeley.

Lenin, V. I. 1970. *Staten och revolutionen*. Rabén och Sjögren, Stockholm.

Lenski, Gerhard. 1966. *Power and Privilege*. McGraw-Hill, New York.

Lenski, Gerhard and Lenski, Jean. 1974. *Human Societies*. McGraw-Hill, New York.

Lerner, Daniel. 1958. *The Passing of Traditional Society*. Free Press, Glencoe.

Lewin, Leif. 1970. *Folket och eliterna*. Almqvist & Wiksell, Stockholm.

1977. *Hur styrs facket?* Rabén & Sjögren, Stockholm.

1988. *Det gemensamma bästa. Om egenintresset och allmänintresset i västerländsk politik*. Carlssons Bokförlag, Stockholm.

Lijphart, Arend. 1977. *Democracy in Plural Societies. A Comparative Exploration*. Yale University Press, New Haven.

1984. *Democracies. Patterns of Majoritarian and Consensus Government in Twenty-one Countries*. Yale University Press, New Haven.

Lindblom, Charles. 1977. *Politics and Markets. The World's Political-Economic Systems*. Basic Books, New York.

Linz, Juan J. 1975. 'Totalitarian and Authoritarian Regimes' in Greenstein, F. I. and Polsby, Nelson W. (eds.), *The Handbook of Political Science*. Addison-Wesley, Reading, Mass.

1978. *The Breakdown of Democratic Regimes. Crisis, Breakdown and Reequilibration*. The Johns Hopkins University Press, Baltimore and London.

Lipset, Seymour M. 1959. 'Some Social Requisites of Democracy: Economic Development and Political Legitimacy'. *The American Political Science Review* 53:69–105.

Lipset, Seymour M. 1960. *Political Man. The Social Bases of Politics*. Doubleday, New York.

Lipset, Seymour M. and Rokkan, Stein (eds.) 1967. *Party Systems and Voter Alignments: Cross-National Perspectives*. Free Press, New York.

Lissak, Moshe. 1976. *Military Roles in Modernization: Civil–Military Relations in Thailand and Burma*. Sage, Beverly Hills.

Lively, Jack. 1975. *Democracy*. Basil Blackwell, Oxford.

Lofchie, Michael F. 1970. 'Representative Government, Bureaucracy, and Political Development: The African Case', in Doro, Marion E. and Stultz, Newell M. (eds.), *Governing in Black Afrika. Perspectives on New States*. McClelland & Stewart, Toronto.

Long, David E. and Reich, Bernard (eds.) 1986. *The Government and Politics of the Middle East and North Africa*. Westview Press, Boulder.

Mackenzie, W. J. M. 1958. *Free Elections*. George Allen & Unwin, London.

Macpherson, C. B. 1966. *The Real World of Democracy*. Oxford University Press, Oxford.

1977. *The Life and Times of Liberal Democracy*. Oxford University Press, Oxford.

Mann, Michael. 1986. *The Sources of Social Power*, Vol. I. Cambridge University Press, Cambridge.

Mansbridge, Jane J. 1980. *Beyond Adversary Democracy*. Basic Books, New York.

Marshall, T. H. 1977. *Class, Citizenship and Social Development*. University of Chicago Press, Chicago.

May, John D. 1978. 'Defining Democracy: A Bid For Coherence and Concensus'. *Political Studies* 26:1–14.

May, K. O. 1982. 'A Set of Independent, Necessary and Sufficient Conditions for Simple Majority Decision', in Barry, Brian and Hardin, Russell (eds.) *Rational Man and Irrational Society?* pp. 299–303. Sage, Beverly Hills.

Mayo, H. B. 1960. *An Introduction to Democratic Theory*. Oxford University Press, New York.

Migdal, Joel S. 1988. *Strong Societies and Weak States. State–Society Relations and State Capabilities in the Third World*. Princeton University Press, Princeton N.J.

Mill, John Stuart. 1958. *Considerations on Representative Government*. Liberal Arts Press, New York.

Moore, Barrington Jr. 1967. *Social Origins of Dictatorship and Democracy. Lords and Peasants in the Making of the Modern World*. Beacon Press, Boston.

Mozaffari, Mehdi. 1987. *Authority in Islam. From Muhammad to Khomeini*. M. E. Sharpe, New York.

Muller, Edward N. 1985. 'Dependent Economic Development, Aid Dependency on the United States, and Democratic Breakdown in the Third World'. *International Studies Quarterly* 29:445–70.

1988. 'Democracy, Economic Development, and Income Inequality'. *American Sociological Review* 53:50–68.

Myrdal, Gunnar. 1968. *Asian Drama*. Pantheon, New York.

Needler, Martin C. 1968. 'Political Development and Socioeconomic Development: The Case of Latin America'. *The American Political Science Review* 62:889–97.

Nemeth, Roger J. and Smith, David A. 1985. 'International Trade and World-System Structure: A Multiple Network Analysis'. *Review* 8:517–60.

Neubauer, Deane E. 1967. 'Some Conditions of Democracy'. *The American Political Science Review* 61:1002–9.

Nord, Lars. 1987. 'Att motivera rösträtt' in Lewin, Leif (ed.) *Festskrist till professor skytteanus Carl Arvid Hessler*, pp. 96–107. Almqvist & Wiksell International, Stockholm.

Norlinger, Eric A. 1972. *Conflict Regulations in Divided Societies*. Center for International Affairs, Harvard University, Occasional Papers, No. 29. Cambridge, Mass.

1977. *Soldiers in Politics: Military Coups and Governments*. Prentice-Hall, Englewood Cliffs, N.J.

O'Donnell, Guillermo. 1973. *Modernization and Bureaucratic Authoritarianism: Studies in South American Politics*. University of California Berkeley, Institute of International Studies. Berkeley.

O'Maolain, Ciaran. (ed.) 1985. *Latin American Political Movements*. Longman, Essex.

Okun, Arthur M. 1975. *Equality and Efficiency. The Big Tradeoff*. The Brookings Institution, Washington, D.C.

Ostheimer, John M. (ed.) 1975. *The Politics of the Western Indian Ocean Islands*. Praeger, New York.

Palmer, R. R. 1959/64. *The Age of the Democratic Revolution. A Political History of Europe and America, 1760–1800*. (Vol. I–II) Princeton University Press, Princeton.

Pateman, Carole. 1970. *Participation and Democratic Theory*. Cambridge University Press, Cambridge.

Pennock, Roland J. 1979. *Democratic Political Theory*. Princeton University Press, Princeton.

Perlmutter, Amos. 1980. 'The Comparative Analysis of Military Regimes: Formations, Aspirations, and Achievements', *World Politics* 33:96–120.

Perry, Charles S. 1980. 'Political Contestation in Nations: 1960, 1963, 1967 and 1970'. *Journal of Political and Military Sociology* 8:161–74.

Peterson, John E. 1988. *The Arab Gulf States: Steps Toward Political Participation*. Praeger, New York.

Philip, George. 1984. 'Military-Authoritarianism in South America: Brazil, Chile, Uruguay and Argentina', *Political Studies* 32:1–20.

Plamenatz, John. 1973. *Democracy and Illusion. An Examination of Certain Aspects of Modern Democratic Theory*. Longman, London.

Poulantzas, N. 1979. *Politisk makt och sociala klasser*. Coeckelberghs Partisan-förlag, Falköping.

Powell, G. Bingham Jr. 1982. *Contemporary Democracies. Participation, Stability, and Violence*. Harvard University Press, Cambridge, Mass.

Pridham, Geoffrey. (ed.) 1991. *Encouraging Democracy: The International Context of Regime Transition*. Leicester University Press, Leicester.

Rabushka, Alvin and Shepsle, Kenneth A. 1972. *Politics in Plural Societies: A Theory of Democratic Instability*. E. Merrill, Columbus.

Rae, Douglas W. 1969. 'Decision-Rules and Individual Values in Constitutional Choice'. *The American Political Science Review* 63:40–56.

Rae, Douglas W. and Taylor, Michael 1970. *The Analysis of Political Cleavages*. Yale University Press, New Haven.

Ragin, Charles C. 1987. *The Comparative Method. Moving Beyond Qualitative and Quantitative Strategies*. University of California Press. Berkeley, Los Angeles and London.

Randall, Vicky. and Theobald, Robin. 1985. *Political Change and Underdevelopment. A Critical Introduction to Third World Politics*. Macmillan, London.

Randall, Vicky. (ed.) 1988. *Political Parties in the Third World*. Sage, London.

Riggs, Fred W. 1963. 'Bureaucrats and Political Development: A Paradoxical View', in LaPalombara, Joseph, *Bureaucracy and Political Development*. Princeton University Press, Princeton.

Riker, William H. 1982. *Liberalism Against Populism. A Confrontation Between the Theory of Democracy and the Theory of Social Choice*. Freeman and Company, San Francisco.

Ronen, Dov. (ed.) 1986. *Democracy and Pluralism in Africa*. Lynne Rienner, Boulder.

Ross, Alf. 1963. *Varför demokrati?* Tiden, Stockholm.

Rouquié, Alain. 1978. 'Clientelist Control and Authoritarian Contexts', in Hermet, Guy, Rose, Richard and Rouquié, Alain (eds.), *Elections Without Choice*. Macmillan, London.

Russet, Bruce M. 1964. 'Inequality and Instability: The Relation of Land and Tenure to Politics'. *World Politics* 16:442–54.

1965. *Trends in World Politics*. Macmillan, New York.

Rustow, Dankwart A. 1967. *A World of Nations. Problems in Political Modernization*. Brookings, Washington, D.C.

1970. 'Transitions to Democracy: Toward a Dynamic Model'. *Comparative Politics* 2:337–63.

Sartori, Giovanni. 1962. 'Constitutionalism: A Preliminary Discussion'. *The American Political Science Review* 56:853–64.

1976. *Parties and Party Systems. A Framework for Analysis. Vol I*. Cambridge University Press, Cambridge.

1987. *The Theory of Democracy Revisited*. Chatham House, Chatham, N.J.

Schmidt, Steffen W., Scott, James C., Landé, Carl H. and Guasti, Laura. (eds.) 1977. *Friends, Followers and Factions. A Reader in Clientelism.* University of California Press, Berkeley.

Schumpeter, J. A. 1947. *Capitalism, Socialism and Democracy.* Harper, New York.

Schweinitz, Karl de. 1964. *Industrialization and Democracy.* Free Press, Glencoe.

Sejersted, Francis. 1988. 'From Liberal Constitutionalism to Corporate Pluralism: the Conflict Over the Enabling Acts in Norway After the Second World War and the Subsequent Constitutional Development', in Elster, Jon and Slagstad, Rune (eds.) *Constitutionalism and Democracy.* pp. 275–302. Cambridge University Press, Cambridge.

Seligson, Mitchell A. 1987. 'Costa Rica and Jamaica', in Weiner, Myron and Özbudun, Ergun (eds.), *Competitive Elections in Developing Countries.* Duke University Press, Durham, N.C.

Shefter, Martin. 1977. 'Party and Patronage: Germany, England, Italy'. *Politics and Society* 7:403–53.

Sklar, Richard L. 1979. 'The Nature of Class Domination in Africa'. *Journal of Modern Africa Studies* 17:531–52.

1983. 'Democracy in Africa'. *African Studies Review* 26:11–24.

Smith, Arthur K. Jr. 1969. 'Socio-Economic Development and Political Democracy: A Causal Analysis'. *Midwest Journal of Political Science* 30:95–125.

Smith, Tony. 1978. 'A Comparative Study of French and British Decolonization', *Comparative Studies in Society and History* 20:70–102.

1985. 'Requiem or New Agenda for Third World Studies?' *World Politics* 37:532–61.

Snyder, David and Kick, Edward L. 1979. 'Structural Position in the World System and Economic Growth, 1955–1970: A Multiple-Network Analysis of Transnational Interactions'. *American Journal of Sociology* 84:1096–126.

Tangri, Roger. 1985. *Politics in Sub-Saharan Africa.* Currey/Heineman, London.

Taylor, Charles Lewis and Hudson, Michael C. 1972. *World Handbook of Political and Social Indicators.* Yale University Press, New Haven.

Taylor, Charles Lewis and Jodice, David A. 1983. *World Handbook of Political and Social Indicators.* Yale University Press, New Haven.

Taylor, Michael. 1969. 'Proof of a Theorem on Majority Rule', *Behavioral Science* 14:228–31.

Therborn, Göran. 1977. 'The Rule of Capital and the Rise of Democracy', *New Left Review* no. 103:3–41.

Thomas, Clive Y. 1984. *The Rise of the Authoritarian State in Peripheral Societies.* Monthly Review Press, New York.

Timberlake, Michael and Williams, Kirk R. 1984. 'Dependence, Political Exclusion, and Government Repression: Some Cross-National Evidence'. *American Sociological Review* 49:141–6.

Tingsten, Herbert. 1965. *The Problem of Democracy*. Bedminster Press, New Jersey.

Tocqueville, Alexis de. 1969. *Democracy in America*. Anchor Press, Garden City.

Usher, Dan. 1981. *The Economic Prerequisite to Democracy*. Columbia University Press, New York.

Valenzuela, J. Samuel and Valenzuela, Arturo. 1974. 'Modernization and Dependency: Alternative Perspectives in the Study of Latin American Underdevelopment'. *Comparative Politics* 6:535–59.

Vanhanen, Tatu. 1984. *The Emergence of Democracy. A Comparative Study of 119 States, 1850–1979*. Societas Scientarium Fennica, Helsinki.

    1987. *The Level of Democratization Related to Socioeconomic Variables in 147 States in 1980–85*. European Consortium for Political Research, Amsterdam.

    1989. 'The Level of Democratization Related to Socioeconomic Variables in 147 States in 1980–85'. *Scandinavian Political Studies* 12:95–127.

Vedung, Evert. 1982. *Political Reasoning*. Sage, Beverly Hills.

Verba, Sidney, Nie, Norman H. and Kim, Jae-on. 1978. *Participation and Political Equality. A Seven Nation Comparison*. Cambridge University Press, Cambridge.

Wallerstein, Immanuel. 1974. *The Modern World System: Capitalist Agriculture and the Origins of the European World Economy in the Sixteenth Century*. Academic Press, New York.

Weiner, Myron. 1987. 'Empirical Democratic Theory' in Weiner, Myron and Özbudun, Ergun (eds.), *Competitive Elections in Developing Countries*. pp. 3–36. Duke University Press, Durham, N.C.

Welch, Claude E. 1970. 'Soldier and State in Africa', in Doro, Marion E. and Stultz, Newell M. (eds.), *Governing in Black Africa. Perspectives on New States*. Prentice-Hall, Englewood Cliffs, N.J.

    1971. 'Cincinnatus in Africa: The Possibility of Military Withdrawal from Politics', in Lofchie, Michael F. (ed.), *The State of the Nations. Constraints in Development in Independent Africa*. University of California Press, Berkeley.

Whelan, Frederick G. 1983. 'Prologue: Democratic Theory and the Boundary Problem', in Pennock, Roland J. and Chapman, John W. (eds.) *Liberal Democracy*. pp. 13–48. New York University Press, New York.

Whitehead, Laurence. 1986. 'International Aspects of Democratization', in O'Donnell, Guillermo, Schmitter, Phillippe C. and Whitehead, Laurence (eds.), *Transitions from Authoritarian Rule: Prospects for Democracy*. The John Hopkins University Press, Baltimore.

    1989. 'The Consolidation of Fragile Democracies: A Discussion with Illustrations', in Pastor, Robert A. (ed.), *Democracy in the Americas: Stopping the Pendelum*. Holms and Meir, New York.

Winham, Gilbert R. 1970. 'Political Development and Lerner's Theory: Further Test of a Causal Model'. *The American Political Science Review* 64:810–18.

Wittfogel, Karl 1957. *Oriental Despotism.* Yale University Press, New Haven.

Young, Crawford. 1988. 'The African Colonial State and Its Political Legacy', in Rothchild, Donald and Chazan, Naomi (eds.), *The Precarious Balance. State and Society in Africa.* pp. 25–66. Westview Press, Boulder and London.

Zolberg, Aristide R. 1966. *Creating Political Order. The Party-States of West Africa.* Rand McNally, Chicago.

Zubaida, Sami. 1987. 'The Quest for the Islamic State: Islamic Fundamentalism in Egypt and Iran', in Caplan, Lionel (ed.) *Studies in Religious Fundamentalism.* pp. 25–50. Macmillan Press, London.

Index